G000151303

THE LAST PRABHU

A Hunt for Roots: DNA, Ancient Documents and
Migration in Goa

Bernardo Elvino de Sousa

Cover design by Bernardo Elvino de Sousa

Some reader comments on the first edition:

Valmiki Faleiro, writer and journalist:
This is the story of how the Switzerland-based author, obsessed with a passion to trace his ancestral roots, and thinking out of the box, employed the emerging science of DNA-based genealogy in combination with literature and ancient records to trace his family name some 36 generations, and more.

Prof. Dr. Teotonio R. de Souza, historian and academic:
Bernardo de Sousa's academic formation, professional experience, and personal background make him the right person to handle the theme. I have referred to this book in my recent publication http://amzn.to/1rh1zJ0 and also in a couple of earlier op-ed columns in the Goan daily Herald. Use of DNA testing for the study of deep ancestry certainly comes to rescue when historical documentation ceases to help due to its usual time limitations. I could by chance reach my first ancestor who was converted to Christianity as Diogo de Souza. He was earlier known as Shantappa Kamat. I found his personal note in an archival document of 1619. But in most cases we can hardly go back beyond the past couple of centuries. That is where the DNA testing can come as a supplementary aid. However, it is not a tool that is easily available to many, both by its costs and innumerable generations involved. One should not also over-estimate the importance of DNA for the formation of social identities. These go far beyond family or ethnic linkages. However, there is always a feeling of excitement in knowing some very distant links in time and space. They could help deconstructing the artificiality of many later identity constructions and force us to explore the likely motivations behind them.

Frank Dabreo, a Goan reader in Canada:
The gold standard on the subject: This is an excellent book for anyone seriously interested in investigating their personal ancestry as well as the social /ethnic ancestry. The style is very lucid even though the content is very scientific and deep.
I read it very quickly the first time and since then I have read it two more times and each time have gathered new insights. as well new leads to follow-up.

The information on DNA science and its application to personal ancestry was very illuminating and helped understanding the very significant conclusions contained in this book as well as followup books.
It was delight to read since I am from Goa.
Definitely the gold standard for persons seriously interested in their personal and cultural ancestry.

Amazon customer:
Fantastic book revealing the immigration route followed by Prabhu's ancestors. I never knew that some Saraswat Brahmins had roots in Iraq!
The formation of castes was a complex process and many people of several ancestries were lumped into a caste. All this remarkable knowledge is revealed in this book through genetic tests.
I admire the last Prabhu....I wonder how much maturity it must have taken for him to allow his children to convert but himself remaining steadfast in his vedic tradition.
I have undergone DNA ancestry testing and Bernardo has written about my haplogroup in his book. My ancestry is coastal and my ancestors were one of the earliest inhabitants of India. However I am a Brahmin, a Gaud Saraswat Brahmin at that.

NK, Amazon customer:
This is a fascinating read for anyone interested in knowing about the pre history and spread of humanity around the world, especially in the Indian sub-continent. They say genes don't lie, well that's because it's the best 'truthometer' we have as of now. Very well researched and the writer tells it like it is. This book has convinced me to do a gene test and I'm very excited

ABOUT THE AUTHOR

 Bernardo Elvino de Sousa was born in Cottarbhat – Aldona, Goa, India on 13th August 1945 and did his early schooling at St. Thomas' High School, Aldona and the latter three years at Loyola High School, Margão. After SSC, he joined St. Xavier's College, Mumbai and obtained the B.Sc. (Hons) degree in chemistry (principal) and physics (subsidiary) from Bombay University. He completed his higher education with the title of Dr. of Natural Sciences (Dr. rer. nat.) from the University of Fribourg, Switzerland, with a thesis in organic photochemistry. After post-doctoral research in Fribourg with a Ciba-Geigy research grant, he joined Ciba-Geigy Ltd. in Basel, Switzerland as a research scientist in 1977 and retired from Huntsman Corporation in September 2010 as Director, Global Product EHS Management. During his 34 years serving the chemical industry, the author has held various executive positions notably in the areas of Product Safety and Quality Management. He has many scientific publications to his credit and post-retirement continues to be involved in Quality Management and Product Safety projects and as an auditor for Quality Management systems as well as a Lead Assessor for the Swiss Business Excellence Award.

He is married to historian Vinita née Veloso, from Badem – Salvador do Mundo, Goa, and they have two children, Ranjit and Savitri.

Comments to the author can be posted on his blog:
https://thelastprabhu.blogspot.com

For my ancestor
RAMU PRABHU
with posthumous affection

… and I am proud of being a descendent of *Ramu Prabhu*, the last person of his patrilineage to bear a Hindu surname, The Last Prabhu.

For my wife and co-migrant
VINITA
my constant companion in all evolutionary processes

and our children
RANJIT and SAVITRI
as a constant reminder to them and their descendants of their ancestral roots

This book is being released to coincide with the birth of the most recent descendant of Ramu Prabhu and our first grandchild, born on April 16, 2011, in Zurich, Switzerland,
RAÚL SANJAY DE SOUSA

"It is not the strongest of the species that survives, nor the most intelligent that survives. It is the one that is the most adaptable to change"
- Charles Darwin

FOREWORD TO THE SECOND EDITION

The rapid strides made in the area of genetics since this book was published nearly a decade ago is nothing short of revolutionary.

Tests on Y DNA have evolved to such an extent that the former entry-level 12-marker test is no longer offered since the interpretation of the results is considered to be much too basic to be of significance. *Family Tree DNA* now offers a test called *Big Y 700* that analyses a minimum of 700 *Short Tandem Repeat* or STR markers, a major difference from the past basic 12 marker test as well as millions of nucleotides thereby enabling a deeper and geographically wider understanding of not only migration patterns but also the discovery of very distant matches.

Whereas ten years ago, migration out of Africa up to the Middle East and Europe could be traced, the much more amplified analyses available today allow for a substantially more detailed migration pattern. As always, in the presence of stiff competition between the many testing institutes that have sprung up, prices are falling and this makes DNA testing even more easily accessible to the general public. In the past, interest in DNA testing was restricted to Western countries but we currently witness a boom in tests for example from the Middle East and India. A paper in *Genome Biology* estimated that more than 100 million people will have their DNA tested by 2021. This in turn opens up new avenues of discovering DNA matches that are not restricted to Western countries alone.

Substantial progress has also been made with tests on mtDNA. Whereas just some years ago only a basic test was available, today a complete sequence mtDNA test can be carried out, again enabling the discovery of close and distant maternal cousins.

Yet another very big step is the option to test autosomal DNA, something that was not available some years back. This expansion from Y DNA and mtDNA into the realm of autosomal DNA or the whole genome test that covers all 23 pairs of human chromosomes and not only the Y chromosome greatly expands the possibility of finding previously unknown deep ancestry with significant repercussions for our understanding of past history since mixtures of ancestries can also be determined.

A revolutionary development in genetics is the availability of vast data on what is now termed ancient DNA or aDNA in short. Science now allows the recovery of DNA from skeletons of individuals who left this world many thousands of years ago including Denisovans and Neanderthals and new technology enables even these minute amounts to be analysed thereby making it possible for us to compare the DNA test results of modern humans to ancient ancestors and thus trace not only our descendance but also migration patterns.

Yet another development is in the area of communication. Organisations such as *Family Tree DNA*, *Genographic Project*, *MyHeritage* among many other offer fora in which participants can share their results, thoughts or opinions and seek answers to their queries from experienced and knowledgeable project administrators. Individuals can upload their test results from their testing facility to a site called *GedMatch* thus pooling together results from different testing laboratories into one vast global databank, greatly expanding the data base for comparisons of the results that were previously restricted to the individual testing institutes.

Genetic genealogy has its limitations and cannot in itself offer all the answers that we seek; it needs to be considered as part of a multidisciplinary approach that takes into account written and orally transmitted history, the study of ancient literature and documents, archeological findings and the evolution of languages among other areas.

Genetic genealogy should not be confused with a genealogical tree. DNA cannot tell us the name of our great grandfather or in which village our great grandmother was born; it has to be considered in parallel with a genealogical tree and not as a replacement.

We also have to understand that ancestors transmit a segment of their genome to their descendants and the further away the generation, the smaller this segment will be. In the first generation each one of us has two ancestors: our parents. In the second generation, our ancestry increases by four because it now includes our grandparents, in the next generation it increases by eight with our great grandparents and so on. Each generation multiplied by two gives us the number of our ancestors of the previous generation. Our ancestry increases exponentially and with 10 generations we have 1024 ancestors, with 20 generations this figure grows to 1,048,576. The further back we go, the tinier the segment that we inherit from them, if at all. Thus the information contained in our own genome will necessarily be very small as the number of generations increases.

Genetic genealogy can tell us if our Y DNA or mtDNA matches with another person but it cannot tell us directly if an individual is our first or second cousin. It can, however, do this indirectly by calculating the probability of the degree of relatedness based on mutation rates of the individual chromosomes.

I am privileged to be familiar with Konkani, basic Marathi, Portuguese as well as the Devanagiri script, a combination that was very useful in translating Gajanana Ghantkar's *Tombo de Aldona* that represents a major
section of his book *The History of Goa in Goykanadi Script*. The *Tombo* consists of a compilation of minutes of several meetings of the *Comunidade* of Aldona from the years 1595 to 1605 and provides a first-hand account of the governance of Aldona village during that period. Through these minutes I had already been able to identify the pre-conversion Hindu name of my ancestors and those of the village clans or *vangads* but with a complete translation of this document, it has been possible for me to also learn about the history of my ancestors in addition to their name and many other details on the Aldona villagers and how they lived their lives in the late 16th and early 17th century.

With the globally easy access to the Internet, any reader can effortlessly acquire information on definitions of the terms used in this book. I have therefore chosen to remove the glossary contained in the first edition. I have also listened to the feedback of my readers who found parts of the book to be overly scientific to be understood by laypersons and have attempted to simplify the explanations in a language that will hopefully be more easily understood.

All these developments have brought to light new facts leading me to reassess or even discard some of the previously made assumptions and compelling me to completely rewrite *The Last Prabhu* to reflect the present state of knowledge. As science continues to progress, further revisions will no doubt become necessary but this will have to be left in the hands of future generations.

What the reader can find in this book

- An simple explanation on what DNA really is and why it is important.
- How to easily carry out Y DNA, mitochondrial DNA and autosomal DNA tests to determine maternal and paternal haplogroups as well as ancient origins that divulge the ancestral migration route starting some 60,000 years ago or earlier. These DNA tests are specifically geared towards deep ancestry and do not in any way touch on health-related genetic pre-dispositions unless the user specifically requests this information.
- How deep ancestry DNA results can be helpful in identifying common ancestors going back seven or eight centuries or more.
- A discussion on the peopling of India as well as Goa.
- Approximate year when the settlers migrated from the north to Goa and established the first Gaunkari system
- Discover if Lord Parashurama was a mythological figure or really existed
- Historical aspects related to the village of Aldona as an example of what probably occurred in many other villages of Goa:
- Origin of the name of Aldona village
- DNA-based scientific proof of when Aldona village was settled
- The pre-conversion Hindu names of the 12 founding clans (*vangads*) of Aldona
- Historical assumptions related to the *gaunkari* system of Goa's villages
- The circumstances of the conversion to Christianity and how it was accepted or otherwise by the villagers
- The Church, Temples and deities of the village and the origins of the church
- The condition of women
- The history of the *comunidades* of Aldona
- The origin and an analysis of the caste system and whether there is a basis for its existence from the viewpoint of genetic genealogy
- Important references to assist the reader in the investigation of his or her own deep ancestry, roots and migratory path.

Contents

Annexes

Introduction to the first edition

When my historian wife and I first read about the Genographic Project, we were both highly enthused by the prospect of discovering more about our deep ancestry, she, from the historical perspective and I to understand and marvel at the possibilities offered by large-scale DNA testing. The project addresses some fundamental questions:

"Where do you **really** come from? And how did your ancestors migrate to the geographical location where you live today?

DNA studies suggest that all human males descend from a group of African ancestors who—about 60,000 years ago—began a remarkable journey.

The Genographic Project (initiated by *National Geographic* and IBM) is seeking to chart new knowledge about the migratory history of the human species by using sophisticated laboratory and computer analysis of DNA contributed by hundreds of thousands of people from around the world. In this unprecedented and real-time research effort, the Genographic Project is closing the gaps of what science knows today about humankind's ancient migration stories."

The results of my DNA tests were both exciting because they indicated that my lineage started with humanity's African Adam but also frustrating because the genetic trail ended in the Fertile Crescent.

My father had often mentioned to me that we are *gaunkars* (i.e., descendants of early settlers) of the village of Aldona but I could no longer recall to which "*vangad*" (family clan that claims to be descendant of early settlers) I belonged, since as a teenager, this topic was of little interest to me. The question that I asked myself is: "How and under what circumstances did my ancestors then migrate from the Fertile Crescent to the Indian village of Aldona, Goa?"

Seeking answers to this question has taken me through a fascinating journey. I am not a historian, a student of history or an expert in genetic genealogy but rather just a Goan emigrant to Switzerland seeking enlightenment with regard to his ancestry. And being a scientist by education, profession and inclination, applying the benefits of genetic genealogy, a science that is making rapid and enormous strides, appealed to me enormously.

No single discipline can provide answers to all the questions that continuously arise and genetic genealogy is not an exception; it constitutes an additional implement in the toolbox.

I have benefitted from the works of pre-eminent Goans but also historians from beyond Goa without whose tremendous contributions genealogical research of any significance would not be possible. The Internet was also a source of meaningful information that aided to address new questions that kept arising and will continue to arise. I was also supported by conversations with many knowledgeable persons and have had the privilege of developing ties of friendship with some of them.

Acquiring source literature from Goa was found to be an insurmountable task and I am indebted to many who have assisted me to obtain the books and information that I needed for this project.

My strenuous effort to obtain a copy of Ghantkar's *History of Goa in Gōykanadi Script* and in particular the *Tombo de Aldona* contained in this book is illustrative of the difficulties involved. The modest but highly knowledgeable ex-President of the *Comunidade* of Aldona, Hector Fernandes, who as I have discovered in the meantime, is also a distant relative, made available a photocopy of the *Tombo de Aldona* that is indispensable for anyone who wishes to become acquainted with the history of this village. He additionally furnished details on many other historical aspects and offered his time and assistance to understand and translate the *Tombo*.

I wish to express my sincere appreciation to Hector for his unstinting support.

Unfortunately, some of the pages of the *Tombo* were missing. My phone calls and email to the publisher for copies of these missing pages were ignored and my pleas to many friends and acquaintances in Goa who could effortlessly have sent me copies from the book remained at the stage of enthusiastic promises.

A visit to the Goa State Archives in January 2010 ended in deep frustration. Finally, after discovering from the internet that the University of Texas Library in USA kept a copy of Ghantkar's book, I was able to obtain a copy of the *Tombo de Aldona* through an American colleague and his niece who live in the area. I wish to thank Richard Bennett and Rhonda Hankins for their tremendous help.

The discussions primarily by email but also by phone with another newly discovered distant cousin Errol Pinto were equally stimulating and (hopefully mutually) beneficial. Errol Pinto, Hector Fernandes, Rohit Menezes and Fr. Nascimento Mascarenhas unhesitatingly gave me permission to use their DNA test results in this project.

My sister in law Prof. Sharmila Veloso procured a very informative book by Chandrakant Keni and copied by hand documents from the library that were not permitted to be photocopied.

I am indebted to Valmiki Faleiro and Frederick Noronha to whom I turned in desperation after my telephone and email appeals to acquaintances and publishers in Goa were met with one big deafening silence.

My wife Vinita and daughter Savitri were both enthusiastic supporters of my efforts but also hapless victims of my enthusiasm, subjected as they were to my unsolicited explanations. To all a very big thank you.

This monograph could be entitled *The genealogy of the de Sousa family from Quitula, Aldona, Goa* but in deference to my paternal grandfather, the focus on the surname Elvino de Sousa is more pertinent.

The name de Sousa is written in different ways e.g. de Souza or D-Souza and is as ubiquitous in Goa as this territory's red laterite soil. In what today would be called a strategy of differentiation by rebranding, my grandfather Dr. Honorato Elvino de Santana de Sousa, decided to grace the surname of his progeny with the addendum "Elvino," thereby initiating the Elvino de Sousa patrilineage that is the subject of this genealogy.

A second reason is the fact that my grandfather was given the property at Cottarbhatt, Aldona, where I was born, by his eldest brother and in exchange was required to relinquish his rights to the familial house in Quitula.

When, as a teenager, I expressed the opinion that I did not find this exchange equitable, my father explained that for my grandfather's generation, the decision of the eldest of the family was final and non-negotiable and the question of whether the exchange was equitable or not did not arise. Thus, he effectively became a "Elvino de Sousa" from Cottarbhatt and no longer a "de Sousa" from Quitula.

To borrow a term from the toxicological vocabulary, at the start of this project, there were two end-points that could be considered as firmly established. The first one, based on the results of my DNA analysis within the scope of the Genographic Project, charts the migratory path of my ancestors from Africa to the Fertile Crescent and the other, based on documentary evidence, proves that my ancestors were Bardezkars and early settlers of the village of Aldona.

I have related the path that my ancestors treaded from Africa to the Fertile Crescent and attempted to elucidate their most probable route from there to their final destination Aldona. My conclusions have been based on a number of elements: analyses carried out on my DNA, literature search on research related to the migration of my haplogroup, historical research published by many eminent historians both from Goa and elsewhere, documentary evidence available in the archives in Goa, discussions with historians and experts knowledgeable in matters related to the *Comunidade* of my village Aldona, as well as a family tree handed down to my family by a church historian.

References to caste and caste affiliations are frequent in this book and indissociable from any research in Goan and Indian genetic genealogy. This is due to the fact that Indian history, haplogroup testing as well as *Comunidade vangads* (family clans) and related literature are all closely linked to them. It is very unfortunate that cast considerations have led to the creation of two *Comunidades* in my village, Aldona. It is to be hoped that better sense will prevail and today's Aldonkars will work towards a reunification. I wish to emphasise that my references in this book to caste affiliations and the caste system in general are purely for purposes of research and in no way indicate my adherence to, or support of, the caste system.

Many gaps still exist, some that will never be closed because documentary evidence has been lost forever to the elements and negligence. Others related to my DNA analysis will hopefully be filled by our descendants as science continues to progress. Data on the haplogroups to which Goans belong is cruelly missing; projects sponsored by the University of Goa or Goa's authorities or appropriate foundations would be a great boon to understand the rich history of the ancestry of Goa and its linkages to the Indian sub-continent.

This book is all about roots and its release has been planned to coincide with the month of the birth of our first grandchild. Such a planning constitutes a burden and imposes time-pressure on the publisher. My very special thanks go to Goa, 1556 and publisher Frederick Noronha for his painstaking editing, cooperation and flexibility in developing — with Bina Nayak – a cover design as well as his value-adding advice on various aspects pertaining to this book.

I made a commitment to myself to elucidate the truth in this project, no matter what it takes or where it leads. There were times of pleasant introspection trying to revive childhood memories but also frustrating moments when the truth seemed to become elusive and source books were simply not accessible or, for example, additional testing would be required. The pursuit of this genealogical truth was like the irritant in an oyster that would hopefully produce the pearl; it is left to the reader to judge if I have succeeded in obtaining that pearl.

PART I: DNA AND MIGRATION

1. The African Connection, DNA and Useful Terminology

"Light will be thrown on the origin of man and his history" – Charles Darwin[1]

It was an exciting and very plausible story to the ears of a credulous three-year old, backed-up as it was by a song. I do not remember asking the question but the explanation on my origin is vividly engraved in my mind:

I was sent in a basket by Baby Jesus to the St. Thomas' Church, Aldona, Goa, from where my aunt who lived in our household and everyone called Madrinha (godmother in Portuguese) collected me.

When she reached *Tercena*, the playground in the immediate vicinity of our home, she shouted out for help because I was heavy. Carrying me up the slope from the church was no mean feat, especially for her who had been afflicted with polio in her childhood.

I felt vaguely responsible for having subjected her to this ordeal; but it did not occur to me to challenge the explanation as a child today may probably have done. The song, that addresses me by my pet name Babasha, the tune of which I still clearly remember, went like this:

Quando Babasha era pequenino
(When Babasha was tiny)
Vindo num cestinho
(He arrived in a basket)
Mandado por Jesus Menino
(Sent by Baby Jesus)
Trazido por Madrinha
(Brought by Madrinha)

My efforts to try to recall the rest of the song have been unsuccessful — the brain of a child has its limitations.

Today, some 70 years later, I know that my origin can be traced back not to the St. Thomas' Church in Aldona but to an African, the common male ancestor of the world's population whose descendants started migrating from Africa.

Africa could thus be called the basket of humanity as Charles Darwin had proposed in the 19th century[2] and therefore the basket in which I was supposedly delivered is not completely off the mark! This common male ancestor referred to as "African Adam" or just "Adam" evolved along with other hominid and *Homo erectus* species that, however, became extinct and only modern humans *Homo sapiens* survived.

We know this from fossil and archeological data and also because of our DNA, first discovered in 1869 by a Swiss scientist Friedrich Miescher who called the molecule *nuclein*. The word *nuclein* evolved to *nucleic acid* and finally *deoxyribonucleic acid* or DNA. Many other scientists subsequently continued to research DNA most notably the Russian biochemist Phoebus Levene and Austrian scientist Erwin Chargaff culminating in the proposal in 1953 of the double helix structure of DNA by James Watson, Francis Crick, Maurice Wilkins and Rosalind Franklin.[3,4]

Although it is generally accepted that early modern humans originated in Africa, the precise region where they first arose is a matter of debate: south or east or north Africa. There are two theories that are debated today: the afore-mentioned recent single origin or "out of Africa" theory and the "multi-regional evolution" that postulates an intermingling of the African *homo sapiens* with other existing homo species populations that they encountered.

A team of scientists led by DNA expert Svante Pääbo, Director of Germany's Max Planck Institute for Evolutionary Anthropology partially analysed a Neanderthal genome isolated from 38'000 to 44'000 years old bone fragments of three Neanderthal females excavated from a cave in Croatia and compared the results with the genomes of a *San* from southern Africa, a *Yoruba* from West Africa, a Papua New Guinean, a *Han* Chinese and a French individual.[5]

The Neanderthal DNA is not present in the genomes of the two Africans but it is prevalent to an extent of one to four percent in the other three. This suggests that non-African humans intermingled with Neanderthals after they had migrated out of Africa. This discovery has led to the modified "Out of Africa" theory that postulates that a first northward migration of hominids through the Middle East, to Europe and parts of western Asia took place around 400'000 years ago.

A second migration took place about 60'000 years ago, and the two populations intermingled possibly in the Middle East – thus explaining the absence of Neanderthal DNA in today's Africans – before spreading to all the other regions of the globe.

It appears from more recent research that the evolution of mankind is much more complex than previously imagined. In 2008, paleoanthropologists excavated from the Denisova cave in the Bashelaksky Range in the Altai Mountains, Southern Siberia, an adult tooth that was found to be 40 thousand years old and a pinkie bone that belonged to a five to seven year old girl. DNA extracted from this bone revealed that this young girl was related but distinct from the Neanderthals and she probably had brown hair and eyes and a brown skin. This new hominin was named a Denisovan after the Denisova cave where it was found. Scientists have found Denisovan genes in Melanesians living in Papua New Guinea to an extent of up to 6 percent (about 410 CentiMorgans) indicating that they coexisted and bred with modern-day humans though where this interbreeding took place is yet to be determined.[6]

In May 2019, Fahu Chen *et al.* reported the discovery of a Denisovan mandible, identified by ancient protein analysis, found by a monk who had come to pray on the Tibetan Plateau in Baishiya Karst Cave, Xiahe, Gansu, China. The scientists dated the bone to be at least 160 thousand years old. This specimen proves that Denisovans existed not only in the Altai Mountains but even more than a thousand miles away from there in Tibet.[7,8]

The genome of the Asian and European populations also contains genetic contributions from both the Neanderthals and Denisovans but in minute amounts. For example, my genome matches with the 50 thousand year old Altai Neanderthal on chromosomes 1, 6 and 11 for a total of 3.8 CentiMorgans and to Denisova on chromosome 19 to an extent of 1.1 cM. A Centimorgan cM is a measure of genetic linkage, with each chromosome containing different amounts of information. For example, chromosome 1 contains 281.5 cM, chromosome 2 contains 263.7 cM and chromosome 21 just 70.1 cM of information.[9] By comparison, the total genome in cM is 6770cM and a match of a child with a parent would be expected to measure in the range of 3385cM.

We now know that Neanderthals and Denisovans are extinct groups of distinct hominins that co-existed, interbred including with modern-day humans, and separated from each other more than 390 thousand years ago.

Excavations in the Denisova cave are continuing. In 2012, a long bone belonging to a 13-year–old female was recovered from the cave. To the astonishment of the scientists, the genome of the 50 thousand year old specimen baptised Denisova 11 was found to contain equal amounts of Neanderthal and Denisovan DNA, establishing the female as being a first generation offspring of a Denisovan father and a Neanderthal mother.[10] That the population of Neanderthals to which the mother of this female belongs migrated between eastern and western Eurasia around 120 thousand years ago is borne out by the fact that she was found to be closely related to Neanderthals who lived later in Europe.

Researchers have determined using highly sophisticated dating techniques that Denisovans lived in the cave between 287,000 and 55,000 years ago and overlapped with the Neanderthals occupying the cave between 193,000 and 97,000 years ago. They also discovered that the oldest fossil occupied the cave 195,000 years ago and the youngest Denisovan fossil dated between 76,000 and 52,000 years. The DNA of the daughter of the Neanderthal and Denisovan reveals that the two met and interbred 100,000 years ago.[11]

All the above findings have led to yet another theory that proposes that Neanderthals, Denisovans and modern-day humans are all descendants from the ancient human *Homo heidelbergensis* that migrated out of Africa at different times. About 300 or 400 thousand years ago, a group migrated out of Africa, split, one group evolved to Neanderthals, the other to Denisovans. In the meantime *Homo heidelbergensis* left behind in Africa evolved to *Homo sapiens* and migrated out of Africa some 60 thousand years ago no doubt interbreeding with Neanderthals and Denisovans that they encountered en route. But both these theories appear to be rather simplistic as will be discussed later.

There is a general consensus that anatomically modern humans first emerged in Africa. There are 3 questions, however, that are still being debated based on fossil, archeological, climatic and genetic data:

- Did they first arise in east, south or north Africa?

- Which geographical routes did they take when dispersing out of Africa?
- When and how did they migrate out of Africa?[12,13]

The oldest modern human fossil to date was found in Ethiopia thereby lending support to an East African origin. Since the genetically most diverse of all human populations has been found in Southern Africa, this region has also been proposed as the origin of anatomically modern humans but alternate explanations to this finding exist. The importance of North Africa has also been recently proposed in this debate but without any conclusive proof.

There are two potential routes that anatomically modern humans could have taken, namely, the Northern route, across the Sinai Peninsula to the Levant and the Southern Route across the strait of Bab el Mandeb at the mouth of the Red Sea. The former is supported by the oldest fossils found outside Africa in the Levant – the Skhul and Qafzeh hominins — dated to 120 and 100-90 ybp (years before present). The latter route appears more probable based on mitochondrial DNA, *Short Tandem Repeat* STR and linkage disequilibrium (LD) decay analysis studies.

Both these routes are not mutually exclusive and could have been used at different times.

Two proposals dominated the discussions with regard to the timing of the dispersal. The first one posited that anatomically modern humans first migrated out of East Africa via the Southern route across the Red Sea basin around 74 – 60 kybp (thousand years before present). The second claimed that there was a much earlier dispersal around 100-130 kybp, prior to the eruption of Mount Toba in Northern Sumatra dated to 74kybp, since stone implements associated with modern humans were found in the volcanic ash. Several other findings seem to confirm the earlier dispersal, one of them being the discovery of 47 teeth in the Funyan cave in Southern China dated to 80-120 kybp. A skull belonging to *Homo sapiens* dated to 210 kybp discovered in the Apidima Cave in southern Greece has very recently been reported making it the oldest *H. sapiens* fossil found to date outside of Africa.[14] The oldest *hominin* fossils found in Africa were discovered in the north African site of Jebel Irhoud in Morocco and date back to 315 ± 34 kybp.[15]

Whole genome data from ancient DNA (aDNA) that is increasingly playing a pivotal role in all these studies has now shed more light on this topic. This ancient DNA revolution was pioneered primarily by Svante Pääbo, Director of the Max Planck Institute for Evolutionary Anthropology in Leipzig, Germany and David Reich, Professor of the Department of Genetics at Harvard Medical School and the Howard Hughes Medical Institute, Boston, USA and their teams. Scientists have succeeded in extracting and analysing the DNA of ancient skeletons from different parts of the world and compare them with each other as well as present day populations with surprising results.

In order to do that, they had to surmount several major challenges. It is known that DNA from skeletal remains can survive for hundreds of thousands of years but in very small amounts and not only isolating it is difficult but the amounts are very small and difficult to separate from other organic material. Scientists found methods to do this efficiently and also concentrate the tiny amounts.[16]

They automated the tests using robots and found ways to minimise contamination, a major problem in aDNA recovery, by using clean rooms adapted from the IT chips manufacturing industry.

Ancient DNA recovery in the past was concentrated in Europe because the skeletons are better preserved in colder climates. Scientists discovered that DNA density of the Cochlea, our inner ear hearing organ, located in the petrous bone, has a very high DNA density and thus analysing DNA from ancient bones from warmer countries became possible.

Based on genome-wide data of four very different hominin populations namely modern humans, Neanderthals, Siberian Denisovans, Australo-Denisovans i.e., ancestors of Siberian Denosivans who separated from the Denisovan population and that interbred with new Guineans, as well as the extinct population of the 100 to 90 thousand years old small humans — named „hobbits" — of the Flores Island in Indonesia and evidence for an archaic human population that separated from modern humans, Neanderthals and Denisovans well before they separated from each other, David Reich proposes that there were at least four Out of Africa migrations:
- Prior to 1.8 million years ago, a first migration of humans from Africa to Eurasia
- About 1.4 million to 900'000 years ago, a second migration from Africa to Eurasia giving rise to a superarchaic human lineage

- After 770'000 to 555'000 years ago, a third migration from Africa to Eurasia giving rise to the ancestors of the Neanderthals and Denisovans
- About 50'000 years ago, a fourth migration out of Africa of modern humans, the one that is discussed the most today.

David Reich also suggests an alternative possibility that instead of the third migration out of Africa mentioned above, it is possible that about 300'000 years ago, ancestors of modern humans returned to Africa before migrating again out of Africa 50'000 years ago corresponding to the fourth migration.

In 2013, fossil skeletons were discovered in the Gauteng province of South Africa in a chamber of the Rising Star Cave system. This new species dated to more than 250 thousand years ago was named *Homo naledi* and researchers believe that it is an extinct branch of modern day humans.[17] In the year 2019, Florent Détroit *et al.* reported the discovery of a new species of *Homo* after analysing bones and teeth found in 2007 in Callao Cave in Northern Luzon, the Philippines, dated to 67 thousand years ago.[18] They named this new hominin species *Homo luzonensis*. Thus, we have so far encountered several branches of ancient hominins and modern day humans that have become extinct and only modern day humans have survived. As more ancient DNA is discovered, particularly in Africa, more surprises will no doubt emerge needing an adaptation of the above description.

What are the causes that led to the extinction of these different hominin species? There are several explanations that can be put forward. One of them is connected to natural calamities such as the volcanic super eruption of Mount Toba in Sumatra that occurred about 75 thousand years ago destroying everything in its wake and leading to a volcanic winter that lasted for at least a decade and caused the earth to cool for a minimum of a thousand years. The hominins in Africa were less affected by the Toba eruption and would have survived whereas those in Eurasia would all be annihilated.

Another cause could be the low fertility of hybrids as first proposed by Laurent Excoffier from studies of animals and plants. Sriram Sankararaman, a scientist in David Reich's team found a removal of Neanderthal ancestry by natural selection in two parts of the genome relevant to the fertility of hybrids including the sex chromosome X.[19] Thus, the hybridisation of Neanderthals with modern day humans may have been a major cause for their extinction as a result of low fertility.

There are existential reasons that compelled our African ancestors to migrate. Curtis W. Marean vividly describes[20] how around 195'000 years ago, a long glacial stage made much of the landmass uninhabitable and nearly extinguished the human species.

The few remaining survivors, thanks to whom we now exist, succeeded in surviving on shellfish and edible plants living in caves on the southern coast of Africa. Their descendants migrated out of Africa 70'000 years ago. These were the so-called coastal people, who in their quest for survival defied the elements to populate the world.

There have been at least five major ice ages in the Earth's history namely the Huronian, Cryogenian, Andean-Saharan, Karoo Ice Age, and the Quaternary Ice Age; the one of interest to our discussion in this book is the current Quaternary Ice Age because it is the one that has enormously influenced and shaped humanity's migration patterns.

Beginning 2.58 million years ago, during the quaternary glaciation, ice sheets expanded out of Antartica and Greenland causing dramatic changes such as land erosion, modification of rivers, creation of millions of lakes, abnormal winds and big changes in sea levels. There were periodic fluctuations of the total amount of land ice, sea levels and global temperatures. During the glacials, Europe, North America and Siberia were covered with ice sheets. The glacials were intermingled with warmer spells or interglacials. The fluctuation initially occurred every 41 thousand years but it slowed down to 100 thousand years.

The earth saw a warm period from about 70 thousand to 30 thousand years ago before returning to colder conditions with the Last Glacial Maximum or LGM.

The Last Glacial Maximum occurred 27 thousand to 19 thousand years ago, followed by a warmer and moister interglacial period about 14500 years ago. A few thousand years later, the earth was plunged into a sudden but short-lived ice age known as the Younger Dryas. This cold period ended about 1300 years later giving way to a warmer climate that we experience till today.

These extreme climatic conditions had a profound effect on the size of human populations as modelling studies indicate. A team of scientists from Finland has shown that the simulated range and size of the human population correspond significantly with spatiotemporal patterns in the archaeological data, suggesting that climate was a major driver of population dynamics 30–13 ky ago (ky is short for thousand years).

In Europe, the simulated population size declined from about 330,000 people at 30 thousand years ago to a minimum of 130,000 people at 23 thousand years ago. By 13 thousand years ago, there were almost 410,000 people in Europe. Even during the coldest part of the LGM, the climatically suitable area for human habitation remained unfragmented and covered 36% of Europe.[21] This simulation thus shows that the population size was dramatically reduced with the onset of the last Glacial Maximum and increased in an equally dramatic fashion after the Younger Dryas with the advent of more temperate climatic conditions. The only way for humanity to survive the harsh climatic conditions was to migrate to refugia for as long as these conditions persisted losing a very sizable number of individuals in the process.

A century and a half ago, around the time DNA had barely been discovered and its role in life completely unknown, in his book "The Origin of Species" first published in 1859, Charles Darwin provided evidence that plants and animals, including man, evolved from earlier more primitive forms by slow transformation.

This evolution, he noted, is a necessary pre-requisite for survival thus setting the scene for the "Out of Africa" theory. Darwin proposed, "probably all organic beings which have ever lived on this earth have descended from some one primordial form, into which life was first breathed".[22] Darwin is more explicit in *The Descent of Man and Selection in Relation to Sex* published in 1883 with his statement "all point in the plainest manner to the conclusion that man is a co-descendant with other mammals of a common progenitor".

For billions of years, life on earth consisted of unicellular organisms that could replicate themselves, a process that involves the correct orientation of the mitotic spindle. Using a technique called ancestral protein reconstruction, scientists studied how the ability to position the spindle evolved over time, going back into the deep past. The scientists found that hundreds of millions of years ago, a mutation that involved a single amino acid transformed an enzyme that facilitates reactions inside the cell into a protein that could communicate and interact with other proteins of other cells. This single change allowed unicellular organisms to evolve into the complex multicellular organisms that we are today.[23,24] This could be the primordial form that Darwin was alluding to.

Current pioneering research in genetics seems to confirm, if confirmation is still needed, Darwin's genius and gives credence to his theory of a common progenitor.

Having thus evolved from a unicellular organism, it is not surprising that all living cells share their DNA.

All living organisms are made up of cells and all cells contain DNA whether a banana, cabbage, chimpanzee or humans. Thus, humans share DNA with a banana or cabbage to the extent of about 50%. Cat-lovers will be happy to know that they have 90% of their genes in common with their pets and the genetic similarity between a human and a cow is about 80%. The genetic difference between humans and a bonobo or chimpanzee is just 1.2% making them our closest cousins in the world. It is even more interesting that the genetic difference between one human and another is just 0.1% on an average.[25] Since a human genome consists of about 3 billion base pairs, that difference of 0.1% amounts to about 3 million base pairs that contain a massive amount of information.

The analysis of any human DNA, in any event, including mine, traces its origin to an African common male ancestor that migrated from Africa thousands of years ago.

Many readers are discouraged with a discussion of the chemistry of DNA and it may dissuade them from continuing to read this and possibly some other chapters of this book but an understanding of the concept can be greatly facilitated by using the building of a wall as an analogy as discussed below.

Any tourist to the beautiful city of Amsterdam cannot fail to admire the slim, tall and colourful canal houses that other than their colour display very similar architecture. A Dutch colleague recounted to me that the houses were once painted in the same colour and there is a reason why this was changed. The Dutch are very hard working and also very sociable, therefore after investing a lot of effort in their work during the week, they relaxed on weekends by visiting the many restaurants and pubs located along the canal and returned home quite inebriated. At a time when the doors of the houses were never locked, they mistook a neighbour's house for their own and ended the night sleeping in someone else's bed next to someone else's wife.

This led to a lot of acrimony until it was decided to get the houses painted in different colours because even a drunk can remember a colour, in any event sufficiently to identify his home. An added advantage is that the colourful buildings have become a big tourist attraction.

Let us assume that the Ministry of Tourism of a country having witnessed the attraction that Amsterdam's canal houses command over tourists, decides to promote tourism in its own country by using a similar strategy. In order to encourage the people to construct colourful houses, it decides to offer bricks in the colours Amethyst (A), Turquoise (T), Crimson (C) and Green (G) at highly subsidised rates. The only condition is that the bricks are to be chosen at random so that the walls would be very colourful. The project was hugely successful and we could now see walls with different brick arrangements e.g.

ATGCATGCATGCATGCAATTGC
GACTAGCTGCTTTCCAGTGTAA
CGTAGCCTTAACGATGTCAACT

And so on and on in all possible combinations, the country saw very colourful buildings and no two were identical.

Inevitably, there was work involved in hauling, lifting and positioning the bricks. And cement was also required to hold the bricks in place when placing them next to, below or above each other and insulate the joints between the bricks.

This is exactly the way our DNA functions. All we have to do is replace the colours Amethyst, Turquoise, Crimson and Green with the chemicals *Adenine*, *Thymine*, *Cytosine* and *Guanine* that are also called a base. The "cement" and "work" are provided by the sugar *deoxyribose* and phosphate that attach themselves to these chemicals. In a wall, bricks have to be attached to one another to form a long chain. Similarly, in DNA, the *deoxyribose* and phosphate bond themselves with one of the bases A, T, C or G to form a *nucleotide*, the basic brick or building block of nucleic acids. Even though a *nucleotide* contains one of the bases, *deoxyribose* and phosphate, it is generally shortened for simplicity to the letters A, T, C. or G. The sugar *deoxyribose* of one nucleotide bonds itself with the phosphate group of an adjacent nucleotide and forms the sugar-phosphate backbone composed of alternating sugar and phosphate groups. This backbone is responsible for the directionality. Two linear sugar-phosphate backbones run opposite each other and twist themselves to form the double helix structure of DNA.

The structure of a cell, that as we have seen earlier is so crucial to our existence, is complex but all we need to retain for our discussion is the fact that DNA is found in our cells: in small amounts in the **mitochondria** of the cell as well as in the nucleus, tightly packaged in **chromosomes**.

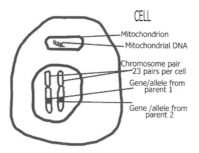

Image 1: Location of chromosomes in a cell

The total amount of genetic information in a cell that is contained in the approximately 25 thousand **genes** that we possess is stored in these chromosomes. This total complement of genes is called a **genome**. A genome is thus the instruction manual that contains genetic information in about 3 billion bases and 25 thousand genes. The DNA contained in the genes contains the instructions for an organism to develop, survive and reproduce. It is this instruction manual that ensures that humans can only produce human babies and elephants can only produce baby elephants.

A chromosome is made up of a single DNA helix on which these genes are located. Humans have **23 pairs of chromosomes**, one from each parent with a total of **46**.

The number of chromosomes is specific to a species; for example, cats and lions have 38 chromosomes and a mouse has 40.

These 23 pairs of human chromosomes are numbered from 1 to 23 according to the amount of information each pair contains. Chromosome 1 is the largest and is over three times bigger than chromosome

22; chromosome 23 contains the smallest amount of genetic information.[26]

When a child is conceived, both the mother and the father contribute equally towards the chromosomes of the offspring. A set of chromosomes containing only one member of each chromosome pair is denoted as a **haploid.**

Thus, the sperm and egg are haploid. Of the 23 pairs of chromosomes that humans possess, 22 pairs are essentially identical, one originating from the mother and the other from the father as already mentioned, and are called **autosomes**. The 23rd pair differs from the rest: females possess two similar chromosomes called "X" whereas in males they are dissimilar with one being an "**X**" and the other a "**Y**". Only males have a XY chromosome: thus, if the father's contribution is an "X" the offspring will be a girl and if it is a "Y," it will be a boy. By tracing the history of an individual's Y-chromosome, male heredity can be elucidated since the Y chromosome can only be passed on from father to son.

The location of a gene on a chromosome is called its **locus.** Each locus of a gene on a chromosome contains one **allele**; alleles are different versions of the same gene, they are sequences that code for a gene, for example ATCGAATCCCGC. Humans have two alleles at each genetic locus, with one allele inherited from each parent.

An individual's unique genome, the complete genetic identity that the person has inherited is called a **genotype**. For example, we inherit the HERC2 and OCA2 genes, which are next to each other on chromosome 15 that play a major role in determining eye colour.[27,28,29]

An individual's **phenotype**, on the other hand, describes the actual physical traits of that person, for example eye or skin colour or height or our pre-dispositions to certain illnesses, our likes and dislikes and so on. Our phenotype results partly from our genotype — inherited from nature — but also by our environment and other circumstances that have influenced our life — acquired by nurture.

A *Single Nucleotide Polymorphism* **SNP** is a rare mutation — another word for polymorphism — that occurs at the rate of approximately one mutation every few hundred generations. As the description indicates, in such a case, a single base A, T, C or G in the genome sequence is replaced or substituted by another. For example, in the following sequence

ATGG**C**ATC

if the fourth base **C** of the sequence would be replaced by **G** to form
ATG**GA**TC

we would have a SNP at that specific position or locus. The two variants C or G are alleles for this position. The nucleotide C would appear in most populations but a minority would have this single mutated SNP.

The base C could also be replaced by any of the other bases thereby
producing different versions of the same sequence.

A SNP marks a branch in the **Y chromosome phylogenetic tree**.
Pronounced "snips," they are very valuable to trace **ancient or deep
ancestry** because as mentioned earlier, a mutation or polymorphism
of this type occurs only once every few hundred generations and is
inherited by the descendants of the individual in whom this mutation
first occurred.

A human genome contains 4 to 5 million SNPs and these mutations
may be unique affecting just one individual or they may affect many.
Not all single nucleotide substitutions are therefore classified as
SNP's; for this purpose, two or more versions of the SNP must each
be present in at least one percent of the general population.[30]

Some SNPs are associated with a disease leading scientists to
study these SNPs to discover ways of treating it, something that is already happening at the present time. Today, it is possible to modify a
genome by incorporating a gene from one species into a different one
through genetic engineering.

That specific traits in plants and animals can be enhanced by cross-
breeding is known since the Moravian monk Gregor Johann Mendel
published the results of his experiments on pea plants in the nine-
teenth century that later became known as Mendel's Principles of
Heredity. These principles have been widely applied to for example
augment milk production by interbreeding different breeds of cows in
Switzerland to maximise the quantity and quality of milk produced per
animal. It is interesting to note that pure local Swiss breeds have practically disappeared and been replaced by local breeds cross-bred with
the Canadian Holstein cows.

In addition to naturally induced genetic variation as the one mentioned above, nature has also provided us with naturally occurring genetic engineering: the sweet potato that is in fact a root and not relat-

ed to the potato. Researchers of the University of Ghent discovered that the plant pathogenic bacteria *Agrobacterium rhizogenes* and *Agrobacterium tumefaciens* have the ability to transfer their DNA fragments into the host plant genome. They discovered that all the cultivated sweet potato samples they analysed contained *Agrobacterium* DNA fragments in their genome and that this naturally occurring genetic modification occurred in evolutionary times.[31]

In the agricultural sector, plums have been made virus-resistant and corn rendered insect-resistant through genetic modification.

In 2018, FDA approved a new drug, the first of its kind, introduced by the pharmaceutical company Novartis, known as CAR-T therapy, intended for use in patients afflicted with a specific type of childhood leukaemia known as ALL, in whom chemotherapy and radiation have failed. ALL has a very low survival rate since less than ten percent of the patients survive for up to 5 years. In this treatment, the patients T-cells (certain type of white blood cells) are extracted from the patient and their genetic code modified by inserting a special receptor called a CAR, an acronym for *chimeric antigen receptor*, that has the ability to attack and destroy the cancer cells. The modified T-cells are now multiplied in a laboratory and the re-engineered T-cells finally re-introduced into the patient. The therapy is highly customised for a specific patient, production of the modified T-cells is complex, the therapy requires close monitoring because of the possibility of severe side effects and the whole process takes more than 3 weeks, all of which explains its very high cost. But there is a big race now to produce similar therapies that will no doubt make it more financially accessible to the general public as time goes by.

Teams of researchers that include virologists, immunologists, molecular biologists, pharmacologists, and pharmaceutical experts from the Lewis Katz School of Medicine at Temple University and the University of Nebraska Medical Center (UNMC) announced in a paper published on July 2, 2019, in *Nature Communications* that the virus responsible for AIDS had for the first time been eliminated from the genomes of living animals. HIV in infected patients is kept from replicating by the lifelong use of antiretroviral therapy ART; if the therapy is discontinued, the virus that lies dormant rebounds. The researchers developed a novel therapy called long-acting slow-effective release (LASER) ART delivered in nano-crystals followed sequentially by a new CRISPR-Cas9 gene-editing technology to cut out large fragments of HIV DNA from infected cells. CRISPR is an acronym for *clustered regularly interspaced short palindromic repeats* and Cas9 *CRISPR-associated protein 9* enzyme; together with *guide RNA*, it can be programmed to target any DNA sequence for cleavage and removal. Using this strategy, they found that HIV DNA had been completely eliminated in about one-third of the HIV-infected mice used for the experiment. Trials in non-human primates will now follow and if successful, clinical trials in human patients and hopefully a complete cure of AIDS will be the next step.[32]

In a daring experiment that has invited universal condemnation, a team led by Chinese scientist He Jiankui at the Southern University of Science and Technology, in Shenzhen, China, used the CRISPR technique to genetically modify human embryos in a laboratory and then transfer them into women's uteruses. Humans carry two copies of the CCR5 gene and it is well known that if both these copies are deleterious, it imparts a high resistance to HIV. Jiankui and his team deleted the gene CCR5, located on the short (p) arm at position 21 on chromosome 3, in hopes of rendering the offspring resistant to HIV, smallpox, and cholera. The gene-edited twin babies are known to have been born.

Even though the addition of such a powerful new method to eradicate disease is to be welcomed and should in principle be allowed, this approach is fraught with danger because it could lead to the creation of designer babies or unintended consequences of gene modifications which is why the method is strictly prohibited world-wide, including in China. On December 30, 2019, the Shenzhen Nanshan District People's Court sentenced He Jiankui to three years behind bars and a 3 million yuan ($430,000) fine, China's state-run news agency Xinhua reported. In a study published in June 2019, Xinzhu Wei and Rasmus Nielsen could demonstrate that deleterious CCR5 genes lead to a 21 percent increased risk of early mortality.[33] The protein made by CCR5 has a highly significant influence on the immune system and altering it therefore affects our immune system and mortality rate. It is very rare that a gene has only one single effect, altering it can therefore be beneficial on one count but cause other unintended negative impacts, as in this case. This is also an example where gene-editing science has progressed much more and faster than legislation that is urgently needed to regulate it.

Genetics is also being now applied to resolve what I would call medical cold cases, diseases for which the medical profession has not been successful in identifying the culprit causing it.

Deborah Balz from Switzerland realised from the time she was a child that her arms and legs were weak and that exercise brought her relief.[34]

As a primary school teacher, she bicycled to school, trained as a marathon runner and won several races. But very soon, it became apparent to her that she could no longer continue in the profession she loved because her voice muscles started failing, she therefore moved to a new job where she could sit longer. Since the new position involved night shifts, she could no longer practice sport as before and her health deteriorated rapidly. She lost her job and became wheelchair-bound.

The numerous doctors and clinics she consulted could not find a cause for her sickness and finally attributed it to psychological distress, panic attacks and other psyche-related afflictions. This diagnosis had financial consequences because under these circumstances she did not qualify for financial support from the invalidity insurance. Deborah Balz claims it was inspirational when one day she woke up and suddenly felt that the cause of her problems must be genetic. A Google search led her to the Genetikzentrum in Schlieren, Canton Zurich.

After studying her case history, the doctors collected her saliva for DNA extraction, along with that of her parents. In a first step, her DNA was extracted, the cell was enzymatically destroyed, the negatively charged DNA captured using magnetic batons and treated with a drop of pure DNA in a test tube. This was followed by sequencing i.e., the DNA alphabet is read using special equipment. This generates about 150 to 200 Gigabytes of data that is saved. Finally, this data was analysed by a computer that compared this data with a reference DNA and identified the differences between the two that amount to about 3 million mutations in an individual. Interpretation software combed through these mutations and identified between 100 and 1000 that could be responsible for the disease.

This is where the role of the computer ends. Specialists now had to painstakingly analyse each of these mutations, compare them with those of her parents and other known cases, a process that took 4 years until the culprit was finally discovered. Deborah Balz had mutations in the gene CLCN1, an autosomal recessive form of *Myotonia Congenita* (Becker Type). With this disease, patients can relax their muscles only with great difficulty, especially if they are not warmed up. With treatment, today Deborah Balz still needs crutches to move around but is no longer wheel-chair bound.

Increasingly, genetics will be playing an important role in medical diagnosis and it is not a surprise that pharmaceutical companies are investing billions of dollars in this area.

Another term that the reader will encounter frequently in this book is *Short Tandem Repeat* **STR,** also known as microsatellites. They are short sequences of DNA normally consisting of two to five base pairs repeated in tandem.

For example AGCT repeated 18 times gives a marker value or allele of 18. A STR occurs more frequently than SNP and is therefore indicative of **recent ancestry.** For the Y chromosome, STR is used synonymously with DYS, which is simply a different way of describing the same phenomenon wherein D stands for DNA, Y for the Y chromosome and S for Segment i.e., the segment of the Y chromosome where this repeated pattern appears. STRs are used extensively in forensic science and paternity testing.

A **haplotype,** a word derived from haploid genotype — we recall, that haploid refers to only one member of the set of chromosomes in a chromosome pair — is the combination of DNA sequences or alleles at different loci on the chromosome that has been transmitted together to an individual. For example, my Y DNA test results are my haplotype because these tests analyse my alleles at specific loci or markers on only one member i.e., Y-chromosome in the XY chromosome pair. Individuals that match exactly on all markers have the same haplotype.

The following example shows the difference between genotype and haplotype:

Locus 1 - 5 / SNP 1-5 / for 1 individual
Haplotype 1 : A   C   A   G   C
Haplotype 2 : G   C   G   T   A
Genotype   : AG CC AG GT CA

1.1 Haplogroups (Hg)

Now that we are acquainted with some important definitions, we can turn our attention to the meaning and importance of haplogroups.

Family Tree DNA defines a haplogroup as "a major branch on either the maternal or paternal tree of humankind. Haplogroups are associated with early human migrations. Today these can be associated with a geographic region or regions".[35]

1.1.1 Y-Chromosome DNA Haplogroups

are determined by analysing the SNPs of a male individual's Y chromosome located on chromosome 23. When SNPs are identified that are found in more than one percent of the population, they are grouped together in the same haplogroup. All those belonging to the same haplogroup share a common ancestor who was the first male individual in whom that specific *single nucleotide polymorphism* or mutation occurred and who transmitted it to future generations of his descendants.

A haplogroup is associated with the alleles on different loci or positions of the chromosomes transmitted to an individual i.e., it consists of similar haplotypes, it is possible to infer or predict a haplogroup with 99 percent certainty from the haplotype but a SNP test is required to confirm the prediction.

During the course of their long migration out of Africa to inhabit all parts of the world, our ancestors moved in groups at a different pace and choosing different routes leading them to acquire differing traits caused by mutations or small changes in their chromosomes that are then transmitted from father to son; these mutations may have been random (genetic drift) or the result of evolutionary requirements or natural selection needed to enhance their chances of survival as postulated by Darwin's theory of natural selection. For example, the original black colour of the skin lightened as a result of genetic mutations accompanying migrations towards the North, a region where the amount of sunlight decreases. By reducing the amount of skin pigmentation, the skin can absorb more UV radiation that is necessary for the synthesis of the very important Vitamin D from the cholesterol in the skin when it is exposed to sunlight.

Population geneticists study these mutations and are in this manner able to trace the genetic ancestry or tree. This in turn enables us to explore the historic migration patterns of our ancestors.

The Y chromosome consortium YCC introduced a **nomenclature** naming major haplogroup branches with capital letters A through T with each Hg originating from a preceding one. Thus, Hg B originated from A and Hg C from B and so on. Since additional mutations occurred in each of these branches, the sub-groups were attributed numbers and lower case letters. For example, J2b2 designates haplogroup J that has undergone further mutations leading to the sub-groups J1 and J2 and J2 has mutated further leading to the branch J2b that again underwent additional changes starting the sub-group J2b2. A haplogroup is also commonly referred to as a clade and a sub-group a sub-clade. With the ever expanding number of individuals testing their DNA and the greatly increased analytical depth, the number of SNPs being discovered has increased exponentially leading to nomenclatures such as, for example, R1a1a1b1a2b3a that are very cumbersome, confusing and sometimes inconsistent. For this reason, *Family Tree DNA* has introduced a shorthand version that lists the main branch followed by a dash and the terminal SNP i.e., the last SNP identified at the level of testing. In our example, Hg R1a1a1b1a2b3a can now be described as R-L365 in the shorthand version. If a more detailed test is carried out, it is possible that a more down stream terminal SNP is identified; it is therefore useful to mention the level of testing that has been carried out when describing a person's haplogroup in the shorthand version. Once we have the main branch and the terminal SNP, it is easy to trace the lineage starting from Hg A if one so wishes by consulting the **ISOGG Y Haplogroup tree** that includes abbreviations.[36,37]

In the above example, a search in Y Full for L365 gives the following information:

R-L365 YP242/FGC19227 * L365/S468 * YP241/FGC19226+6 SNPs formed 2700 ybp, TMRCA 2100 ybp

where the different mutations leading to the classification are mentioned as well as the TMRCA, an abbreviation for Time to Most Recent Common Ancestor. For definitions of abbreviations in Y Full cf.[38]

1.1.2 Mitochodrial DNA (mtDNA) Haplogroups

Modern humans descend from Mitochondrial Eve, the first female who stands at the beginning of humankind and from whom we have inherited our mitochondrial DNA along with all the subsequent mutations.

Only females can pass on their mitochondria to their children because the egg contains their mitochondria but the male sperm does not. Thus we all inherit the mitochondrial DNA of our mothers because males due to the absence of mitochondria in their sperm cannot transmit it further, only females can.

MtDNA consists of 16569 SNPs divided into the control region and the coding region, the part of the mtDNA genome that contains the genes. The control region, also called the hypervariable region i.e. the fast changing region, is further divided into two regions:
- Hypervariable Region 1 HVR1 from nucleotide 16001 to 16569 and
- Hypervariable Region 2 HVR2 from nucleotide 00001 to 00574

The coding region runs from nucleotide 00575 to 16000.

In the coding region, mtDNA mutates very slowly at about one mutation every 10 to 12 thousand years at any specific locus or position. It therefore gives us very useful information on our matrilineal ancestry including the migration patterns.

As in the case of Y DNA, mtDNA haplogroups run from A to Z in the order of their discovery. More details on my mtDNA haplogroup and its significance is discussed in Part I, Chapter 5.

2. The Patrilineal Trail: From Africa to the Fertile Crescent

As discussed earlier, there is increasing evidence that anatomically modern humans migrated out of Africa in several waves using mainly two dispersal routes namely via the Nile Valley and Sinai (Northern route) or Bab al Mandab strait (Southern route).

Modern humans started to leave Africa between 50'000 and 70'000 years ago. They travelled in groups, choosing different routes and arriving at different destinations. These migrations can be traced back by analysing the "markers" or mutations left behind in the human phylogenetic tree. Based on these markers, every individual can be assigned to a specific haplogroup that is a branch of the phylogenetic tree.

What is a **marker**? A genetic marker is a gene or DNA sequence with a known location on a chromosome that can be used to identify individuals or species. Each of us carries DNA that is a combination of genes passed from both our mother and father, giving us traits that range from eye color and height to athleticism and disease susceptibility. As part of this process, the Y-chromosome is passed directly from father to son, unchanged, from generation to generation down a purely male line. As mentioned before, Mitochondrial DNA, on the other hand, is passed from mothers to their children, but only their daughters pass it on to the next generation. It traces an exclusively maternal line.

As we have also seen earlier, the sex-determining chromosome pair number 23 in a male consists of a Y and an X chromosome, the Y being passed down the patrilineal line from father to son to grandson.

A comparison of the markers for exact matches between two or more individuals can give an indication of how many generations ago these individuals shared their most recent common ancestor i.e., the Time to the Most Recent Common Ancestor **TMRCA**, by calculating the assumed rates of mutation associated with the specific chromosome.

The test results normally include the identification of the **haplogroup**. The basic haplogroup determination does not always suffice to trace the migratory path of one's ancestors with acceptable precision and therefore, a **deep clade testing** is carried out in which the sub-clade to which one's haplogroup belongs is determined with greater precision. For more detailed information cf.[39,40,41,42,43]

The DNA is passed on unchanged, unless a mutation—a random, naturally occurring, usually harmless change—occurs. The mutation, known as a marker, acts as a beacon; it can be mapped through generations because it will be passed down for thousands of years.

When geneticists identify such a marker, they try to determine when it first occurred, and in which geographic region of the world. Each marker is essentially the beginning of a new lineage on the family tree of the human race. Tracking the lineages provides a picture of how small tribes of modern humans in Africa tens of thousands of years ago diversified and spread to populate the world.

By looking at the markers we carry, we can trace our lineage, ancestor by ancestor, to reveal the path they traveled as they moved out of Africa.

There are numerous laboratories that carry out tests on Y DNA at different depth levels. In my case the following tests have been carried out:

The Genographic Project: Y DNA 12 markers

Family Tree DNA: Y DNA 37 markers
Y DNA 111 markers
Deep Clade - J
J2 - M172 SNP Pack
Big Y-700

The 12-marker test by The Genographic Project determined my haplogroup to be **J-M172** starting with the marker P305 and ending with M172:

P305   M42   M168   P143   M89   M578   M304 M172

2.1 The Origin and Age of Y Haplogroup J and its Subclades

The many conflicting reports on the different aspects of genetic genealogy notwithstanding, a remarkable consensus emerges that haplogroup J originated in the Fertile Crescent.

To quote from the International Society of Genetic Genealogy ISOGG, this haplogroup "evolved in the ancient Near East and was carried into North Africa, Europe, Central Asia, Pakistan and India. J-M172 (in YCC nomenclature: J2) lineages originated in the area known as the Fertile Crescent."

The Fertile Crescent that gets its name from its very rich soil and crescent shape, incorporates the Levant (Eastern Mediterranean) as well as Mesopotamia (the Tigris-Euphrates region) that is considered to be the cradle of civilization and includes present day Iraq, Syria, Lebanon, Israel, Kuwait, Jordan, Southeastern Turkey and West and Southwest Iran.

Haplogroup J is further subdivided into subclades J1, J2 that are further subdivided into many additional subclades e.g. in the case of J2 we have J2a, J2b, J2a1 and so on.

Most experts agree that haplogroup J arose 25 to 30,000 years ago. Semino *et al.* who have studied the origin, diffusion and differentiation of Y-chromosome haplogroups E and J provide an estimate of the age of both these haplogroups as well as their subclades.[44]

Sengupta *et al.*[45] found that J2 is nearly absent among Indian tribals; in fact, only the Lodha tribals, who are Austro-Asiatic speakers, show a predominant J2b2 occurrence. The frequency of the J2 clade in Pakistan is about 12% and similar in both Dravidian and Indo-European castes whereas in India, it is significantly higher in the Dravidian (19%) than among Indo-European castes. This in itself is indicative of the northwest entry into India and further migration towards the south and east. The authors relate Haplogroup J2a-M410 and J2b-M12 with an exogenous origin i.e., exogenous to India and link it to the Indus Valley.

Sahoo et al.[46] who have studied regional distributions found that the haplogroup J2 is more pronounced in Northwest India. Their findings are "consistent with an influx of a subset of J2 lineages to India from the Near East, followed by their subsequent diffusion from India's northwest toward the south and east".

It is of interest to note that both the Sumerians as well as Israelites have been linked to Y haplogroup J2 including the traditional Kohanim families.

The following description of the migration of my ancestors out of Africa starting with the marker P305 (A1) and ending with M172 (J2) is largely taken from the report of the results of my Y DNA 12 marker test by the Genographic Project corresponding to Y DNA haplogroup J2 according to the following sequence:

P305 (A1) —> M42 (BT) —> M168 (CT) —> P143 (CF) —> M89 (F) —> M578 (HIJK) —> M304 (J) —> M172 (J2)

P305
Age: More than 100,000 years old
Location of Origin: Africa

The common direct paternal ancestor of all men alive today was born in Africa between 300,000 and 150,000 years ago. Dubbed "Y-chromosome Adam" by the popular press, he was neither the first human male nor the only man alive in his time. He was, though, the only male whose Y-chromosome lineage is still around today. All men, including your direct paternal ancestors, trace their ancestry to one of this man's descendants. The oldest Y-chromosome lineages in existence, belonging to the A00 branch of the tree, are found only in African populations.

Around 100,000 years ago the **mutation** named P305 occurred in the Y chromosome of a man in Africa. This is one of the oldest known mutations that is not shared by all men. Therefore, it marks one of the early splits in the human Y-chromosome tree, which itself marks one of the earliest branching points in modern human evolution. The man who first carried this mutation lived in Africa and is the ancestor to more than 99.9% of paternal lineages today. In fact, men who do not carry this mutation are so rare that its importance in human history was discovered only in the past two years.

As P305-bearing populations migrated around the globe, they picked up additional markers on their Y chromosomes. Today, there are no known P305-bearing individuals without these additional markers.

Branch: M42
Age: About 80,000 Years Ago
Location of Origin: East Africa
Around 80,000 years ago, the BT branch of the Y-chromosome tree was born, defined by many genetic markers, including M42. The common ancestor of most men living today, some of this man's descendants would begin the journey out of Africa to the Middle East and India. Some small groups from this line would eventually reach the Americas, while other groups would settle in Europe, and some would remain near their ancestral homeland in Africa.

Individuals from this line whose ancestors stayed in Africa often practice cultural traditions that resemble those of the distant past. For example, they often live in traditional hunter-gatherer societies. These include the Mbuti and Biaka Pygmies of central Africa, as well as Tanzania's Hadza.

Branch: M168
Age: About 70,000 years ago
Location of Origin: East Africa
When humans left Africa, they migrated across the globe in a web of paths that spread out like the branches of a tree, each limb of migration identifiable by a marker in our **DNA**. For male lineages, the M168 branch was one of the first to leave the African homeland.

The man who gave rise to the first **genetic marker** in my lineage probably lived in northeast Africa in the region of the Rift Valley, perhaps in present-day Ethiopia, Kenya, or Tanzania. Scientists put the most likely date for when he lived at around 70,000 years ago. His descendants became the only lineage to survive outside of Africa, making him the common ancestor of every non-African man living today.

My nomadic ancestors would have followed the good weather and the animals they hunted, although the exact route they followed remains to be determined. In addition to a favourable change in climate, around this same time there was a great leap forward in modern humans' intellectual capacity. Many scientists believe that the emergence of language gave us a huge advantage over other early humanlike species. Improved tools and weapons, the ability to plan ahead and cooperate with one another, and an increased capacity to exploit resources in ways we hadn't been able to earlier allowed modern humans to rapidly migrate to new territories, exploit new resources, and replace other hominids such as the Neanderthals.

Branch: P143
Age: About 60,000 years old
Location of Origin: Southwest Asia

This mutation is one of the oldest thought to have occurred outside of Africa and therefore marks a pivotal moment in the evolution of modern humans. Moving along the coastline, members of this lineage were some of the earliest settlers in Asia, Southeast Asia, and Australia.

But why would man have first ventured out of the familiar African hunting grounds and into unexplored lands? The first migrants likely ventured across the Bab-al Mandeb strait, a narrow body of water at the southern end of the Red Sea, crossing into the Arabian Peninsula and soon after developing mutation P143 — perhaps 60,000 years ago. These beachcombers would make their way rapidly to India and Southeast Asia, following the coastline in a gradual march eastward. By 50,000 years ago, they had reached Australia. These were the ancestors of some of today's Australian Aborigines.

It is also likely that a fluctuation in climate may have contributed to my ancestors' exodus out of Africa. The African ice age was characterised by drought rather than by cold. Around 50,000 years ago, though, the ice sheets of the Northern Hemisphere began to melt, introducing a short period of warmer temperatures and moister climate in Africa and the Middle East. Parts of the inhospitable Sahara briefly became habitable. As the drought-ridden desert changed to a savanna, the animals hunted by my ancestors expanded their range and began moving through the newly emerging green corridor of grasslands.

Branch: M89
Age: About 55,000 Years Old
Location of Origin: Southwest Asia

The next male ancestor in my ancestral lineage is the man who gave rise to M89, a marker found in 90 to 95 percent of all non-Africans. This man was likely born around 55,000 years ago in Middle East.

While many of the descendants of M89 remained in the Middle East, others continued to follow the great herds of wild game through what is now modern-day Iran, then north to the Caucasus and the Steppes of Central Asia. These semiarid, grass-covered plains would eventually form an ancient "superhighway" stretching from France to Korea. A smaller group continued moving north from the Middle East to Anatolia and the Balkans, trading familiar grasslands for forests and high country.

Branch: M578
Age: About 50,000 Years Old
Location of Origin: Southwest Asia

After settling in Southwest Asia for several millennia, humans began to expand in various directions, including east and south around the Indian Ocean, but also north toward Anatolia and the Black and Caspian Seas. The first man to acquire mutation M578 was among those that stayed in Southwest Asia before moving on.

Fast-forwarding to about 40,000 years ago, the climate shifted once again and became colder and more arid. Drought hit Africa and the Middle East and the grasslands reverted to desert, and for the next 20,000 years, the Saharan Gateway was effectively closed. With the desert impassable, my ancestors had two options: remain in the Middle East, or move on. Retreat back to the home continent was not an option.

Branch: M304
Age: 18,900 – 44,500 Years Ago
Location of Origin: South Asia or West Asia

Geneticists have found this branch and its descendant lineages in North Africa, where it is 69 percent of male lineages in Tunisia, about 30 percent of male lineages in Egypt, and about 27 percent of male lineages in Sudan. In South Asia, it is 29 percent of male lineages in Pakistan, around 14 percent of male lineages in India, and about 19 percent of male lineages in Sri Lanka.

In Europe, this lineage is most common in Italy (30 percent), Spain (20 percent), and Portugal (18 percent).

Today, descendants of this line appear in the highest frequencies in the Middle East, North Africa, and Ethiopia, and at a much lower frequency in Europe, where it is observed exclusively in the Mediterranean area. Approximately 20 percent of the males in southern Italy carry the marker, along with 10 percent of men in southern Spain.

Branch: M172 (Haplogroup J2)
Age: 15,000 – 22,000 Years Ago
Location of Origin: West Asia

The earliest members of this lineage were nomadic hunter-gatherers who weathered the last glacial maximum in the comparatively mild climate of West Asia. As the Earth warmed, groups containing this lineage were positioned ideally for participation in the Neolithic Revolution in the Fertile Crescent of the Middle East. They thrived in the emerging agricultural societies and expanded into new lands, carrying farming technology with them.

This branch is a major lineage, and it has many descendants. Today, people from this lineage live as far east as China (1 to 2 percent) and as far west as Ireland (2 to 3 percent) and Spain (10 to 11 percent). Geneticists have found the highest frequencies in Bahrain and Iran, where it is over 33 percent of male lineages.

Today, descendants of this line appear in the highest frequencies in the Middle East, North Africa, and Ethiopia, and at a much lower frequency in Europe, where it is observed exclusively in the Mediterranean area. Approximately 20 percent of the males in southern Italy carry the marker, along with ten percent of men in southern Spain.

The following table shows the times when the markers discussed above were formed as well as the Time to the Most Recent Common Ancestor TMRCA as determined by YFull.

Branch	Formed ybp	TMRCA ybp
P305 (A1)	161300	133400
M42 (BT)	130700	88000
M168 (CT)	88000	68500
P143 (CF)	68500	65900
M89 (F)	65900	48800
M578 (HIJK)	48500	48500
M304 (J)	42900	31600
M172 (J2)	31600	27900

Table 1: Branches and TMRCA for the migration from Africa to the Fertile Crescent

The formed and TMRCA dates are estimates based on an average mutation of one SNP every 144.41 years and an assumed age of 60 years for living providers of YFull samples. On average one male generation is 32.5 years, which is about 4.44 generations per mutation.

3. The Patrilineal Trail: From the Fertile Crescent To The Indus Valley

The 12-marker test with The Genographic Project enabled me to trace the migratory route of my ancestors from African Adam in the region of the Rift Valley right up to the Fertile Crescent. But the question remained as to how and why my ancestors pursued their long journey from there to finally set down their roots in the village of Aldona in Goa.

A more detailed test for downstream subclades of haplogroup J2 could perhaps yield a response or at least bring me closer to what I was seeking. Additional tests with Family Tree DNA with 37 markers placed me in haplogroup **J2b2** and with 111 markers as well an SNP confirmation with a J2 - M172 SNP Pack unequivocally in haplogroup:

J – Z2433

J-Z2432, the subclade preceding J-Z2443 is one of the main sub-clades of J2b2 (J-M12) that separated from L283 some 10,000 years ago, during the Early Neolithic. This branch is found almost exclusive-ly in South Asia today, apart from a few reported samples from the Middle East (Syria, Iraq, Arabian peninsula, Egypt). In all likelihood it represents the descendants of Iranian Neolithic farmers toward the Indian subcontinent, although it cannot be ruled out at present that some clades migrated later from Iran, during the Chalcolithic period or the Bronze Age.[47]

Starting from M172 where The Genographic Project's 12-marker test's determination left off, described in the previous chapter, we can see below the further downstream mutations up to J-Z2443. The YCC nomenclature is given in brackets wherever it could be determined:

J-M172 (J2) —-> J-M12 (J2b2) —-> J-M241 (J2b2a) —-> J-Z2432 —-> J-Z2433 (—-> J-Z2449 or further downstream?)

A genetics expert and moderator of the J-M241 Project on Family Tree DNA, Hunter Provyn, has developed an algorithm called *phylo-geographer*[48] that can trace the migration based on an individual's SNPs. Accessible for free as a public service, all one is required to do is to key in the terminal SNP and it produces a migration map based on all the relevant data available on YFull; he admits that the map is approximate but provides a good general indication. Hunter Provyn studied my SNPs as available after the 111 marker test and predicted that my haplogroup would be J-Z2449 or further downstream and per-suaded and supported me to carry out a Big Y-700 test and send the BAM file to YFull for a complete interpretation to determine the most downstream subclade. This approach would yield the most detailed information and interpretation that current scientific knowledge in this area has to offer. The results of this approach as well as a migration map obtained from Provyn's Phylogeographer are discussed in the sub-chapter below.

Big Y-700 and YFull Next Gen Sequence Interpretation

Early 2013, Family Tree DNA launched **Big Y**, its most advanced Y chromosome test of the time that explored deep ancestral links on our common paternal tree. This test performed next-generation sequencing with Illumina HiSeq 2000 equipment and the analysis uses Arpeggi genome analysis technology.

In 2018, FTDNA decided to replace Big Y with a product named **Big Y-500** to take into account the vastly expanded knowledge base in this area and increase the overall coverage of the Y chromosome.

Chromosome Y has roughly 57,200,000 nucleotides or base pairs (57.2 Mbp). Of these, there are regions that are of genealogical relevance since they contain the genetic information that is transferred practically unchanged from father to son. There are other regions that are inaccessible to next-generation sequencing technology or subject to recombination with the X chromosome with which the Y chromosome is paired. These latter two regions are therefore not of interest for testing purposes and after removing them from consideration, approximately 23,600,000 nucleotides (23.6 Mbp) remain as a target for sequencing. The sample submitted for testing is enriched for regions of interest within these 23.6 Mbp.

The Big Y-500 actually consists of two tests with two different kinds of DNA markers namely Short Tandem Repeats (STRs) that are useful to determine closer relations of about 10 generations as well as Single Nucleotide Polymorphisms (SNPs) that serve to learn about human migrations and more distant relationships. The Big Y-500 tested for 500 STRs, a major increase from the maximum of 111 STR markers that could be tested prior to the introduction of this option.

Big Y-700 was introduced in March 2019 and replaces Big Y-500. This test now analyses 700 STRs and uses an improved enrichment of the DNA fragments of the Y chromosome that are most valuable for paternal ancestry. Family Tree DNA's biggest and most informative Big Y yet now allows for the discovery of even more SNPs than the previous tests.

Big Y-700 examines thousands of known branch markers as well as millions of places where there may be new branch markers. Thus, previously unknown SNPs can be discovered and are of interest not only to bring new insights to specific lineages as well as more precision in the migration patterns of our ancestors but also in advancing science.[49,50]

Even though FTDNA provides fairly detailed test results, it is recommended to submit the full Y-chromosome raw data (BAM) files to YFull for a very detailed analysis - called Next Gen Sequence Interpretation - and a very good visualisation of the results in lists and charts. Information on the YFull organisation can be found here:[51]

The Big Y-700 determined that my confirmed Y DNA haplogroup is:

J-FT14628

whereas YFull placed me in:

J-FT14805*

A detailed comparison between the the two reveals that J-FT14628 is equivalent to J-Z8316 and is, in fact, one step upstream from YFull's determination. Thus, the most downstream haplogroup subclade is represented by the results provided by YFull, namely **J-FT14805***. The star symbol indicates the presence of a paragroup, representing chromosomes belonging to a clade and not its subclades. In other words, it is identical with the haplogroup root, and is also referred to as nodal i.e. the chromosomes of the haplogroup J-FT14805* are identical with those of the root J-FT14805 and it does not contain any mutations of one of its subclades.

My Big Y 700 test has led to the discovery of 40 novel SNPs and about 31 of these where identification is unambiguous will eventually be added to the Y DNA haplogroup tree and thus advance the science of genetics.

With this result, it is now possible to analyse the migration of my ancestors from the time they ventured forth from Africa until their arrival in Goa. This long adventure is depicted in the chart below.

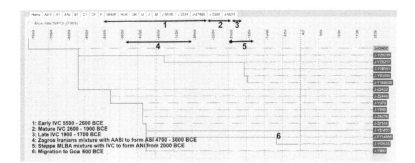

Image 2: Migration chart provided by YFull and annotated by the author

The chart shows the complete evolution starting with haplogroup A. Since the previous migration paths have already been described earlier in detail, the discussion here starts at J-Z2432 and ends with J-Y62635, located one step downstream from my haplogroup J-FT14805*.

During the early Indus Valley Civilisation (IVC) or Harappan phase 5500-2600 BCE (1), my ancestors arrived as Iranians from the Zagros mountains in the
Harappan / IVC region as haplogroup J-Z2432, that has a TMRCA of 8200 ybp based on all samples on YFull. Haplogroup J-Y28235 branched out from it and subsequently split into several other sub-clades.

Subclade	TMRCA based on author's YDNA	TMRCA based on all samples
J-FT14805	2700	2600
J-Z8316	5800	6300
J-Z8326	5800	6300
J-Y958	5800	6300
J-Y978	6900	6300
J-Z2449	7500	7500
J-Z2433	7700	7500

Subclade	TMRCA based on author's YDNA	TMRCA based on all samples
J-Z2432	8700	8200

Table 2: TMRCA chart of the subclades leading to J-FT14805 as calculated by YFull

My ancestral Iranians migrated further, mutated to J-Z2433 and stayed this way until the beginning of the early Indus Valley Civilisation IVC or Harappan phase, when they interbred with the local Ancient Ancestral South Indian (AASI) population leading to the formation of Ancestral South Indian ASI people. They continued to migrate, mutated to J-Y978 that branched into other subclades J-Y958 and J-Z8326, all with the same TMRCA of 6300 ybp. These fast mutations indicate a rapid expansion most probably triggered by favourable climatic conditions. After a short spell as J-Z8316, still in the early IVC phase, they migrated further as J-FT14805 and spent the whole of the remaining early IVC and mature IVC phases until its extinction without further mutations. This is understandable in view of the stable and flourishing IVC culture during this time. Coinciding with extinction of the IVC culture, they mixed as ASI with the Yamnaya-related pastoral Middle Late Bronze Age MLBA population from the Steppe to form the Ancestral North Indian ANI population assimilating this new culture before migrating further. The AASI, ASI, Steppe MLBA and ANI populations are discussed in more detail in Part II, Chapter 1, Peopling of India.

A new migration now took place: J-FT14805 with a TMRCA of 2600 to 2700 ybp migrated to Goa whereas its branch J-Y62635 migrated further.

Thus, around 700 - 600 BCE, my ancestors belonging to J-FT14805 imbibed with a mixture of ASI and ANI cultures arrived in Goa as settlers where they found their permanent abode.

We have to keep in mind that these dates are calculated by making assumptions on the rates of mutations and therefore approximate but they are sufficiently close to establish a window that may vary by a few decades.

Were they the first settlers who arrived in Goa with their leader Parashurama or were they more recent migrants following in the foot-steps of earlier settlers? The above results cannot answer this question. It would be necessary to carry out whole genome tests on more *gaunkars* settlers in the Goan villages from the different *vangads* or clans to confirm the approximate year of their arrival in Goa. It is my sincere hope that more Goans will become interested in genetic ge-nealogy and analyse their DNA in the future.

We can nevertheless make an educated guess. Since people typi-cally migrated in groups, we must assume that my early settler ances-tors arrived as part of a group. Additionally, the population sizes were small; we know for a fact that even a thousand years later in 1601, the total population of the prosperous village of Aldona including Calvim, that could boast of surplus agricultural produce, numbered around 2500. Thus, we would expect that this group would be the first settlers with an ANI/ASI cultural mix to migrate to and populate Goa.

One approach to understand the migration pattern and direction is to analyse the frequency of occurrence of all the upstream hap-logroups. Even though the number of samples available in YFull are presently limited to be of statistical relevance, they are nevertheless significant and combined with other sources of information offer a ra-tional migration path.

YFull reveals the geographical locations as far as known to it of all the participants whose samples the organisation has analysed. Of the two branches of J-Z2433, one individual from Punjab, India, tested positive for J-Z2449* and another person, also from Punjab, India, be-longed to J-Y978. The fact that the only two samples for these sub-clades on YFull are both located in Punjab, India, leave little doubt that my ancestors were settled in the Punjab region of the IVC. It also explains why so many Saraswat Brahmins settled in the Kashmir re-gion, it being in the immediate vicinity of Punjab. It must be recalled that the first major settlement of this extraordinary Harappan / IVC cul-ture was discovered in Pakistani Punjab, namely Harappa, after which site the culture continues to be known synonymously with the Indus

Valley Civilisation. As discussed in the following chapter, 147 IVC sites have been discovered so far in Indian Punjab. The small number of Y DNA samples tested so far do not allow an exact specification of the location of the IVC site in the Punjab where my ancestors settled during the early Harappan / IVC phase but it is certainly exciting to be able to locate the region and the year with the help of this detailed Y DNA analysis.

Moving further downstream, there is only one participant belonging to J-Y958 and he is from India but the location is unknown. The next downstream branch J-Z8326 is shared by two samples, one from India, exact location unknown and another who comes surprisingly from the Portuguese autonomous region of Azores. The latter's ancestors certainly migrated from India, probably from a coastal area, with the involvement of the Portuguese. We then come to J-FT14805 to which I belong as the only sample that has tested positive for that haplogroup so far.

One step downstream from this haplogroup is J-Y62635 with a TM-RCA of 2000 ybp that was tested positive by 3 participants, one from Afghanistan, a second from Bahrain and a third from Goa. Unfortunately, I was unable to contact this fellow Goan because it would have been of great historical value to learn more about his ancestry. He was part of a scientific study entitled *The South Asian Genome*[52] but my email to one of the lead authors requesting contact information has remained unanswered. At least one of the descendants of my ancestors with haplogroup J-FT14805 back-migrated towards the north - Afghanistan - from wherever they were located, probably a coastal region since that would be the most plausible way from a person to travel from India to Bahrain.

It is equally very interesting to note the migration of this branch to Goa around the year 1BCE or 1AD. It must be surmised that more than 600 years after the arrival of my ancestors as settlers, migration of settlers to Goa continued thus establishing that Goa was settled by multiple waves of immigrants over a big span of time.

To complete the picture, we find 3 persons who tested positive for the next downstream subclade J-Y960. Two of them are located in Andhra Pradesh and the third one in Sri Lanka, thus confirming what both genetics and historians have claimed that after the arrival of the Steppe MLBA population, migration occurred from the north - in the case of my ancestors, Punjab Harappan region - towards the south.

Not surprisingly, my results yield SNP matches with 41 shared SNPs with the 3 samples belonging to downstream haplogroup J-Y62635 directly descended from J-FT14805.

Historians have in the past referred to the Gaunkari system in vague terms as an ancient institution established thousands of years ago but now thanks to genetic genealogy and my detailed Big Y 700 DNA analysis we are for the first time able to attribute a more specific date to their arrival - around 700 to 600 BCE - bringing with them a mixture of IVC and Yamnaya-related Sintastha cultures described in the Vedas.

Entering the SNP FT14805 in Provyn's *Phylogeographer* provides the following migration map based on 14452 samples including 78 samples of ancient DNA:

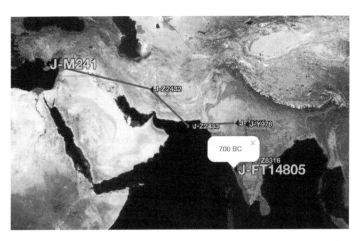

Migration map 1: Migration from J-M241 to J-FT14805 to Goa

Starting from the Fertile Crescent, the migration towards the east leads to Iran, further towards the northwest of South Asia, today's Afghanistan and Pakistan, and then to Punjab. From there, we find a southward migration that then veers towards the west to Goa.

The reader will immediately notice that up to J-Y978, the area covered is identical with the Harrapan or the Indus Valley Civilisation region visualised in a map of the region by one of the foremost Indian Harappa archeological experts and Vice Chancellor of Deccan College, Pune, India, Dr. Vasant S. Shinde et al.[53] From there, the migration southwards begins until the final destination shown on the Phylogeographer migration map, Goa, India, arriving around 700BCE.

Thus, it can be unequivocally confirmed that my ancestors were part of the Indus Valley Civilisation prior to their further migration southwards and finally to Goa.

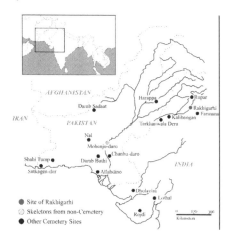

Migration map 2: Indus Valley Civilisation (Source: Vasant S. Shinde et al. [53])

3.1 The Indus Valley Civilisation (IVC)

The Indus Valley Civilisation was established during the Bronze Age in the northwestern region of South Asia. Spread over nearly 1.5 million square km, it extended from Sutkagen-dor in the west on the Pakistan–Iran border to Shortugai (Afghanistan) in the north, Alamgirpur (UP, India) to the east and Daimabad (Maharashtra, India) to the south.[54] It is also referred to as Indus Ghaggar-Hakra or the Indus-Sarasvati civilisation.

Due to the efforts of a large number of scholars and organisations, approximately 1000 IVC sites in India in the Ghaggar-Hakra Basin

and half that number in Pakistan have been identified. This number will increase as research in the region continues. The highest number of IVC
sites to date are located in Haryana (350 sites), followed by Gujarat (230
sites), Punjab (147 sites), Uttar Pradesh (133 sites),
Rajasthan (75 sites), Chandigarh (4 sites), Himachal
Pradesh (3 sites), Delhi (1 site) and Jammu (1 site).[55]

The various phases are dated as follows:
- Early Harappa /Ravi Phase: 3300 – 2800 BCE
- Early Harappa / Kot Diji Phase: 2800 – 2600 BCE
- Harappa Phase: 2600 – 1900 BCE
- Harappa / Late Harappa Transitional: 1900 – about 1700 BCE

Recent excavations in the Ghaggar Basin have extended the beginning of the IVC to 5500 BCE.[56]

The Early Harappa phase thus started approximately during or before the Ubaid period, a migration of inhabitants from Mesopotamia to the Indus Valley can therefore be considered to be feasible.

There is evidence that trade was carried out between inhabitants of the Indus Valley and Mesopotamia from the Harappan seals and jewellery that have been found at that location. In response to wars and climatic upheavals in the Mesopotamia region, it would therefore not be unusual for the people of that region to seek refuge in the Indus Valley in the same manner as Goans migrated to Karnataka and other neighbouring regions to escape the perils of the Portuguese inquisition, famines, or the attacks of the Maratha forces.

No evidence of warfare in the Harappa region has been unearthed so far rendering the proposed theory of an Aryan invasion (AIT) highly questionable. Prototypes of Hindu religious figures have been excavated in Harappa and so-called Shiva seals, depicting the Hindu god Shiva have also been found. We know that uninterrupted Shiva worship has continued for thousands of years, a religious continuity that would be unthinkable if Aryan invaders had conquered the region and imposed their own culture.

The migrants established settlements on the basin of river Sarasvati as well as other adjoining rivers. Did the Sarasvati River really exist or was it just a mythical river? One of the foremost researchers in this area is French-born Indian author Michel Danino, Visiting Professor Indian Institute of Technology, Gandhinagar, whose thoroughly researched book *The Lost River: On The Trail of The Sarasvati*,[57] and subsequent publications are indispensable reading for any person interested in this topic.

India's ancient Vedic texts praise the goddess Sarasvati as "*Ambitame, Naditame, Devitame, Sarasvati*" - the best of mothers, the best of rivers, best of goddesses, Sarasvati (Rigveda 2.41.16). In the Rigveda hymn 10.75 *Nadi Stuti* - an Ode to the Rivers - the Sarasvati River is positioned in verse 5 between the Yamuna and the Sutlej. The goddess Sarasvati is also mentioned along with Indra and Chitra in Rigveda 8.21.17 and 8.21.18.[58] The fact that the goddess Sarasvati is included in the Vedas raises a very puzzling question that is discussed in Part II, chapter 4.

Danino provides compelling evidence based on topographical and archeological studies, both old and recent, from many published sources that leave little doubt as to the past existence of the mighty Sarasvati River identified as modern day Ghaggar- Hakra system, that once flowed through Haryana, Punjab, Northern Rajasthan and Rann of Kutch. Satellite imagery of the last thirty years has provided a map of numerous dried-up beds of rivers and streams, known as palaeochannels, in the Sutlej-Yamuna interfluves.

The river was fed in pre-historic times by Himalayan glaciers, monsoons and the Yamuna and Sutlej. The glacial sources eventually stopped and the contributions from the Yamuna and Sutlej ceased as well. The Sarasvati River continued, however, to be fed by the intense monsoons and the densely forested Shivalik slopes until aridity set in due to reasons that are still being elucidated by researchers and the once mighty river dried up.

For a civilisation dependent on agriculture and trade, the Indus Valley / Harappa Civilisation could only flourish with access to abundant water and waterways. Harappa was located on the banks of the river Ravi, Mahenjo-daro on the Indus and Rakhigarhi was situated between two paleobeds of the Chautang river. Kalibangan, Banawali and Bhirrana were all located on the banks of the Sarasvati River or its channels. Thus, when we discuss the Indus Valley Civilisation, it includes not only the Sarasvati River or its banks, but also the surrounding rivers and their banks and the basins of all these rivers. In fact, as the Sarasvati dried up and declined, mature Harappan shifted northeast towards the Sutlej and Yamuna.

Sometime around 2000 BCE, a major cataclysm caused the river to dry up. Some authors have attributed this to tectonic changes but it is, again, possible that in addition to the aridity, continuous monsoon shortfalls led the river to gradually dry up, resulting in the migration of its inhabitants and extinction of the Indus Valley Civilisation.

A team led by geologist Liviu Giosan mapped the land forms of the region covering the Indus Valley/Harappan Civilisation using photographs taken by shuttle astronauts and images from the Shuttle Radar Topography Mission and then searched for corroboration of their findings on the ground using drilling, coring and manually dug trenches.

The team concluded that initially powerful monsoons caused extensive flooding of the Indus River and its tributaries depositing rich silt that was ideally suited for agriculture. The monsoons then moved eastward, flooding ceased, but provided sufficient water overflows for a successful development of inundation agriculture and large agricultural surpluses. This is how the Harappan Civilisation could evolve and prosper starting around 5200 years ago. The monsoons, however, continued their eastward drift, became weaker and less regular and the large cities could no longer be sustained. Around 3900 years ago, the population started migrating eastwards towards the moister monsoon regions of the upper Punjab, Haryana, and Uttar Pradesh in the direction of the monsoon shift and also diversified the crops to adapt to the changes but these rains were no longer sufficient to produce surpluses and enable the development of large cities of the type that existed during the Harappan period. The Indus Valley Civilisation thus became extinct.[59,60]

The drying up of the Sarasvati drastically curtailed the ability of the inhabitants to grow food; ensuing hunger called for innovative solutions and fish that was surely available became a viable supplement and alternative in order to survive. This is a possible explanation of why the Sarasvat Brahmins are fish eaters deviating from the custom of all other Brahmins in India.

My ancestors were therefore in the region around the time the Indus Valley Civilisation was firmly established. Clearly, evidence emanating from ancient DNA retrieved from skeletons of inhabitants of IVC would serve as a definitive proof: if Y DNA J2b or one of its subclades would be identified, it would corroborate the fact that they were indeed inhabitants and co-founders of this ancient civilisation.

That this is indeed the case has been shown by research carried out by the teams of David Reich and Vasant S. Shinde albeit focused on whole genomes rather than Y DNA haplogroups. This topic is discussed extensively in Part II, chapter 1, Peopling of India.

3.2 Sumerian and Semitic Populations

It is well established that Sumer had an active trading relationship with the Indus Valley Civilisation.

What do we know of the people who inhabited Mesopotamia / Fertile Crescent some 6,000 years ago? How did they live, what were their customs, how were they organised? And why would they migrate to the Indian sub-continent?

Several lifetimes would be needed to read and dissect the ample literature available on the inhabitants of this region, namely, the Sumerians followed by Semitic Akkadians and others; Wikipedia, however, offers a succinct and useful description[61] from where the following is an extract.

Sumer was a civilisation located in Mesopotamia that lasted from the late 6th millennium BCE until the rise of Babylon in the early 2nd millennium. The cities of Sumer introduced agriculture ca. 5300 BCE and produced surplus food thus enabling the population to change its nomadic mode of life as hunter-gatherers and adopt sedentary ways by settling in one location. The population increased, requiring a labour force and division of labour. The need to keep records led to the development of writing ca. 3500 BCE.

"By the late 4th millennium BCE, Sumer was divided into about a dozen independent city-states whose limits were defined by canals and boundary stones. Each was centred on a temple dedicated to the particular patron god or goddess of the city and ruled over by a priestly governor (ensi) or by a king (lugal) who was intimately tied to the city's religious rites".

"The Sumerian city states rose to power during the prehistorical Ubaid (5300 - 4100 BCE) and Uruk (4100 – 2900 BCE) periods. Sumerian history reaches back to the 26th century BCE and earlier. But the historical record remains obscure until the Early Dynastic III period, ca. the 23rd century BCE, when a now deciphered syllabary writing system was developed, which has allowed archaeologists to read contemporary records and inscriptions.

Classical Sumer ends with the rise of the Akkadian Empire in the 23rd century (ca. 2334 – 2218 BCE). Following the Gutian period, there is a brief "Sumerian renaissance" in the 21st century, cut short in the 20th century BCE by Amorite invasions. The Amorite "dynasty of Isin" persisted until ca. 1700 BCE, when Mesopotamia was united under Babylonian rule".

The following is a chronology of the various dynasties that had a major influence on Mesopotamia during that period:

- **Ubaid period:** 5300 – 4100 BCE (Pottery Neolithic to Chalcolithic)
- **Uruk period:** 4100 – 2900 BCE (Late Chalcolithic to Early Bronze Age_I)
  Uruk XIV-V: 4100 – 3300 BCE
  Uruk IV period: 3300 – 3000 BCE
  Uruk III / Jemdet Nasr period: 3000 – 2900 BCE
- **Early Dynastic period (Early Bronze Age II-IV)**
  - Early Dynastic I period: 2900 – 2800 BCE
  - Early Dynastic II period: 2800 – 2600 BCE (Gilgamesh)
  - Early Dynastic IIIa period: 2600 – 2500 BCE Early Dynastic IIIb period: ca. 2500 – 2334 BCE
- **Akkadian Empire period:** ca. 2334 – 2218 BCE (Sargon)
- **Gutian period:** ca. 2218 – 2047 BCE (Early Bronze Age IV)
- **Ur III period:** ca. 2047 – 1940 BCE

Migration waves from this region could have been a result of several events: The city-states were constantly at war with each other. The Sumerians during the Uruk period are known to have captured slaves as workers possibly inciting inhabitants of the region to flee in order to escape such a fate.

A dry period from 3200 to 2900 BCE reduced the amount of food available. Further, many wars were fought, with Lagesh, who was known to use terror as a matter of policy, annexing Sumer followed by the conquest of the region by the Semitic king Sargon, whose dynasty was in turn overthrown by the Gutians.

Sumer recovered from the semi-barbaric Gutians and the city-states became independent again during the 3rd dynasty of Ur. After 1900 BCE, the Amorites conquered the whole of Mesopotamia thus ending the separate identity of the Sumerians. Additionally, the salinity of the soil continuously increased encouraging the inhabitants to replace the cultivation of wheat by barley but also making food scarce. All these events could not have failed to trigger waves of migrations to the neighbouring regions including the Indian sub-continent.

There appear to be many parallels between the customs of the Sumerians and those of Goan villages. The Sumerians established temple-centred cities which may have served as a model for the *gaunkari* system.

A priest-king was assisted by a council of elders during the Uruk period, which could translate to the chief headman of the first family clan or *vangad* assisted by a council, the members of which are the headmen of all the other *vangads* of the village. The civilisation was male-dominated but women played an important role and were protected, a tradition that sadly disappeared in Brahmin society.

They were accomplished agriculturists and very familiar with irrigation which may explain their knowledge of how to reclaim land (*khajan* land) for agricultural purposes. They used the lunar calendar, worshipped some major deities and hundreds of minor gods whilst maintaining animism, all this could have developed into a sophisticated Hindu philosophy on the banks of the Sarasvati.

The migrants could not only have been Sumerians but could also have consisted of Semitic tribes. The latter are defined as follows:

"**Semite**, member of a people speaking any of a group of related languages presumably derived from a common language, Semitic. The term came to include Arabs, Akkadians, Canaanites, Hebrews, some Ethiopians, and Aramaean tribes. Mesopotamia, the western coast of the Mediterranean, the Arabian Peninsula, and the Horn of Africa have all been proposed as possible sites for the prehistoric origins of Semitic-speaking peoples, but no location has been definitively established".

By 2500 BCE Semitic-speaking peoples had become widely dispersed throughout western Asia. In Phoenicia they became seafarers. In Mesopotamia they blended with the civilization of Sumer. The Hebrews settled with other Semitic-speaking peoples in Palestine.[62]

Tests on ancient DNA would be an approach to confirm or disprove an eventual migration of Sumerians to the Indus Valley region but unfortunately such a study does not yet exist.

The genetic ancestry of the Marsh Arabs of Iraq considered to have strong links with the Sumerians has been studied and found to belong to Y DNA haplogroup J1-M267*. The fact that they rear water buffalo and are adept at rice farming are strong indicators of their links to India from where these were introduced. But whether they are indeed Sumerians descendants is yet to be demonstrated.[63]

Furthermore, a prevalent Middle Eastern ancestry of the modern population of the marshes of southern Iraq implies that if the Marsh Arabs are descendants of the ancient Sumerians, they were most likely autochthonous and not of Indian or South Asian ancestry.

4. The Patrilineal Trail: From the Indus Valley To Goa

Professor Shinde has described the decline of the Harappan Civilisation.[64] The reasons for the decline and extinction of Indus Valley Civilisation is a matter of conjecture. There are several studies that substantiate the aridity that descended on various parts of the world including the Indian Subcontinent and the Harappa region. The revered and mighty Sarasvati River dried up. It is possible that the aridity of the times contributed to this catastrophe. It is equally possible that the river Sarasvati, presently represented by Ghagger-Hakra and its main tributary the Drishtvati deviated from its course and merged with other rivers as a result of a tectonic upheaval.

Having lost their fertile land as well as the resulting surplus food grains, the IVC population had no other choice than to migrate. A further contributing factor is that a number of IVC ports on the Makran coast were no longer viable and the flourishing trade with Mesopotamia and Egypt had to cease. The IVC population shifted to other areas such as the western part of Uttar Pradesh, Punjab and more fertile areas in Gujarat in India but also in all other directions towards the Middle East.

As will be discussed more extensively below, genetic studies published in a paper jointly by the teams of David Reich and Vasant Shinde, coinciding with the decline of the IVC in the 2nd millennium, the Harappan population encountered Yamnaya-related pastoral groups with whom they mixed to form the Ancestral North India *ANI* population.

Other Harappan groups moved south and east and mixed with a population labelled Ancient Ancestral South Indian *AASI* groups to form the Ancestral South India *ASI* population.

We know from the fact that the Y DNA haplogroups linked to the Harappans can be found in countries such as Saudi Arabia, Bahrain and United Arab Emirates that members of this population migrated also to the Middle East after the Indus Valley Civilisation collapsed. In fact, genetics expert Hunter Provyn calculated that a Y DNA match from Saudi Arabia and I shared a common ancestor exceeding 3000 years ago which would coincide with the time the IVC/Harappa civilisation became extinct.

To summarise, circa 1900 BCE or later, with the drying up of the Sarasvati river, my Sarasvat ancestors who in the meantime had thankfully developed a taste for fish, a trait that is deeply and firmly anchored in my genes, were forced to seek a new abode that eventually brought them as settlers to Goa.

A. R. S. Dhume[65] argues that Goa was formed as a result of seismic activity and became habitable ca. 8,500 BCE

Both Dhume and Keni postulate that *Parashurama*, the sixth avatar of Lord Krishna, who is credited with the creation of *Parashurama Kshetra*, of which Goa forms a part, was not a mythological figure but actually existed in reality; Dhume proposes the window 2550 and 2350 BCE for his existence. This dating corresponds to before the extinction of the Harappa period (around 2100 to 1900 BCE) and the intermingling of the Steppe and IVC populations and is thus not plausible.

In *Medieval Goa*, historian Teotonio R. de Souza discusses the theories that deal with the ethnic origin of the first settlers and has the following to say[66]: "The pauranic tradition recorded in the *Sahyadri-Khanda* of the *Skanda Purana* refers to Sarasvat Brahmins migrating from Bengal-Bihar region to Goa c. fourth century AD at the invitation of the king Mayuravarma in order to support his throne. The late D. D. Kosambi has upheld this tradition with arguments from religion, linguistics and ethnology. According to another theory, the Senvi Sarasvat Brahmins of Goa must have migrated from the Kutch-Saurashtra region sometime around the eighth century AD, probably under the pressure of the early Arab invasions of that area."

The late historian Chandrakant Keni, on the other hand[67] offers evidence that the Gaud Sarasvats had settled in the Kashmir region. This raises the interesting question on whether my ancestors, escaping from the dried-up banks of the Sarasvati River, migrated to the Bengal-Bihar region and lived there until the 4th century AD before arriving in Goa or took the shorter route to Kashmir from where they finally migrated to Goa. Genetic genealogy results now reveal, as we have seen earlier, that neither of these occurred.

Sharma et al.[68] offer a clue on this issue; their study analysed the Y haplogroups of regional population groups of India and in 51 samples of J&K Kashmiri Pandits (Brahmins) found a percentage of 9.80 of haplogroup J2 and the following percentages for the different R haplogroups: R* 1.96, R1* 11.76, R1a* 3.92, R1a1 19.61, R2 13.73.

In the 30 samples of West Bengal Brahmins, they found no J2, but 72.2 percent of R1a1 and 22.22 percent of R2. The 38 Bihari Brahmins samples yielded the following results: J2 2.63%, R1* 5.26%, R1a1 60.53% and R2 5.26%.

We have seen earlier that along with H, Y haplogroup R1a1 is one of the most abundant in India, including Western India, in both caste and tribal populations.

These results indicate that all the hypotheses could be correct: Brahmins belonging to haplogroup R1a1 migrated earlier to Goa from the Bengal-Bihar region, the Senvi could have migrated later from the Kutch-Saurashtra region but since J2 was not found in Bengali Brahmins and only at low levels in Bihari Brahmins, it is improbable that my ancestors belonging to haplogroup J2 migrated to Goa from either of these places.

About ten percent of the Kashmir Pandits belong to haplogroup J2, but also 21.4% of Punjabi Brahmins in the North, 23.8% of Madhya Pradesh Brahmins in Central India and 16.7% and 15.6% respectively, of Brahmins from Maharashtra and Gujarat in Western India. Based on the research published by Chandrakant Keni, there is a high probability that some members of the population to which my ancestors belonged spread northwards towards Kashmir whereas my ancestors migrated eastwards from Punjab towards Uttar Pradesh, further south to Madhya Pradesh where they would have been welcomed by the Candellas.

Brower & Johnston, Barbara Rose claim that "Kashmiri Hindus are all Saraswat brahmins, known by the exonym Pandit (the endonym being Batta), a term first reserved for emigrant Kashmiri Brahmins in Mughal service."[69]

Chandrakant Keni has conducted in-depth research[70] that greatly contributes to enlighten us on this matter.

The author states with confidence that Sarasvats from Kashmir migrated to Konkan, basing his assertion on examples of illustrious

Kashmir Sarasvats such as the poet Bilhana and author Soddhala who both settled in the Chalukyan capital of Kalyan at different times as well as records and inscriptions, for example pertaining to land grants.

He further establishes the links between Gujarat and Goa as well as the patronage that Sarasvat Brahmins received from rulers at various times, the main thrust of this benevolence being "with the advent of Madhava, the Prime Minister (*Sira Pradhana*) of Marappa of the Vijayanagara Empire" as proven by an inscription of 1347.

Concurrently, economic, social and political upheavals imparted a strong impetus to the Kashmiri Sarasvats to depart from Kashmir: five catastrophic famines from the 9th to the 12th century, despotic rulers some of whom adopted anti-Brahmin policies, and political upheavals in the form of rebellions, uprisings and a civil war due to the poor leadership of "weak, unstable and helpless rulers".[71]

This combination of a highly hostile environment in Kashmir and a welcoming and benevolent attitude of the rulers of Aparant provided a compelling reason for them to migrate. The Kashmiri Sarasvats were closely connected with Gujarat; they may have transited in Gujarat on their way to Goa and other southern regions by the sea route. Thus, Kashmiri Saraswats would have been a part of the several migration waves that occurred from the North to Goa.

The names of the districts Tisvadi and Salcete derived from the Sanskrit *Tis vadi* (thirty settlements) and *Sasasth* (sixty-six) lend credence to the puranic traditions that Parashurama invited ninety-six families to settle in Goa.

This is not incompatible with the findings from genetic genealogy discussed above except that these settlements could not have occurred simultaneously but rather in many successive waves.

The district of Bardez, from the Sanskrit *Bara desa* (twelve regions), and consequently the village of Aldona was settled at a later stage, as confirmed by genetic genealogy findings, since the *Bardezkar* Brahmins are of Sasashtikar origin who may have been forced to leave Salcete because of overpopulation, in-fighting or some other reason.

This would explain why Sasashtikar Brahmins tended to look down on their Bardezkar counterparts.

In the case of my ancestors, they migrated from the Punjab IVC region, transited through Uttar Pradesh and Madhya Pradesh as borne out by genetic genealogy as well as the relatively high frequency of haplogroup J2b in these regions.

We are now in a position to summarise the migratory path that brought my ancestors from their origin in Africa to Goa with a very good degree of precision. The explanation as to why Calvim has been proposed as their final destination in Goa is provided in Part III, Chapter 15: Population of Aldona in 1601:

African Rift Valley North Africa ——-> Middle East Fertile Crescent ——-> Indus Valley Basin / Punjab ——-> Uttar Pradesh ——-> Madhya Pradesh ——-> Goa, possibly Salcete ——> Calvim (Kaluve)–Aldona, Goa.

5. The Matrilineal Trail through Mitochondrial DNA

Women, as mentioned earlier, do not possess a Y-chromosome but they transmit their **mitochondrial DNA (mtDNA)**, the genetic material found in mitochondria, to their offspring, both sons and daughters; sons, however, cannot pass down their mother's mtDNA to their children because sperm does not contain mitochondria in contrast to the egg, the transmission is therefore exclusively maternal. Thus, a mtDNA analysis of both men and women can provide information on their maternal ancestry.

My mother, Ana Rita, née Cordeiro, hailed from Mapusa, the eldest daughter of Filipe Cordeiro, physician and professor of anatomy of the Goa Medical College and Maria Correia Afonso from Benaulim.

My maternal grandmother was the daughter of José Joaquim Roque Bras Correia Afonso and Claudina Pacheco; thus, my mitochondrial DNA has been handed down to me by Claudina Pacheco and to her by her maternal ancestors, the earliest known maternal ancestor being **Ana Maria Pereira**, married to Dr. Antonio do Rosario Gonzaga Alvares, who had an only daughter Maria Esperança Josefa Alvares.

A mtDNA analysis carried out on my DNA sample by *Family Tree DNA* determined that it belongs to the **mt-DNA haplogroup U5**.

As discussed earlier, a haplogroup is a major branch of our descendance tree, defined by the mutations present in the genome and linked with early human migrations. The mutations that define haplogroup U5 are C16192T, C16270T. The mutations that are used to attribute mtDNA results to a specific haplogroup can be found using the appropriate link provided by Family Tree DNA.[72]

This resource lists all the mtDNA haplogroups and their subclades that exist today and the mutations that are used to define them.

Mitochondrial Eve is defined as the woman who is the matrilineal most recent common ancestor (MRCA) of all human beings. It is generally admitted that she lived some 200'000 years ago.

MtDNA Haplogroup L is the oldest and it is one of its branches, L3, that emigrated out of Africa about 60'000 years before present to populate the rest of the world.[73]

More than a decade ago, Kivisild *et al.* found that more than 80% of the Indian mtDNA lineages belong to either Asian-specific haplogroup M (60.4%) or western-Eurasian-specific haplogroups H, I, J, K, U and W (20.5%).[74]

Gail Tonnesen, an expert genetic genealogist has provided a comprehensive description of haplogroup U that is extensively reproduced here.[75]

Haplogroup U is estimated to have originated in the Near East or Southwest Asia around 50,000 years ago, about 15,000 years after modern humans expanded out of Africa. Haplogroup U appears to have lived during a period of rapid population growth and expansion because it has nine major surviving daughter groups, U1 through U9, which are now found among people who have ancestral origins throughout Europe, Asia, and Africa.

Haplogroup U5 is estimated to be about 30,000 years old, and it is primarily found today in people with European ancestry. Both the current geographic distribution of U5 and testing of ancient human remains indicate that the ancestor of U5 expanded into Europe before 31,000 years ago. A 2013 study by Q. Fu *et al.*[76] found two U5 individuals at the Dolni Vestonice burial site in the Czech Republic that have been dated to 31,155 years ago. A third person from the same burial was identified as haplogroup U8. The Dolni Vestonice samples have only two of the five mutations (C16192T and C16270T) that are found in the present day U5 population. This indicates that the U5 - (C16192T and C16270T) mtDNA sequence is ancestral to the present day U5 population that includes the additional three mutations T3197C, G9477A and T13617C.

Bryan Sykes, author of the bestseller "The Seven Daughters of Eve" calculated that it is the oldest subclade of mtDNA haplogroup U and named the originator of haplogroup U5 *Ursula* (she-bear). U5 has been found in human remains dating from the Mesolithic in various European locations and its subclades U5a and U5b form the highest population concentrations in the far north of Europe.

Because there are five additional mutations (T3197C, G9477A, T13617C, C16192T and C16270T) that distinguish present day U5 from U, we can conclude that U5 experienced a long period of very slow population growth or a population bottleneck in Europe. The earliest branching of U5 is its two subclades U5a and U5b that have been dated to about 27,000 years ago by Pedro Soares *et al.*[77] while Behar *et al.* have a younger estimate of about 22,000 years. U5a is defined by two additional mutations A14793G and C16256T, while U5b is defined by three additional mutations C150T, A7768G and T14182C.

During the Last Glacial Maximum (LGM), vast ice sheets covered much of North America, northern Europe, and Asia causing drought, desertification, and a large drop in sea level

The ice sheets reached their maximum coverage about 26,500 years ago. Deglaciation commenced in the Northern Hemisphere at approximately 20,000 years BP and in Antarctica approximately at 14,500 years BP.[78]

The Last Glacial Maximum forced U5a and U5b into ice age refugia in southern Europe and perhaps Ukraine and the Near East in order to survive the cold and extreme arid conditions. U5a has only two known subclades, U5a1 and U5a2, both estimated to be about 20,000 years old. U5b has only three known subclades, U5b1, U5b2 and U5b3, also estimated to be about 20,000 years old. However, age estimates for these subclades from Behar and from Soares vary over a range of 16,000 to 24,000 years. While there is uncertainty in the age estimates of these subclades, it seems likely that a population decline during the LGM is the cause of the lack of ancient diversity or branching in haplogroup U5. It also seems likely that U5a1, U5a2, U5b1, U5b2 and U5b3 were each present in ice age refugia in southern Europe.

As the ice began to retreat about 15,000 years ago, haplogroup U5 was among the first people to repopulate central and northern Europe. We know this because U5 is the dominant haplogroup in ancient remains of early hunter-gatherer populations in Europe with U5 and its sister group U4 representing about 90% of the earliest Mesolithic hunter-gatherers. The 2013 Fu *et al.* study found haplogroup U5 in both pre-ice age Palaeolithic remains and post-ice age Mesolithic remains, and they conclude: "Because the majority of late Palaeolithic and Mesolithic mtDNAs analysed to date fall on one of the branches of U5, our data provide some support for maternal genetic continuity between the pre- and post-ice age European hunter-gatherers from the time of first settlement to the onset of the Neolithic."

Also beginning around 15,000 years ago we begin to see increasing expansion and diversity in the daughters of U5a1, U5a2, U5b1, U5b2 and U5b3. Each of these has eight or more surviving subclades, and this increase in diversity is consistent with a growing population as U5 expanded from ice age refugia into central and northern Europe. However, U5 was largely replaced by early farmers and other Neolithic immigrants to Europe, and currently U5 represents only about 9% of European mtDNA. Some of the very old subclades of U5 are extremely rare today, perhaps because they represent the remnants of hunter-gatherers who were mostly replaced by Neolithic immigrants.

On the other hand, some U5 subclades are much more common in present populations than others. While we know that U5 was the dominant mtDNA group among early Mesolithic Europeans, it is possible that some U5 subclades might also have been present in early farming or herding populations in the Near East and West Asia, so the present day population of U5 could include a mix of early hunter-gatherers and more recent U5 Neolithic farmer/herder immigrants. Alternatively, certain U5 subclades in southeastern Europe could have adopted farming or been incorporated into farming and herding communities at an early date, perhaps at the beginning of the Neolithic when farmers from the Near East began their expansion into Europe. If certain U5 subclades adopted farming and animal husbandry at an earlier date, their population size could have expanded more rapidly and this could explain their larger distribution today. Testing of ancient remains also shows that U5 was present in the Pontic-Caspian Steppe region, which may have been the home land of Indo-European speakers. It seems likely that certain subclades of U5 expanded from the Steppe into both Europe and south Asia during the Bronze age migrations that brought Indo-European languages to these regions.

Even though haplogroup U is not uncommon in India, the subclade U5 is Europe-specific and rare on the Indian sub-continent. Kivisild *et al.* propose that haplogroup U split possibly in Ethiopia, with some subclades e.g. U5, migrating towards Europe and others e.g. U2i and U7, towards the Indian subcontinent; they found a frequency of just

1.2% of U5 in India after having investigated 550 Indian mtDNA samples.

Concluding that mtDNA U haplogroup subclades migrated from the Near East, Richards *et al.* summarise the situation as follows: "Haplogroup U, which is >50,000 years old in the Near East and which harbours both specific European (U5), northern African (U6), and Indian (U2i) components, each dating to approx. 50'000 ybp, occurs both in Arabia and the northern Caucasus and, indeed, throughout the Near East".[79]

The question therefore arises as to how my maternal ancestry bearing a European-specific haplogroup subclade U5 migrated to India. The study of Richards *et al.* on mtDNA haplogroups U5 and V found a high rate of 10% — 20% of back-migration from Europe to the Near East, the estimate falling to 6% — 8% for the core zone of the Fertile Crescent.

They offer the following possible explanation for these back-migrations: "...include the Philistine migrations from the Aegean into the Levant during the Bronze Age; the expansion of Greek, Phrygian, and Armenian speakers into western Anatolia, central Anatolia and Armenia, respectively ~1200 b.c.; and the importation of European as well as African slaves by the Islamic caliphs of Syria and Iraq during the medieval period".

The inability to identify a more precise picture regarding the migration of my maternal ancestors persuaded me to carry out a more detailed mtDNA analysis that would hopefully shed more light and precision to the migration patterns of my early maternal ancestors. A mtDNA Full Sequence test, the most comprehensive mtDNA analysis that exists having become available, I ordered this test that was completed by *Family Tree DNA* in August 2017.

A mtDNA Full Sequence test investigates the HVR1, HVR2 and Coding Region. Mitochondrial DNA has two major parts:
- the fast changing control region that is also known as the hypervariable region HVR, further subdivided into two regions HVR1 running from nucleotide 16001 to nucleotide 16569 and HVR2 that runs from nucleotide 00001 to nucleotide 00574
- the coding region that contains genes, mutates slowly and runs from nucleotide 00575 to nucleotide 16000.

Typically, the HVR regions might mutate every 400 years whereas one could expect a mutation in the coding region every 1600 years.

The results show that I belong to the

mtDNA haplogroup U5a1a2a

This haplogroup is estimated by Behar *et al.* to have originated about 3000ybp. A female skeleton code-named RISE 496 carrying this mtDNA haplogroup that was exhumed from Arban 1 cemetery in Russia and discussed below in detail was found to be 3070 years old. An ancient mtDNA of this haplogroup from Benzingerode-Heimburg, Germany tested as sample BZH12 dated at 3758 ± 33, therefore the Behar *et al.* estimate needs to be corrected to ca. 4000ybp.

The detailed mtDNA findings are generally presented as Reconstructed Sapiens Reference Sequence as well as revised Cambridge Reference System, the former being the preferred presentation and given below in tabular form for my mtDNA. The results are presented as the difference from the reference sequence.

In the year 2012, Behar *et al.* proposed to use a new reference sequence, the so-called Reconstructed Sapiens Reference Sequence (RSRS), to replace the revised Cambridge Reference Sequence (rCRS) of human mitochondrial DNA. While the rCRS belongs to the peripheral European haplogroup H2a2a1, the RSRS represents the deepest root in the known human mtDNA phylogeny and corresponds to the bifurcation of haplogroups L0 and L1'2'3'4'5'6, after combining information from all available mitochondrial Neanderthal genomes. In other words, it uses both a global sampling of modern human samples and samples from ancient hominids.

Extra Mutations: A200G   309.1C   315.1C   522.1A   573.1C
573.2C   573.3C   573.4C   C16286T   A16309G
T16362C
Missing Mutations: 573.XC   C16189T

HVR1 DIFFERENCES FROM RSRS				
A16129G		T1618 7C	T1622 3C	G1623 0A	C1625 6T

C16270T		T1627 8C	C1628 6T	A1630 9G	C1631 1T
T16362C		A1639 9G			

HVR2 DIFFERENCES FROM RSRS

C146T		C152T	C195T	A200G	A247G
309.1C		315.1C	522.1A	522.2C	573.1C
573.2C		573.3C	573.4C		

CODING REGION DIFFERENCES FROM RSRS				
A769G	A825t	A1018G	T1700C	A2758G
C2885T	T3197C	T3594C	G4104A	T4312C
A5319G	A6629G	T6719C	G7146A	T7256C
A7521G	T8468C	T8655C	G8701A	G9477A
C9540T	G10398A	T10664C	A10688G	C10810T
C10873T	C10915T	A11467G	A11914G	A12308G
C12346T	G12372A	T12705C	G13105A	G13276A
T13506C	T13617C	T13650C	A14793G	A15218G

Table 3: HVR1, HVR2 and Coding Region for mtDNA U5a1a2a

No close matches to my mtDNA have been found to date in the FTDNA database. This can be explained in part because it is not a commonly found haplotype. It is, however, possible to join one of the many projects to compare details and discuss issues and this is what I did by joining the FTDNA U5 project. Of the many individuals belonging to the U5a1a2a haplogroup who have joined this project and whose results have been published in FTDNA's U5 project, one from

India in addition to my own have been grouped together with a pro-posal for a new subclade. There are 7 differences between the two "Indian" results, which indicates that we are *distant* relatives. Since the other member of Indian origin chose to remain anonymous despite my having contacted him or her through the good offices of the project administrator, I could not further investigate this link. What distin-guishes our "Indian" results from the remaining samples is the extra polymorphism A16309G that none of the others feature.

Wolfgang Haak *et al.* published the SNPs of 105 ancestral DNAs.[80] The paper reports on an ancestral Late Neolithic sample BLH 12 be-longing to the same haplogroup U5a1a2a found in Germany but after comparing the mutations to mine, it was found not to contain the extra mutation A16309G.

Another list of mtDNA U5a1a2a can be encountered on the website of Ian Logan (ianlogan.uk.com) along with the sources. Again, a care-ful examination of the published results reveals an absence of the mu-tation A16309G in all the samples.

On its own, this finding is not particularly useful to determine the ori-gin of my maternal ancestor other than the conclusion that a branch of haplogroup U5a1a2a must have existed bearing the extra mutation A16309G that migrated to India. It is at this stage as I was research-ing further on this subject that I came across a publication in the jour-nal *Nature* entitled "Population Genomics of Bronze Age Eurasia" pub-lished in June 2015 and coauthored by 66 scientists.[81] In this fascinat-ing work, in a project called RISE, the authors used advanced tech-niques to sequence 101 ancient humans across Eurasia and demon-strate that the Bronze Age of Eurasia (around 3000 – 1000 BCE) in-volved large-scale population migrations and replacements including the spread of Indo-European languages. When studying supplemen-tary Table 14 of this study that contains an overview of the mtDNA haplogroups of the 101 genomes along with their polymorphisms, RISE 496 immediately caught my attention because it is the only one that carries the mtDNA haplogroup U5a1a2a, the same as mine. The sample belongs to an adult female, exhumed from Arban 1 cemetery in Russia, longitude 90,187, latitude 52,954, belonging to the Bronze Age Karasuk culture. The coordinates provided take us to Poltakov, Republic of Khakasiya (also known as Khakassia), Russia. Khakasiya, capital Abakan, consists of the western half of the Minusinsk Basin on the upper Yenisey River and is located in the south-western part of Eastern Siberia. The Republic is rich in natural resources such as copper, molybdenum, iron, gold, silver, coal, oil as well as forested areas.

To my great astonishment, I discovered that RISE 496 shares with me the same extra mutation A16309G that no one else other than one other individual from India does, thus clearly linking my maternal ancestry to the group of people to whom she belonged.

The Karasuk culture (ca. 200 - 700 BCE) evolved from the Andronovo culture (ca. 2000 - 900 BCE), that was preceded by the Sintashta (ca. 2100 -1800 BCE), Abashevo (ca. 2500 - 1900 BCE) and other cultures derived from the Yamnaya.

The Bronze Age Karasuk to which RISE 496 belonged were farmers who practiced metallurgy on a large scale. They lived in pit houses and buried their dead in stone cysts covered by kurgans i.e., pre-historic burial mounds and surrounded by square stone enclosures. The Karasuk culture evolved from previous cultures starting with the Yamnaya culture where kurgan burials were common.

Professor Morten Erik Allentoft and co-author Peter de Barros Damgaard were both kind enough to respond to my queries. The fact that I have the same mtDNA haplogroup and extra mutation does not imply that RISE 496 is my *direct* ancestor because there may have been thousands of people with this mutation in the Bronze Age Steppe region and any of them could have been a direct ancestor. The result confirms, however, that RISE496 and I share a common ancestor. Given that I am from India and the haplogroup with its unique extra mutation is also found in someone else in India, it most likely reflects Late Bronze Age connections to South Asia, which is well established archaeologically and linguistically.

What can thus be concluded is that my maternal ancestors did not arrive in India as the result of a back migration from Europe. They were related to Siberians who inhabited the Siberian Steppe region and migrated from there southwards to India. Since we now know that the Sintashta population migrated to India, it is probable that my maternal ancestors were also Sintashta, common ancestors of the Karasuk RISE 496, who migrated along with the male pastoralist warriors, who arrived in India from the Steppe and are described in detail in Part II: Peopling of India.

My maternal lineage has gifted Goa with many distinguished scholars and can even claim a relationship with a Duchess of Habsburg and Queen Elisabeth of England.[82] It is an awe-inspiring experience to discover that my maternal lineage equally stems from Bronze Age Siberian herders and metallurgists belonging to the Sintashta culture related to the Yamnaya who were involved in the spread of Indo-European languages. Such is the power of DNA.

6. Ancient Origins: Autosomal DNA and Ancient Origins

Information provided by Y DNA arises from the Y strand of the XY chromosome number 23 that contains the smallest amount of information in the human genome. Yet, as we have seen in the earlier chapters, it is very helpful in enlightening us on our patrilineal ancestry and their migration routes. In addition to the X strand of chromosome 23, the biggest amount of information resides in the remaining 22 chromosomes of the human genome, the so-called autosomal chromosomes.

Most genetic testing companies offer the possibility to analyse autosomal DNA. *Family Tree DNA* compares these results with ancient DNA as well as other results in their vast data base to break it up into 3 components for ancient European origins: Hunter-Gatherers, Early Farmers, and Metal Age Invaders. In my case, the results are as follows:

Hunter-Gatherers: 0%
Early Farmers: 12%
Metal Age Invader: 63%
Non-European: 25%

The 25% Non-European cluster breaks down as 98% Central / South Asian:

Central Asia: 45% (about **11.5%** of the total)
South Central Asia: 53% (about **13.5%** of the total)
Traces: 2%

The following is a description of these different components of my ancient ancestry.

Early Farmers 12%:

This covers the period after the last glaciation, the beginning of the Neolithic Era or post-palaeolithic Era, about 8000-7000 years ago when triggered by the warmer weather, modern human populations

75

started migrating from the Near East. The stone tools developed during the Palaeolithic became more refined.

During the Neolithic period, modern humans introduced farming and pastoralism for their subsistence, leading to a more sedentary lifestyle and the emergence of artisan practices such as pottery.

The population started to disperse but they showed a close genetic relatedness indicating that there were relatively few numbers.

Metal Age Invaders 63%:

The Neolithic Era was followed by the Bronze Age covering the period 3000-1000 BCE. Tool making was further refined and stone tools were replaced by copper incorporating bronze and tin. It is around this time that nomadic herding cultures from the Steppes started migrating towards Europe and Central Asia that had more temperate climates. These migrants were the Yamnaya or people closely related to them.

The people of the Yamnaya-related culture brought with them domesticated horses, wheeled chariots, and metal tools and changed the social and genetic makeup of the regions they migrated to. They also brought with them the Proto-Indo-European languages.

Subclades of Y DNA haplogroups R1a and R1b are attributed to the Yamnaya culture, the former predominates in South Asia including India and the latter in Europe.

The reason for a relatively high percentage of this cluster in my ancestry can be attributed to the fact that I have inherited Yamnaya-related genomes both from the patrilineal as well as the matrilineal lineage.

Central Asia:

The Central Asia cluster consists of present day Pakistan, Kashmir, Northern India, and Western Nepal. Populations in Northern India remained linguistically, technologically, and genetically divergent from populations in South India until roughly 4000 years ago.

The Indus Valley or Harappa Civilisation was located in this region, which experienced both a rapid growth as well as a swift fall. Harappa had its own script (which has yet to be deciphered), urban planning, and even a common weight system.

South Central Asia:

The South India cluster is comprised of present-day Southern India, and Sri Lanka. Until roughly the 6th millennium BCE, Peninsular India and Sri Lanka were connected by land.

This cluster is closely linked to the Central Asian cluster. The two clusters were, however, divergent, using different language families, roughly divided by the Narmada river, until about 4000 years ago co-inciding with the extinction of the Indus Valley Civilisation (IVC). The populations of Central and South Central clusters were culturally isolated from one another until the fall of IVC.

The results of the analysis of my origins fits remarkably well with the findings of the Narasimhan *et al.* paper discussed in Part II, Chapter 2: Peopling of Goa. The Early Farmers and Central Asia cluster are the migrants from the Zagros Mountains of Iran, admixed with the local inhabitants and established the Indus Valley or Harappa Civilisation, the Metal Age Invaders are the Yamnaya-related people who admixed with the Indus Valley Civilisation population to form the Ancient North Indian ANI population, the Central Asia cluster represents the IVC population that developed in the Indus Valley and the South Asia cluster represents the IVC population that after the extinction of this civilisation mixed with Ancient Ancestral South Indian population AASI to form the Ancestral South Indian Population ASI.

What was the Yamnaya culture that has left such an enduring imprint on the populations of Asia and Europe and brought the Indo-European languages to the world? A detailed description can be found in Part II, Chapter 1: Peopling of India, Sub-chapter 1.1 Ancient North Indian ANI Ancestry.

6.1 Some Applications of Autosomal DNA

There are several DNA testing companies, each of them offering similar but not necessarily identical DNA tests since they do not test identical markers.[83] Each company also provides its own analyses but restricted to the information in their individual databases, which is clearly a disadvantage.

This is where *GEDMatch* Tools for DNA & Genealogy Research comes in.[84] Users of the different testing companies can upload their results to the *GEDmatch* database thereby expanding exponentially the *GEDmatch* database and allowing the users to share and more importantly compare their results with those of all other companies that have chosen to also upload their results to GEDmatch. This company also offers a number of services to the user under their free basic programme and helps us to greatly expand the knowledge and information base of our ancestry.

6.2 Archaic DNA

GEDmatch has uploaded the whole genome sequences of 55 ancient skeletons and offers a programme called Archaic DNA where a user can check if and the amounts of archaic DNA he or she shares with them. It is also possible to carry out one to one comparisons with individual archaic DNA kits. Since the amount of DNA shared is very small, the one to one programme allows the parameters to be adjusted.

I have compared my DNA with those of a few archaic kits and below are two examples using a SNP count minimum threshold of 500 (default in the programme) and a minimum segment cM size of 3:

Ust-Ishim Siberia 45 thousand years old, matching segments on chromosomes 15 and 20 with a total of 10.1 cM

LBK Stuttgart 7 thousand years old, 1 matching segment on chromosome 1 with a total of 3.4 cM

Decreasing the segment size to for example 1 cM will yield more matching segments. In the above examples

Ust-Ishim 13 matching segments

LBK Stuttgart 5 matching segments

The amounts of DNA I share with these ancient skeletons is minuscule but it shows nevertheless that my ancestry is closer to the Siberian Ust-Ishim than to the German LBK.

Ust-Ishim lived in Siberia 45 thousand years ago and is the first modern human whose archaic whole genome has been decoded. He probably belonged to the first wave of humans to migrate out of Africa and into Asia and Europe and appears to be related more closely to East Asians, which is why I share a bigger amount of DNA with him than with LBK Stuttgart. He belonged to Y DNA haplogroup K2a and mtDNA haplogroup R*. An interesting fact is that the Neanderthal genes that he shared have been found to be in clusters rather than in fragments indicating that he lived not long after Neanderthals and modern humans had exchanged genetic material.[85]

The Linearbandkeramik LBK (Linear Pottery Ceramic Culture) sample was a Neolithic farmer found in an ancient LBK settlement in Stuttgart, Germany; his mtDNA haplogroup was found to be T2.

From the above, therefore, it can be inferred that Ust-Ishim's descendants spread from Siberia towards East Asia leaving their traces as far away as Goa, India.

6.3 Phenotyping

Autosomal DNA can be used to discover specific traits by analysing SNPs of the genome.

Scientists have for example discovered that specific SNPs of the genes APBA2, ASIP, DCT, GRM5, HERC2, IRF4, KITLG, MC1R, OCA2, SLC24A4, SLC24A5 and SLC45A2 determine skin, hair and eye colour.[86]

In 1903, in Gough's Cave in Cheddar Gorge, Somerset, England, Britain's oldest complete human 10 thousand year old fossil was excavated and is now known as the *Cheddar Man*. DNA was extracted from the petrous bone of this fossil in 2018 and using a forensic tool it can be predicted that he probably had blue eyes, lactose intolerance, dark curly or wavy hair, and dark to very dark skin akin to western European Mesolithic hunter-gatherers found in Spain, Luxembourg and Hungary.[87]

Increasingly, autosomal data is being used in forensic science to phenotype criminal suspects and many cases have been solved in recent times using this approach. Data uploaded to *GEDmatch* is public and the site advises those who are not comfortable with this policy either not to upload their data or delete the information if they have already uploaded it.[88] Very recently, *GEDMatch* has started offering the possibility of opting out of giving access to law enforcement but urges all participants not to do so.

Eight-year old April Tinsley was murdered in Fort Wayne, Indiana, USA, in April 1988. Police had recovered the DNA of the murderer but could not identify him in spite of all their efforts.[89]

In 2015, police asked a small company to produce a computer-generated sketch based on the DNA but they could still not identify the criminal.

In the spring of 2018, the company *Parabon NanoLabs*, that had become involved in the case fed the autosomal DNA information into

GEDmatch and could narrow their search to two brothers who were subsequently arrested and one of them confessed to the crime. Thus, using a combination of phenotyping and producing an approximate sketch and finding genetic relatives by matching their autosomal DNA to others whose data can be found in a public database can lead police to criminals that are being sought.

In the same manner as DNA can lead police to identify criminals, it can also serve to exonerate and free innocent persons wrongly accused of having committed a crime. In the United States of America, the first DNA-based exoneration of an innocent individual occurred in 1989 when the conviction of Gary Dotson for aggravated kidnaping and rape was overturned on August 14, 1989, after he had served 10 years in prison.

The case of Kirk Bloodsworth, a former Marine, is even more scary. He was 23 years old when he was wrongfully convicted and sentenced to death for having sexually assaulted and strangled nine-year-old Dawn Hamilton in a wooded area of Rosedale, Maryland, in 1984. Kirk Bloodsworth spent nine years in prison, two of them on death row, until it could be proven through DNA tests that he was not at all involved in the crime.

Between 1989 and 2017, 365 wrongly convicted persons have been freed in the Unites States of America after DNA tests could prove their innocence.[90]

Several other cases where DNA results have been successfully used in forensics to identify criminals and bring them to justice are increasingly being published in the daily press. Cf. for example.[91]

Revealing the truth through DNA testing is not always without some discomfort. A story that appeared on Wall Street Journal on February 1, 2019, is a good illustration.[92] Julie Lawson, a daughter of late Sonny and Brina Hurwitz from Boston, USA, took a DNA test and then persuaded her sister Fredda Hurwitz to do likewise. When searching for matches, the name of a man came up as a close genetic match. Neither of the sisters had ever heard of this person. They searched on Facebook and noticed that the photograph of this man closely resembled their late father and was in fact their brother. Their father had a son that had been kept a secret from them. But their ordeal was far from over. Julie Lawson's test showed that she had no genetic links to this man. She was the result of a brief extra-marital affair of her mother and the man who raised her was not her biological father and she and Fredda were actually half-sisters.

Anyone taking a DNA test must be open to whatever the results may show and be prepared to accept the truth. DNA does not lie.

Autosomal DNA is also increasing in popularity with adopted individuals who wish to identify their birth parents. I was contacted by a lady who was adopted and with whom I am a match in both *Family Tree DNA* and *Gedmatch*. The former also indicates the degree of the relationship that in this case is "5th cousin or remote cousin". From the name of her mother that is known to her, I could exclude a relationship on the maternal side. A 5th cousin or remote cousin relationship means that we both shared a common ancestor more than 5 generations ago — a great-great-great grandfather or more remote — and if we assume a generation to be of 32 years, this would add up to more than 160 years which is very distant to be useful for purposes of identification. My great-great-great grandfather had many children and his children and grandchildren as well, so that identifying a specific individual after 5 generations is very difficult. A relationship of 2nd cousin or less is much more promising to elucidate the identity of birth parents. A technique that can be used is *triangulation* in which a person searches for two of his or her matches that are also matches among themselves. If I am a match with *Match1* in a chromosome segment and a match also with *Match2* in the same segment, it cannot be concluded that *Match1* and *Match2* are related because my match with *Match1* may be the result of a segment inherited from my father on one strand of the chromosome pair and the match with *Match2* may have come from my mother on the second strand of the chromosome pair. As discussed earlier, we have 23 chromosome pairs and a DNA test cannot distinguish between the two strands of the pair. If, however, *Match1* and *Match2* match in the same segment as they match me, we have a triangular relationship - *Match1*, *Match2* and myself - and we share a common ancestor and thus the search can be narrowed down. A specific example of triangulation in my case is discussed in the next chapter.

Any adopted person who wishes to go down this track would be well advised to read the story of Randall Howe, a judge on the Arizona Court of Appeals, Division One.[93] Judge Howe who had been adopted received a DNA kit as a birthday gift through which he was able to identify his birth parents and many other details regarding his ancestry. But at the end of his search he drew the following conclusion "But when you sit around the Christmas tree or the Christmas dinner table with your family and friends, remember that what matters is not what blood flows through your veins, but how much love and caring and sacrifice flows between each of you".

In India, the Council of Scientific and Industrial Research CSIR has initiated a project in 2019 to sequence the genome of 1000 rural youth from all over India, men and women, pursuing degrees in the life sciences or biology with the intention of educating a generation of students on the utility of genomics.[94] This approach is to be applauded because it will undoubtedly lead to a heightened interest in this topic and possibly lead to new discoveries and breakthroughs in the area of genetic genealogy in India.

Yet another use of phenotyping using autosomal DNA is the Polygenetic Score prediction algorithm.

In most cases, traits such as eye colour, height, susceptibility to cardiovascular disease, male pattern baldness and so on can be attributed not just to one specific gene but to a number of variants occurring in many genes of small effects. As an example, in addition to the effects of the variations in the well-known BRCA genes, over a hundred other genes have been identified as having an influence on a woman's probability of developing breast cancer. Polygenetic score, also known as polygenetic risk score or genetic risk score, is an algorithm that aggregates the impact of all the variants associated with a complex trait or disease.

With the dramatic increase of databanks with phenotype information, it has become easier to identify variants associated with a specific trait. For example, in the past, women had to rely on family history to determine if they carried a risk of inherited breast cancer. If a polygenic score is available, every woman can now identify this risk without needing to rely on family history alone, information that may not be available in the case of adopted children or orphans.

A polygenetic score is a predictive and not a diagnostic tool. It does not mean that an individual with a high polygenetic risk score will definitely develop a condition, and a low score does not mean that he or she will not. But it does allow the individual with a high score to opt for regular screenings and thus catch a disease at its earliest stages.

Terrie Edith Moffitt is a clinical psychologist who has pioneered research on gene-environment interactions in the areas of psychiatry, psychology, and neuroscience. She is Associate Director of the Dunedin Longitudinal Study, which follows 1037 people born in 1972-73 in Dunedin, New Zealand. She also launched the Environmental-Risk Longitudinal Twin Study, which follows 1100 British families with twins born in 1994-1995. She has studied the twins from birth to age 12 so far.

Moffitt and her team have made use of GWAS - a genome-wide association study — to analyse genetic variants focussing on SNPs in the whole genome of different individuals to see if any variant is associated with a trait. Together with her partner Avshalom Caspi she demonstrated in 2002 that children who carried a mutation in the *MAOA* gene were more vulnerable to developing antisocial behaviour following exposure to maltreatment during childhood. Her next publication showed that a polymorphism in the serotonin transporter gene *SLC6A4* caused greater vulnerability to developing depression.[95]

Based on studies in the United States, Britain, and New Zealand, she and her team reported three consistent findings: "First, education-linked genetics were related to social attainment: Children with higher education polygenic scores tended to complete more years of schooling, build more successful occupational careers, and accumulate more wealth. Second, there was a gene–environment correlation: Children with higher polygenic scores tended to grow up in socioeconomically better-off homes. Third, education-linked genetics were related to social mobility: Regardless of where they started in life, children with higher polygenic scores tended to move up the social ladder in terms of education, occupation, and wealth, even compared with siblings in their own families".

The authors acknowledge that their studies have limitations. The genetic measurement is imprecise and the education polygenic score explains only a fraction of the estimated total genetic influence on education. A second limitation is that the studies are based on data banks in specific locations of the United States, Britain and New Zealand and therefore not necessarily applicable world-wide. The authors also mention incomplete genetic correlation between mothers and their children as well as a lack of complete genetic information on the parents of the people whose lives were studied as additional limitations.[96]

As the data banks with phenotype information increase and expand, it will become easier to predict behavioural traits and disease vulnerability with much more precision in the coming years. This in turn will help immensely to mitigate the effects of many diseases and also allow the introduction of measures to aid the socioeconomically disadvantaged members of society.

7. Matches of Y DNA and Autosomal DNA: Cousin Errol, Cousin Hector, Cousin Eric

7.1 Y DNA Matches

Both the Genographic Project as well as *Family Tree DNA* (FTDNA) offer their customers the possibility to sign a release form whereby the results are placed in a database and compared with the results of other participants taking part in this scheme. FTDNA informs the concerned parties in the event that a match is discovered; the affected individuals then have the choice to contact one another and further investigate their common ancestry.

My results with the Genographic Project for 12 markers and the information that I belonged to haplogroup J2 remained dormant for a few years when quite unexpectedly an email from FTDNA announced an exact match for my twelve markers and furnished the name and contact details of the person concerned: Errol Pinto.

A quick check confirmed that the Pinto surname only appears in the fourth and fifth *vangad* of Aldona's *Comunidade Fraternal* and since I belong to the fourth clan, the indication of a common ancestry was plausible. Thus began a highly interesting and stimulating discussion with Errol. At the same time, my objective of documenting in a monograph whatever I could gather on my genealogy acquired an entirely new dimension, that of a project that would take into consideration the historical perspective of the *gaunkari* system.

I admit without reservation my great excitement at this new development. Clearly, there was a need to extend the DNA testing to 25 and later on 37 markers and still later to 111 markers, thereby fine-tuning the comparison with Errol. A deep clade test would also be necessary to confirm the findings of the Genographic Project and equally to identify the exact subclade.

An obvious consequence of this approach was to enrol in this project another individual with a surname that was different from Pinto or de Sousa but belonging to the same *vangad*, the intention being to scientifically verify the claims that members of a specific *vangad* share a common pre-conversion Hindu surname and ancestry.

My choice fell on my friend, Hector Fernandes, the highly knowledgeable President of Aldona's *Comunidade Fraternal*, with documented credentials with regard to his *vangad* who also belongs to the fourth *vangad*. I was obviously aware of the haplogroups that had been identified in India in general and Western India in particular.

Consequently a blind comparison with a *gaunkar* of a completely different village would be of interest to my project. Again, I was fortunate that a *gaunkar* of the village of Saligão, from where my great grandmother hailed, well-known Church historian late Rev. Fr. Nascimento Mascarenhas, also clearly with documented credentials with regard to his *vangad*, willingly agreed to participate.

The last results became available in the first week of September 2009. Errol, Hector and I all obtain an exact match with respect to twelve markers.

In February 2019, a new message from FTDNA informed me that another match had been discovered with Eric D'Cunha. Again, a check with the surnames that appear in the 4th *vangad* confirmed that Eric belongs to this *vangad*; the family name Cunha figures only in the 4th *vangad* of Aldona's *Comunidade Fraternal*.

Eric D'Cunha, Hector Fernandes and Errol Pinto and myself have all taken the 37-marker test and the discussion below therefore focuses on the results at this level even though Errol and I have also tested for 111 markers and I have additionally taken the YFull 700 test as well.

All four of us are a complete match at a genetic distance of zero at 12 markers and 25 markers except for Hector who shows a genetic distance of 1 with me at the 25-marker level. A genetic distance is defined as the number of alleles that are not identical i.e., of the 25 alleles that have been compared, Hector and I are a mismatch on one of them. Matches are considered to be relevant upto a genetic distance of 7.

At the 37-marker level, all four of us match with a genetic distance of 4. It should be obvious that the greater the number of alleles tested, the greater the chances of finding an allele mismatch or genetic distance.

Family Tree DNA offers a tool FTDNATiP™ that it defines as "a program that predicts the time to the most recent common ancestor for two men based on their Y-chromosome STR matching and STR mutation rates. FTDNATiP™ uses specific mutation rates that have been proven to differ across STR markers. This improves the power and precision of estimates of Time to the Most Recent Common Ancestor TMRCA".

Linked with the results of a mutation rate study conducted by the University of Arizona, and presented by *Family Tree DNA* at the 1st International Conference on Genetic Genealogy on Oct. 30, 2004, it has resulted in an extremely powerful new tool for genealogists that calculates the probability that two individuals shared a common ancestor within a specified number of generations.

Applying this tool to my matches with Eric, Hector and Errol, I obtain the following probabilities that I shared a common ancestor within 24 generations:

Eric and Bernardo:	99.82%
Hector and Bernardo:	99.81%
Errol and Bernardo:	99.78%

If this tool is applied for Hector Fernandes using his kit number we see the following results that are very similar:

Eric to Hector:	99.85%
Bernardo to Hector:	99.81%
Errol to Hector:	99.82%

For added confirmation, the TiP tool returned for Errol and myself at the 67-marker level a value of 98.96%. The probability at fewer generations is much lower as can be expected; for example, the TMRCA that Errol and I shared a common ancestor 4 generations ago is in the vicinity of 30% and 70% at 8 generations ago.

The fact that 4 different members of the same *vangad* bearing four different post-conversion family names indicating that they belonged to different families within this clan and were baptised at different times with different godfathers and yet have a practically identical TMRCA leaves little doubt that they are all descendants of the same common ancestor, the founder of the 4th *vangad* of the *Comunidade Fraternal*. This is a key finding obtained through genetic genealogy that enables us to infer how and when the village of Aldona was settled.

A generation is generally assumed to be 25 to 35 years depending on the family. If we use the value of 32.5 years (see end of Part 1, chapter 2), 24 generations add up to 780 years or we can round it up to 800 years to compensate for the probability values that are below 100%

.

The conclusion that can be drawn from the above findings is that the fourth *vangad* of the *Comunidade Fraternal of Aldona* was founded by a male individual approximately 800 years ago.

This figure is approximate and must be considered as such. The time predictor TiP tool is based on probable average mutation rates of the individual markers tested; these mutation rates in an individual may be equal to but also below or higher than average. We must nevertheless keep in mind that the value of over 99.8 percent when matched with 3 different individuals and of about 99 percent with 67 markers when compared to Errol Pinto is significant and adds to the precision. **The founder event may have occurred 900 or 1000 years ago** but it does provide a very good guideline of roughly when the event took place.

7.2 Autosomal DNA Matches

An individual who tests for autosomal DNA with *Family Tree DNA* or *23andme* or *MyHeritage* or any of the many genetic testing companies available today will be offered the option to discover matches with other users who have tested with this company. It is possible to upload this information to *GEDMatch* or *MyHeritage* and possibly other genetic companies to gain access to a much larger database increasing exponentially the number of matches. Thus, I found 36 matches on Family Tree DNA, 100 on MyHeritage and 1646 on GEDMatch.

Alan Machado, the author of "Sarasvati's children: A history of the Mangalorean Christians," knew from a family history written by his uncle that he is a descendant of Prabhu *gaunkars* from Aldona. The name Machado is not listed in the post-conversion names of the *gaunkars* of Aldona in any of the 12 *vangads* of the *Comunidade Fraternal* but we do encounter the name of Macedo in the 12th *vangad*. When going through Church records, Alan discovered that his family was referred to as Macedo but it was changed to Machado around 1880.[97]

On the public database *GEDmatch*, Alan is shown as belonging to Y DNA haplogroup J-M172 i.e. J2 which is upstream from my haplogroup. *GEDMatch* also shows a genetic relationship of Alan with both Errol Pinto and myself. Since the Y DNA haplogroup is compatible and he is a genetic cousin of both Errol and myself, we can conclude that Alan Machado is a gaunkar of Aldona's 4th *vangad*. **We can also**

conclude from the above that the 12th *vangad* was spun off from the 4th since we are genetic cousins and share the same pre-conversion family name of Prabhu. We can also confirm thanks to genetic genealogy that his original post-conversion name is indeed Macedo and not Machado.

Another one of these matches was with *Donald D'Souza* from Mangalore. We discovered that we share neither a Y DNA haplogroup nor a mtDNA haplogroup; we could thus exclude a *direct* paternal or maternal relationship.

We also found out through *GEDmatch* that Donald was a genetic cousin not only of myself but also of Errol Pinto and Alan Machado who are both my patrilineal genetic cousins, an example of triangulation discussed earlier. The relationship therefore had to be an *indirect* patrilineal.

This is where a paper trail can be of significance. Looking closer at the family names on both sides, we discovered that the family name of Donald's father's grandmother's father was D'Souza Prabhu, a combination of my post and pre-conversion names, which is the indirect patrilineal link we were searching for. For a definitive confirmation, we would need to determine the Y DNA haplogroup of a direct descendant of D'Souza Prabhu who is probably a member of Aldona *Comunidade's* 4th *vangad* and can be predicted to belong to Y DNA haplogroup J-M172 (J2) or one its subclades. In this context, it is very wise of some of the Mangalorean Christians to have preserved their pre- and post-conversion names unlike Goans who have lost their historical links by simply ignoring their pre-conversion Hindu names.

Yet another match is with USA-based Mangalorean *Anil Ferris* whose Y DNA haplogroup is J-M241 (J2b2b, one step downstream from J-M172). GEDmatch shows that he is also linked with Errol Pinto and even more so with Alan Machado. His name probably evolved from Faria that is found only in the 4th *vangad* of Aldona's *comunidade* and he can therefore be classified as a Prabhu of Aldona's 4th *vangad*.

Errol is a Christian from Mangalore who has since emigrated to the United States. He was able to trace his ancestry to an ancestor living in Mangalore in mid 19th century. Additionally, his family tradition transmitted orally claimed descent from a Prabhu.

Tipu Sultan not only decimated the Mangalorean Christian population but also destroyed Churches and records that could have been helpful in tracing their ancestry as described by Alan Machado in his book Sarasvati's Children. With the help of genetic genealogy, it can now be confirmed that his ancestors were *gaunkars* of Aldona village belonging to the fourth *vangad* who migrated to Mangalore at a time that is still to be determined.

Eric D'Cunha, Alan Machado, Anil Ferris, D'Souza Prabhu are also Goans belonging to the 4th *vangad* of Aldona's *Comunidade Fraternal* whose ancestors chose to migrate to Karnataka.

It is well established that in medieval Goa, many Hindus preferred to migrate to the surrounding Muslim-held territories or neighbouring Karnataka rather than renege on the religion of their ancestors and embrace an alien God imposed on them by the Portuguese conquerors. But what is the explanation for this exodus from Aldona of Christian converts who enjoyed many advantages under the Portuguese as a result of their conversion compared to their Hindu brethren?

According to written family history transmitted by the ancestors of Anil Ferris, the migration of his ancestors from Goa to Karnataka occurred around 1735 because the incessant wars between the Portuguese and Marathas resulted in their crops being stolen. At least one family tried to return to Goa about 1760 but was afraid to face the possible perils of the Portuguese inquisition and consequently returned to the Mangalore region.

For the newly baptised Christians after the advent of the Portuguese, life in Goa was a bed of bougainvillea, beautiful flowers for some but mostly thorny for the rest. The Christians were shunned by their non-converted Hindu brethren on the one hand and on the other persecuted by the inquisition introduced in 1560 by the very same authorities that had coerced them into converting.

They faced additional hardships in the form of natural calamities: a great famine in 1630, severe cyclones accompanied by earthquakes in 1649 and 1654. Invasions of Bardez and Salcete by Adil Shah in 1654, invasion of Bardez by Shivaji in 1667 and renewed Maratha attacks in 1683 were additional calamities.[98] Errol's family must therefore have undertaken a perilous migration to Karnataka in the 16th or 17th century.

In 1567 the first Provincial Council of Goa passed an ecclesiastical edict — one of 115 — requiring newly baptised Christians to forego their ancestral Hindu name in favour of that of their Portuguese baptismal godfather. The inquisitorial edict of 1736 introduced 52 prohibitions that intended to eliminate all traces of customs that were even remotely reminiscent of Hindu traditions.[99] It is for this reason that the Prabhus of the 4th *vangad*, just like their entire fellow converts from other Goan villages were forced to forsake the ancestral Hindu names of their ancestors and acquire alien Portuguese family names.

These results derived from genetic genealogy are a triumph over the bigotry of the Catholic Church in 16th century Goa and demonstrate that all the attempts at what could be called identity cleansing have finally ended in failure. Thus a Pinto, Fernandes, D'Cunha and de Sousa can now hold their heads high and backed by scientific proof state with pride that they are in reality distant genetic cousins Errol Prabhu, Hector Prabhu, Eric Prabhu and Bernardo Prabhu.

8. Who Was First: Adam Or Eve?

Chapter 2 of the Genesis relates how man was created:
"Then the Lord God formed the man out of the dust of the ground and blew into his nostrils the breath of life, and the man became a living being".[100] We read further that God said that "it is not good for the man to be alone. I will make a helper suited to him". God then "cast a deep sleep on the man, and while he was asleep, He took out one of his ribs and closed up its place with flesh. The Lord God then built the rib that he had taken from the man into a woman".

In keeping with the age old adage that nobody gets something for nothing, Adam had to sacrifice a rib to acquire a female companion.

As we have seen earlier, humans possess 23 pairs of chromosomes of which 22 are autosomal and the 23rd pair is sex-determining. Sex is thus determined by the Y chromosome located on chromosome 23 with females possessing two XX chromosomes and males one X and one Y.

In order to confirm the story of the creation of man and woman as related in the Genesis, we would expect that the XY chromosome pair evolved first, since man was created first and subsequently from the XY pair, a XX pair specific to females emerged.

The reality is exactly the opposite. Human sex chromosomes XY evolved from autosomes XX. In other words, the default pathway is female and the Y chromosome acts as a switch that overrides this default pathway.

Lahn and Page identified nineteen ancestral autosomal genes that continue to exist on the X and Y chromosomes that pre-date the change of XX to XY. These pseudoautosomal regions at the ends of the X and Y genes in chromosome 23 still recombine during male meiosis but the rest of the regions on this pair do not because recombination has been suppressed.[101] They discovered that the evolution of the human sex chromosomes was marked by four events that occurred in four strata of one of the X chromosomes of the XX pair.

The first event occurred about 240 to 320 million years ago after the divergence of the mammalian and avian lineages creating stratum 1 and the emergence of the sex-determining region Y gene SRY as the primary sex determinant. This event was an inversion, i.e., a segment of DNA turns upside down on the chromosome. Recombination i.e., the exchange of bits of genetic material between a pair of chromosomes was suppressed as a result of the inversion allowing the Y chromosome to evolve independently of its X homologue. Stratum 2 underwent a similar process 130 to 170 million years ago, stratum 3, 80 to 130 million years ago and finally the evolution on stratum 4 began less than 50 million years ago when the simian and prosimian lineages diverged.

With the lack of recombination, the Y chromosome experienced a massive decay and only about 3 percent of the original genes persist today. This explains why the XY chromosome 23 is the smallest of all the chromosome pairs. The Y chromosome could not evolve to acquire new or additional functions because they would require two copies to function as in the case of the remaining 22 other pairs, a situation know as dosage constraint.[102]

The massive decay of the Y chromosome has led to speculation that with continuing degeneration the Y chromosome will eventually become extinct. This would indeed be expected in a linear degeneration model. Analytical approximations and computer simulation models suggest, however, that non-recombining chromosomes degenerate rapidly initially, but gene decay slows down over time and stops altogether once a threshold is reached.[103] Thus, there is hope that human males will continue to exist and not become extinct.

How was sex determined in our evolutionary ancestors before the SRY gene emerged? It could be through species that have separate sexes where the sex of the offspring is triggered by environmental conditions. For example, the sex of most turtles, alligators, and crocodiles is determined after fertilisation by the temperature of the developing embryos. This could also have arisen as species that have both male and female sex organs or hermaphrodites; many types of snails, earthworms, slugs, some fish species and most plants are hermaphrodites.

Jessica K. Abbott *et al.* have provided a useful retrospective of the sex chromosome evolution that an interested reader may wish to consult.[104]

It is known that when a foetus develops in the uterus, our internal organs have the potential to develop into either male or female. Only at weeks 9-13 of pregnancy is the differentiation between female or male take place; this is when the Y chromosome switch in males is turned on and overrides the default pathway which is female. This in itself is indicative of a subsequent evolutionary sexual differentiation.

Charles Darwin furnishes numerous examples of vestigial characteristics in various species, i.e., characteristics that lost all or most of their original function through evolution. In humans and other tailless primates, the coccyx is the remnant of a vestigial tail, wisdom teeth are vestigial third molars that human ancestors used to help in grinding down plant tissue and the appendix is a vestige of the cecum, an organ that would have been used to digest cellulose by humans' herbivorous ancestors.[105]

The mammae in males are vestigial remnants of a pre-evolutionary condition prior to a specialisation to male and female and these were rendered rudimentary and vestigial due to disuse as Charles Darwin explains below.

In *The Origin of Species*, in Chapter XIII, at the very beginning of the section on "rudimentary, atrophied, or aborted organs," Charles Darwin was simply stating an observation when he said that: "Organs or parts in this strange condition, bearing the stamp of inutility, are extremely common throughout nature. For instance, rudimentary mammae are very general in the males of mammals..."

In the same chapter, he offers an explanation: "I believe that disuse has been the main agency; that it has led in successive generations to the gradual reduction of various organs, until they have become rudimentary — as in the case of the eyes of animals inhabiting dark caverns, and of the wings of birds inhabiting oceanic islands, which have seldom been forced to take flight, and have ultimately lost the power of flying".

From all the above explanations, therefore, there is no doubt that in the ancestors of humans, Eve evolved first and Adam developed from Eve after an autosomal X chromosome changed to a Y chromosome.

Why did the XY chromosome pair with a SRY switch to override the XX default pair emerge? One can only speculate. We know that natural selection has often triggered mutations that are beneficial to humans in order to ensure their survival. It is well known that in some regions in Africa, a mutation on chromosome 11 provides partial immunity against malaria. We have also read that a mutation reduced skin pigmentation in regions with lower incidence of sunlight to enable the skin to absorb more UV radiation necessary for the synthesis of Vitamin D. It would therefore not be surprising that natural selection triggered the changes in the XX chromosome pair resulting in better prospects for our survival because perhaps too many genetic errors occurred in the pre-evolutionary stages due to climatic or other reasons. In view of the evolutionary development of the sex chromosomes in several stages, it can be expected that genetic combinations other than XX and XY that is prevalent in most cases will occur and, in fact, they do, leading occasionally to an atypical number of chromosomes. For example, some males may have missing genes in the Y chromosome, a condition that is linked to reduced fertility. Cases of a partially developed Y chromosome can lead to incomplete testicular development. In some cases, a genetic change can consist of an additional X chromosome leading to the presence of not a XY pair but a XXY. Researchers have also found an additional Y chromosome leading to the presence of XYY. Cases of the SRY gene shifting from the Y chromosome to the X chromosome have also been discovered. Thus, genetic divergences in the Y chromosome and intersex are inherent to the human condition and are to be expected from the evolutionary standpoint.

Intersex can be divided into four categories:[106]
- 46, XX Intersex: The person has the chromosomes of a woman, the ovaries of a woman, but external (outside) genitals that appear

male. The causes are generally attributed to specific enzyme deficiencies or hormonal problems.

- 46, XY Intersex: The person has the chromosomes of a man, but the external genitals are incompletely formed, ambiguous, or clearly female. Again, as above, the causes can be enzyme or hormone-related.
- True Gonadal Intersex: Here the person must have both ovarian and testicular tissue. The true causes of this condition are unknown.
- Complex or Undetermined Intersex: Many chromosome configurations other than simple 46, XX or 46, XY can result in disorders of sex development. These include 45, XO (only one X chromosome), and 47, XXY, 47, XXX -- both cases have an extra sex chromosome, either an X or a Y.

The figures change from one study to another, but it is believed that between 0.1% and 0.2% of the population may be born with an intersex condition.

PART II: Peopling Of Goa

If ever there was a melting pot, then it is certainly India. The diversity of the country's population is unique with regard to its cultural and genetic diversity. How this has come to be is helpful in understanding the context that led to the migration of my ancestors to Goa. No published literature exists on the genetics of Goa but a discussion on the peopling of India is very useful to set the stage for a discussion on the peopling of Goa.

1. Peopling of India

In the past, two main theories have been proposed to explain how India has been populated:

1. The Out of India Theory

This theory posits that Aryans and the Indo-European languages are indigenous to India, and it is these Indian Aryans who spread these languages to Eurasia. Genetic support for this theory came from studies by

Thangaraj, Singh *et al.* on mtDNA.[107]

The authors found that mtDNA haplogroup M, to which 60 percent of India's female population belongs, originated in South Asia and most likely in India. Extrapolating this finding to the entire male and female population would indicate that it is India that spread the Indo-European languages to the rest of the world.

An obvious difficulty with this theory is the fact that Y DNA haplogroups of the Indian population are quite varied and not indigenous and thus in contradiction to the conclusions drawn from mtDNA. For example, Sengupta *et al.*[108] studied 728 Indian samples representing 36 populations, including 17 tribal populations, from six geographic regions and different social and linguistic categories.

They comprised Ho, Lodha, Santal (Austro-Asiatic), Chakma, Jamatia, Mog, Mizo, Tripuri (Tibeto-Burman), Irula, Koya Dora, Kamar, Kota, Konda Reddy, Kurumba, Muria, Toda (Dravidian), and Halba (Indo-European).

The 18 castes included Iyer, Iyengar, Ambalakarar, Vanniyar, Vellalar, Pallan (Dravidian) and Koknasth Brahmin, Uttar Pradhesh Brahmin, West Bengal Brahmin, Rajput, Agharia, Gaud, Mahishya, Maratha, Bagdi, Chamar, Nav Buddha, and Tanti (Indo-European)

whereas T. Kivisild *et al.*[109] investigated 325 samples from Chenchu, Koya tribals as well as of W. Bengali, Konkanastha Brahmins, Gujerati, Lambadi, Punjabi and Sinhalese subjects.

The Y DNA haplogroups that the two authors identified belong to C, F, G, H, J, K, T, L, O, P, Q and R, the main ones being **C, F, H, J, L and R**.

Sahoo *et al.*[110] have extended their analysis by investigating a population sample of 936 Y-chromosomes, representing 32 tribal and 45 caste groups from all four major linguistic groups of India.

This study detected a total of 18 haplogroups in the sampled population out of which C, H, J2, L, O and R1, R2 encompassed in excess of 90 percent and included the haplogroups already identified as the major ones in the two studies mentioned earlier.

It can thus be concluded that even though the majority of the mtDNA found in India is autochthonous, Y DNA is not and the Out of India theory has therefore serious limitations.

2. The Aryan Invasion Theory

The proponents of this theory claim that a population from the Caucasus speaking Indo-European languages migrated east towards India and west towards Europe spreading their language along their path. In India, they invaded and violently subdued the indigenous population. They then spread to the rest of the Indian subcontinent from the north to the south. This theory was enthusiastically embraced by Nazi Germany who adopted a modified version of the Swastika as their emblem to emphasise their belief.

No signs of violence as would be expected from a major invasion proposed by this theory have ever been discovered in the Indus Valley Civilisation region.

In his pioneering work "The History and Geography of Human Genes", published in 1994, Luca Cavalli-Sforza and his team proposed at least four major components for India's genetic structure.[111]

- An almost extinct first component (Australoid or Veddoid), older substrate of Palaeolithic occupants
- A second major migration of early Neolithic Caucasoid proto-dravidian speaking farmers from Western Iran responsible for most of the genetic background of India
- Indo-European speaking Aryans, who entered India about 3500 years ago, from their original homeland north of the Caspian sea

(the largest enclosed body of water on earth bounded by Northern Iran, southern Russia, western Kazakhstan and Turkmenistan, and eastern Azerbaijan).

- Austro-Asiatic and Sino-Tibetan language speakers in the North East and centre.

In their seminal work entitled *Peopling of India*, Gadgil *et al*. have studied mtDNA results, a well as linguistic and anthropological information to draw very interesting and relevant inferences on how India has been populated since pre-historic times.[112]

The authors postulate that at least four major lineages are represented by the four language families spoken in India: Austric, Dravidian, Indo-European, Sino-Tibetan.

Since the great majority of Austric speakers, who in India are exclusively tribal, inhabit Southeast Asia, they suggest that they may have entered India from the Northeast some 50 kybp (thousand years before present) and are thus the oldest inhabitants. They were followed by the Dravidian speakers, 6 to 10 kybp from the Middle East, who were wheat cultivators and bred cattle entering India from the Northwest. The rice-cultivators from China and Southeast Asia speaking Sino-Tibetan languages arrived in India 8 to 10 kybp using the northeastern corridor. The last to arrive were the Indo-European speakers around 4 kybp and brought with them the knowledge of iron technology and domestication and use of horses.

The limitation of all these studies is that in addition to archeological and linguistic data, they are based exclusively on either Y DNA or mitochondrial DNA and are therefore restricted in scope. They are no doubt very useful to establish the patrilineal and matrilineal ancestry but we miss a massive amount of information from our autosomal genes.

Our ancestry consists of fragments of DNA that have been passed on to us since times immemorial by our successive paternal and maternal ancestors. Each of us has inherited DNA from our parents, they in turn from their parents who got their genetic material from their parents and so on. Each of these has contributed to our individual genetic makeup and all this resides in our 23 chromosome pairs. The key therefore lies in a full genome analysis i.e., an analysis of all 23 chromosomes. It would be particularly helpful if whole genome tests of ancient skeletons or bones from the population of the Indus Valley Civilisation could be carried out because they would reveal not only their Y

DNA and mtDNA haplogroups but more importantly the ancestry of the ancient inhabitants as well as their migration paths.

David Reich and his team were interested in verifying Luca Cavalli-Sforza's speculation that the inhabitants of the Andaman Islands could possibly be descendants of the earliest out of Africa migrants dating back to even prior to fifty thousand years ago.

Having read a paper by Lalji Singh and Kumarasamy Thangaraj, Center for Cellular and Molecular Biology, Hyderabad, India on an analysis of the mitochondrial and Y DNA of Andaman Islanders, they proposed to these scientists to carry out whole genome analyses of the Andaman Islanders. Singh and Thangaraj not only accepted to collaborate but suggested expanding the project to include mainland Indians as well and offered access to their vast collection of DNA.

David Reich runs if not the most than certainly one of the most advanced genetics laboratories in the world. The DNA was analysed by SNP microarray, a technology not available in India at that time. They found that that the frequencies of genetic mutations found in all Indians could be explained by a mixture of two very different ancient populations, one related to Europeans, central Asians and Near Easterners and the other distantly related to East Asians. They initially called the former „West Eurasian," a term that led to what Reich says were „the tensest twenty-four hours of my scientific career".

Thangaraj and Singh threatened to call off the project because they objected to the term „West Eurasian" since it could imply that West Eurasian people had migrated into India and it could very well have been the other way around as indicated by their mitochondrial DNA data. The problem was resolved by changing the terms West Eurasian and East Asian-related to „Ancient North Indian" ANI and „Ancient South Indian" ASI, a terminology that has now been universally adopted, and avoids all reference to their homeland or migrations.[113,114]

Further analysis showed that ANI/ASI mixture applied to all Indians irrespective of caste including the tribals and the ANI component ranged from 20 percent to 80 percent. In short, all Indians are a mixture and there is no such thing as a pure Indian race.

People belonging to higher castes have on average a higher proportion of ANI ancestry and speak an Indo-European language whereas the lower castes have a lower proportion of ASI and speak a Dravidian language. This is indicative of a social stratificatiℴ. duced by the mixing of the two ancestries and that the Indℴ languages was brought into India by ANI.

These studies could not reveal when the mixing occurred; to this end, new methods had to be developed. The Reich team measured the size of the DNA fragments from the ANI and ASI ancestry in the Indian samples and calculated how many generations would be needed to inherit a fragment of that specific size keeping in mind that with each generation, the DNA we inherit gets increasingly fragmented. The results showed that the mixture occurred between four thousand and two thousand years ago and that there had been multiple waves of ANI mixture.

We now had a good picture: all Indians are a mixture of ancient populations, this mixture started around 4000 years ago around the time the IVC/Harappa civilisation became extinct and it occurred in multiple waves. A more detailed and precise finer picture would be possible by analysing ancient DNA and this is exactly what eminent archeologist and Indus Valley Civilisation expert Professor Vasant S. Shinde and his team undertook in the IVC region. From such a study, it would be possible to discover the ancestry of the people who lived in IVC and if they shared any ancestry with a population from the North. In short, if would either confirm or disprove the Aryan Invasion Theory.

Professor Shinde's team attempted unsuccessfully to retrieve DNA from an Indus Valley site during an excavation at Farmana, Haryana in 2007–2010 because not being geneticists, they failed to work swiftly and take precautions to avoid contamination of the samples.[115]

The team did not repeat the same mistakes when an excavation was carried out at the IVC site of Rakhigarhi, also in the Indian State of Haryana, during the period 2013-2016. The fascinating archeological and anthropological findings were published in February 2018 but there is no allusion to the retrieval of DNA in that article.[116] It has, however, been documented in a India Today cover story published in September 2018 and elsewhere.[117,118] that in 2014, DNA was retrieved from four skeletons at the Rakhigarhi cemetery: a couple, a boy and a man who lived approximately 4600 years ago during mature Harappa. A paper with the results eagerly awaited by the international scientific community expected in September 2017 is yet to be published, apparently due to their non-conformity to political expectations but hopefully science will finally prevail and the information will soon be available. If the studies would reveal that the Y DNA of the skeletons does not show ANI descent, the Aryan Invasion Theory would have to be revisited and this seems indeed to be the case. In an essay published in Caravan Magazine on April 27, 2018, Niraj Rai, the head of the Ancient DNA Laboratory at Lucknow's Birbal Sahni Institute of Palaeosciences (BSIP), where the DNA samples from the Harappan site of Rakhigarhi are being analysed, is quoted as saying that the Harappan population do not have any Steppe ancestry and the results will soon to be published in *bioRxiv*.[119] In yet another article in Outlook India published on August 2, 2018, Niraj Rai is quoted as follows: "The Rakhigarhi samples have a significant amount of 'Iranian farmer' ancestry. You won't find this DNA in the North Indian population today, but only in South Indians".[120]

In the meantime, in March 2018, David Reich and his team at Harvard and Vasant Shinde and his team of scientists leading the Rakhigarhi project found a way to circumvent the absence of IVC ancient DNA and instead analysed outliers that would be expected to be similar to the IVC population and labelled them Indus_Periphery. They jointly published an article tagged as Narasimhan *et al*. entitled The Genomic Formation of South and Central Asia that largely provides the answers even though "we do not have access to any DNA directly sampled from the Indus Valley Civilisation",[121] an astonishing statement considering the fact that the results on the DNA retrieved by Professor Vasant Shinde's team from the 4 samples from the Rakhigarhi cemetery have been completed and are referred to in the press in India as mentioned above.

In their afore-mentioned Narasimhan *et al*. study, the authors generated whole genome studies of previously unreported aDNA from 362 individual and higher quality data of an additional 17 previously reported individuals from Iran and the southern part of Central Asia that the authors label Turan (short for Turkmenistan, Uzbekistan and Tajikistan), from the western and central Steppe and northern forest zone Kazakhstan and Russia and finally from Swat Valley of Northern Pakistan that represents South Asia in this study. The samples cover the Chalcolithic and Bronze Age Eastern Iran and Turan (5600 – 1200 BCE), early hunter-gatherers from the western Siberian forest zone

(6200 – 4000 BCE), Chalcolithic and Bronze Age pastoralists from the Steppe east of the Ural Mountains (4700 – 1000 BCE) and Iron Age South Asians from the Swat Valley of Pakistan (1200 BCE – 1 CE). They compared this information with whole genome data of present-day 246 ethnographically distinct groups in South Asia. The results confirm what was already known from the project with Thangaraj and Singh but provide a more detailed picture of India's ancestors, their migration locations and timings of the events.

From the many highly interesting conclusions proposed in this paper, the following are of particular relevance to this discussion:

- The population of the *Indus_Periphery* – a term the authors use to cover outlier individuals and the Northern fringe of IVC in the absence of aDNA from the IVC region itself — consisted of a mixture of both Iranian migrants from the Zagros Mountains region (58%-86%) and South Asian hunter-gatherers, labelled Ancient Ancestral South Indian (*AASI*)-related (14% — 42%), a lineage deeply linked to present-day indigenous Andaman Islanders. They mixed around 4700-3000 BCE and this population was well established in the region in the 3rd millennium BCE. It is, however, possible that the Iranian ancestry was present even earlier and earlier settlements will be discovered over time. Based on the YFull 700 analysis of my DNA, this appears to be indeed the case.

- Coinciding with the decline of the IVC, Yamnaya-related pastoral groups labelled *Steppe–MLBA* for Middle Late Bronze Age – moved south and mixed with the *Indus_Periphery*-related groups in the 2nd millennium BCE to form the Ancestral North India *ANI* population. To quote from the paper: " A parsimonious hypothesis is that as *Steppe_MLBA* groups moved south and mixed with *Indus_Periphery*-related groups at the end of the *IVC* to form the *ANI*, other *Indus_Periphery*-related groups moved further south and east to mix with *AASI* groups in peninsular India to form the *ASI*." We recall that the decline of the IVC occurred approximately between 2000-1800BCE and the Sintashta culture evolved between 2100 and 1800BCE. The obvious conclusion is, therefore, that the Yamnaya-related population that first arrived on the Indian subcontinent belonged to the Sintashta culture.

- Other *Indus_Periphery*-related groups moved south and east and mixed with *AASI* groups to form the Ancestral South India *ASI* population.
- In this scenario, the IVC population spoke a Dravidian language and was responsible for spreading it in South India when they moved south.
- The language ancestral to all modern Indo-European languages spoken in India and Europe, namely, Late Proto-Indo-European was the language of the Yamnaya-related ancestors who not only spread south to India but also west to Europe.

The major migrations are depicted in detail in the image below:

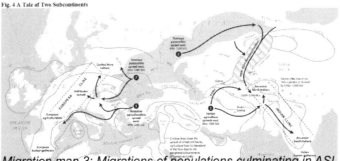

Fig. 4 A Tale of Two Subcontinents

Migration map 3: Migrations of populations culminating in ASI and ANI and their mixtures on the Indian subcontinent.
Source: Narasimhan et al.[121]

A just published study by Shinde, Reich *et al.* reports the results of their investigation of an ancient IVC genome. The authors found that the largest component was related to ancient Iranians and the rest with Southeast Asian hunter-gatherers, a unique profile that matches ancient DNA from 11 genetic outliers from sites in Iran and Turkmenistan who were known to trade with IVC. The ancient Iranians migrated more than 10'000 years ago and were therefore not farmers but rather different groups of hunter-gatherers because their migration occurred much earlier than the introduction of farming in the Fertile Crescent. Farming in IVC could consequently have been the result of local innovation or learning from their connections with trading partners rather than wide scale migration of Iranian farmers. The presence of Steppe-related pastoralist ancestry could also be excluded.[122] Clearly, it is not possible to draw broad conclusions based on the results of one single ancient individual since this would hardly be statistically representative of the millions of people who inhabited the IVC region. It also does not exclude the possibility that other later migrations followed, including of Iranian farmers. Research in this area is continuing and is expected to shed more light on the migrations of our ancient ancestors.

It has already been established in many studies that the Yamnaya Steppe population belong to Y DNA haplogroup R1a in South Asia and R1b in Europe and its subclades. Consequently, we would expect that DNA from the skeletons retrieved on the Harappan site of Rakhigarhi do not exhibit this haplogroup since the Yamnaya-related population was not in the region. In the India Today cover story mentioned above, Niraj Rai, the lead genetics researcher on the Rakhigarhi project is quoted as affirming that this is indeed the case:"R1a is not there".

1.1 Ancient North Indian ANI Ancestry
Who were the Yamnaya?

Allentoft *et al.* have provided a good description of the different cultures that arose and evolved in the Steppes; the following account includes parts that are relevant for our discussion.[123]

The Bronze Age started in Mesopotamia was triggered by the use of copper alloys and bronze to manufacture different kinds of products such as weapons, agricultural tools, ornaments and cooking and drinking utensils. The metal being unavailable in Mesopotamia, it was sourced from the Caucasus and Anatolia, where Mesopotamian groups that came to be known as the Uruk movement established themselves in order to ensure supplies. The finished products were then traded from Mesopotamia to the Caucasus where the Maikop culture developed in northern Caucasus with individualised property and monogamous families. A new concept emerged of burials in individual or family graves in kurgans (barrows) with the graves being covered with a mound of earth that resemble small hills. This culture soon spread to the Steppe where an economy based on pastoralism and cattle herding flourished. The Maikop culture left for posterity figurines of cattle made out of gold to symbolise the use of these animals for the earliest wheeled vehicles.

In the meantime, in the western forest bordering the Steppe a large settlement known as the Tripolje culture emerged. Because of its large size, the settlement could not sustain itself and collapsed. The population migrated to the Steppe where they encountered the Maikop culture; out of this merger, horse domestication and wheeled wagons developed to adapt to the new highly mobile pastoral society. From the meeting of the Maikop and Tripolje cultures, a new expansionist society called the Yamnaya culture evolved around 3000 BCE.

Lazaridis *et al.* show that Early to Middle Bronze Age Steppe groups, including Yamnaya, tagged by them as Steppe EMBA, are best modeled with formal statistics as a mixture of Eastern European Hunter-Gatherers (EHG) and Chalcolithic farmers from western Iran. The mixture ratios are 56.8/43.2, respectively.[124]

They were highly mobile, rode horses, and lived in wagons as a way of managing large herds and did not therefore leave behind any major settlements.

In an incisive article entitled Social Inequality Leaves a Genetic Mark, by eminent professor of genetics at Harvard Medical School David Reich, the author argues that due to the biological differences between the sexes, women have to carry the unborn child for nine months and invest several years in rearing it whereas men have to invest much less time to procreate and are therefore much more efficient in spreading their genes. Consequently, genetic data shows that powerful men have a far greater effect than powerful women as measured by their contribution to the next generation.

This is exemplified by the fact that about 8 percent of the male population in the lands that once belonged to the Mongol Empire that extended to Korea in the east, central Europe to the west and Tibet to the south share a characteristic Y-chromosome sequence and a cluster of similar sequences differing by only a few mutations. This Y-chromosome imprint is attributed to Genghis Khan and his descendants.

The onset of the Bronze Age about 5000 years ago launched a period of great human mobility and wealth accompanied by social inequality, triggered by the domestication of the horse, the invention of the wheel and its application in wheeled vehicles and the accumulation of metals like copper and tin used in the manufacture of bronze. This was the time when the Yamnaya rose to power by exploiting these resources. They and the cultures ensuing from them displaced the farmers from northern Europe and the hunter-gatherers in central Asia in the east leaving a genetic imprint that easily surpasses that of Genghis Khan.

The late archaeologist and anthropologist Marija Gimbutas concluded from her excavations that the Yamnaya culture was a very sex-biased and stratified society. Eighty percent of the kurgans contained male skeletons as also the satellite graves. The skeletons showed marks of violent injuries and were buried with fearsome metal daggers and axes.[125]

Using an admixture model to compare the X chromosome with the autosomes of different populations that migrated to Europe in ancient times, Amy Goldberg *et al.* found no evidence of sex-biased admixture during the migration of Anatolian farmers across Europe during the early Neolithic implying that men and women of this population migrated in roughly equal numbers. For later migrations of the Yamnaya from the Pontic Steppe during the late Neolithic/Bronze Age, however, they found a dramatic male bias, with approximately five to 14 migrating males for every migrating female and in repeated multigenerational cycles.[126] The Yamnaya related Steppe migration to the Indian subcontinent was no doubt a replication of migration of this culture to Europe.

Evidence from ancient DNA shows that in the Yamnaya society, power was concentrated among a small number of elite males. They and their descendants left their Y chromosome imprint in Europe and India in a very big way because where none was present prior to the Bronze Age, their Y DNA predominates today in both regions. David Reich adds that the Y chromosome of the Yamnaya being of a few types, a limited number of males must have been extraordinarily successful in spreading their genes and this expansion could "not have been entirely friendly".

Around 2900 BCE they expanded towards the west to the Hungarian plain as well as north of the Carpathian and to the east to the Urals where they seem to have settled down for a thousand years.

An extension of the Yamnaya in the Ural-Tobol Steppe is the Poltavka culture that interacted with the Abashevo culture from the region of the southern Ural Mountains to evolve to the **Sintashta culture (2100-1800BCE);** genetically this group tagged by Narasimhan *et al.* as Steppe_MLBA harboured a mixture of Steppe_EMBA ancestry described above and European Middle Neolithic Agriculturist ancestry tagged as Europe_MN. Located close to copper mines, the Sintashta constructed highly organised fortified settlements where houses were systematically laid out and the economy was principally pastoral. They built chariots, bred horses, produced new weapons and trained people to use them. They had a warrior aristocracy and warriors and charioteers were often buried with two-wheeled chariots and two horses in kurgans. It would appear that after 1800 or 1700 BCE, the Sintashta expanded eastwards to form the Andronovo culture. They migrated further south and east into northern Iran and Northern India / Pakistan where they became the new ruling elite. The Rig Veda hymns and texts written probably between 1500 and 1000 BCE show many similarities with the Sintashta / Andronovo rituals. The continuation and transformation of this culture is represented by the Karasuk Culture proven to be connected to my maternal ancestry (cf. Part 1, chapter 5.The Matrilineal Trail through Mitochondrial DNA)

From a genetic point of view, the Yamnaya were a mix of European hunter-gatherers and Caucasian hunter-gatherers in approximately equal proportions.[127]

Autosomal DNA studies suggest that the genetic ancestry of the Corded Ware culture of Europe and the **Sintashta** are similar and may imply that Corded Ware groups from Europe migrated eastwards and contributed to their ancestry.[128] But we also know that the ancestry of the Corded Ware is genetically closely linked to that of the Yamnaya implying a euroasiatic Steppe migration into the European heartland.[129]

1.2 Ancient South Indian ASI Ancestry

The whole genome analysis described in the paper by Narasimhan *et al.* found that the ASI ancestry consisted of a mixture of an **Iranian agriculturist** component and an indigenous **Ancient Ancestral South Indian AASI** component, a hunter gatherer population related to the present-day Andaman Islanders. They suggest that ASI may have formed during the Bronze Age with the arrival of Iranian agriculturists around 3000 BCE where they interbred with the indigenous AASI.

The Iranian migrants from the Zagros Mountains harboured a West Eurasian, early Anatolian and West Siberian hunter-gatherers labeled West_Siberian_HG ancestry. The West Siberian people were themselves a mixture of 30 percent Eastern European hunter gatherers, 50 percent Ancestral North Eurasians (i.e., Siberians of 22'000 to 15'000 years ago) and 20 percent East Asian.

Scientists used a programme called qpAdm that is commonly applied today in genetics. In this programme, proposed source populations are compared with a test population to evaluate if the comparison is consistent and if this is indeed the case, in which proportions the test population is mixed. The results show that gene flow occurred into South Asia and not the other way around, thus sounding the death knell to the Out of India theory.

The **Ancient Ancestral South Indian** population were indigenous hunter gatherers and a branch of Asian hominins that split off at the same time as the ancestors of East Asians, the Onge tribes of the Andaman Islands and the Australian aboriginals. The AASI together with the East Asians, Onge and Australian aboriginals are lineages that were formed when the out of Africa humans spread eastward in one single migration event. In this context, it would be of great interest to have access to the genetics of the inhabitants of the North Sentinel Islands, one of the last uncontacted populations of the world. No published data on the genetics of the Sentinelese exists; their traditions are known to be similar to those of the Onge tribe and they are quite possibly linked to the AASI population.

As we can see from the above, there is no such thing as a pure Indian and every Indian has an ancestry that is profoundly mixed in differing proportions:

The Iranians from the Zagros mountains were of a mixed heredity of West Eurasian, early Anatolian and Western Siberian. The genes of the latter Western Siberian consisted of 30% Eastern European hunter gatherers, 50% Ancestral North Eurasians and 20% East Asians.

These migrants from Iran mixed with the local population that they encountered that are closely related to the Onge and are tagged as Ancient Ancestral South Indians AASI to give rise to the Ancestral South Indians ASI.

Around the time the Indus Valley Civilisation became extinct, the Yamnaya related population from the Siberian Steppe, in all probability belonging to the Sintastha culture arrived from the North. They were a mixture of 26% European Middle East neolithic agriculturists and 74% of a Steppe population of Early to Middle bronze age. These migrants mixed with the ASI whom they encountered when they entered the Indian subcontinent to give rise to a population tagged as Ancestral North Indian ANI.

The Sintashta arrived in multiple waves to the north and the proportions of the mixtures therefore vary with a greater ANI component in northern India.

At the same time, the ANI-ASI mixtures migrated further South and mixed with the ASI and AASI that they encountered, thus adding more proportionality to the genetic mixtures.

In fact, Indians are not only mixtures but as we can see from above, they are mixtures of mixtures.

The popular Indian curry was no doubt inspired by the Indian genetic ancestry: a complex mixture of varied spices in variable proportions, sometimes sweetish, sometimes pungent, with different flavours depending on the region, and yet resulting in the same unmistakable unique end product, the Indian curry, akin to Indian ethnicity.

1.3 India's Mitochondrial DNA Landscape

In the year 2000, Toomas Kivisild *et al*. published an interesting paper on Indian ancestry.[130] After analysing about 1000 mtDNA covering 19 different Indian populations they found that the most frequent haplogroup is M (56 to 60%) and the subclades found in India are different from those encountered in East Asia. They calculated the branching off of the Indian subclades from the other branches to 55 thousand to 73 thousand years ago. The same is true of haplogroup U that is frequent in Europe but not in East Asia but the Indian subclades differ from those found elsewhere. They also found that the carriers of mtDNA R*— the star indicates that the haplogroup is nodal and subclades had not yet been formed — arrived in India very early along with M*. They concluded that 90 percent of the mtDNA encountered in India is indigenous and external mtDNA gene flow into India is less than 10 percent.

A more recent study confirms the above findings. Additionally, the authors identified the mtDNA haplogroups M and its subclades M2, M2a, M3, M4, M6, M9, M18, M25; M-DEG. They also found the haplogroups N and R and to a smaller extent T and U1, U2i, U4, U7a.[131] It is noteworthy that the authors do not mention U5 related to my maternal descent.

To summarise, the mitochondrial DNA haplogroups found in India are to a large extent autochthonous.

1.4 India's Y DNA Landscape

Sengupta *et al.*[132] studied 728 Indian samples representing 36 populations, including 17 tribal populations, from six geographic regions and different social and linguistic categories. They found eight haplogroups with frequencies exceeding 5% within India that account for 95.8% of the samples: H and its subclades H1*, H1c, H1a, and H2 (26.4%); R1a1-M17 (15.8%); O2a-M95 (14.6%); R2-M124 (9.3%); J2-M172 (9.1%); O3e-M134 (8.0%); L1-M76 (6.3%); and F*-M89 (5.2%).

T. Kivisild *et al.*[133] investigated 325 samples from Chenchu, Koya tribals as well as of W. Bengali, Konkanastha Brahmins, Gujerati, Lambadi, Punjabi and Sinhalese subjects. Sahoo *et al.*[134] extended their analysis by investigating a population sample of 936 Y-chromosomes, representing 32 tribal and 45 caste groups from all four major linguistic groups of India.

This study detected a total of 18 haplogroups in the population tested out of which C, H, J2, L, O and R1, R2 encompass in excess of 90 percent and include the haplogroups already identified as the major ones in the two studies described above.

A very recent study published in October 2018,[135] 407 unrelated male individuals from 12 states in India were genotyped using a suite covering a wide range of Y-STRs. A total of 14 haplogroups were found namely:

R1a, H, L, Q, J2b, J2a1 x J2a1-bh, J2a1b, J1, G2a, I2a (xI2a1), R1b, E1b1b, E1b1ba and T.

Of these, the following three were the major Y DNA haplogroups present throughout India carried by more than 83 percent of the population:

R1a (51.5%)

H (16.2%)

L (15.8%)

R1a was found to decrease from north to south, the presence of L decreased from south to north and H is evenly distributed throughout the country.

Among the branches of J, J2b and J2a1 x J2a1-bh were the most prominent. All the other Y-STRs were rare in the population submitted to analysis.

It is not surprising that Sengupta *et al.* found haplogroup proportions that differ from the above study because as the whole genome studies have shown, regional admixtures within India vary greatly and the sample sizes are small compared to the total population of the country.

The four main Y DNA haplogroups that are found in India are described in more detail below.

1.4.1 Y DNA Haplogroup R1a – Z93

Haplogroup R originated in North Asia around 30700 ybp according to YFull. This haplogroup has been identified in the 24,000 year-old remains of "Mal'ta boy" from the Altai region, in south-central Siberia whose existence had been predicted by David Reich based on genetic analyses and is today labelled as Ancient North Eurasian ANE. This individual belonged to a tribe of mammoth hunters that may have roamed across Siberia and parts of Europe during the Palaeolithic.[136] R1a was formed 22800 ybp and the subclade R1a-Z93 (YCC nomenclature R1a1a1b2) that is widely present in India emerged about 5000 ybp.[137]

In the past, scientists have proposed a number of possible origins of R1a-Z93 but the ancient DNA revolution has now provided a more specific answer. Narasimhan *et al.* found that whereas R1a was absent in the Yamnaya samples labelled *Steppe_EMBA* tested in their project, 68 percent of the population labelled *Steppe_MLBA* harboured this haplogroup; this population is related to the Sintashta culture. Data published by Allentoft *et al.* reveals that the sample RISE386 belonging to the Sintashta culture belonged to this haplogroup.

Narasimhan *et al.* found that a genetically homogenous population inhabited a vast region of Eastern Europe and trans-Ural Steppe associated with Corded Ware, Srubnaya, Petrovska, Sintashta and Andronovo complexes, all of them genetic mixtures of *Steppe_EMBA* (i.e., Yamnaya) ancestry and European Middle Neolithic agriculturists (*Europe_MN*). Most males analysed harboured the R1a-Z93 Y DNA haplogroup.

Mathieson *et al.* found a direct link between the European Steppe and Central / South Asia by discovering four Srubnaya and one

110

Poltavka males of haplogroup R1a-Z93 which is common in present-day central/south Asians and Bronze Age people from the Altai.[138]

It is now possible to describe the migration from the Steppes to South Asia and India. About 3000 years BCE, Yamnaya pastoralists spread west to Europe and east towards the Altai Mountains, where several cultures such as Srubnaya, Petrovska, Sintashta and Andronovo harbouring the Y DNA haplogroup R1a subclades. Using the Inner Asian Mountain corridor these Yamnaya-related people identified as the Sintashta moved southwards arriving in the Indian subcontinent around 2000-1500 BCE coinciding with the extinction of the Indus Valley Civilisation, and mixed with the ASI they encountered to form the Ancestral North Indians ANI.[139]

1.4.2 Y DNA Haplogroup H

This haplogroup has not been comprehensively studied. This haplogroup was probably formed thirty to forty thousand years ago. It consists of 3 subclades H1, H2 and H3, each of them subdivided into additional subclades.

The vast majority of the people belonging to this subclade can be found in South Asia.

In Western Europe, the bearers of Y DNA haplogroup H are the Romani people who are known to have originated in India.

Interestingly, H2 is commonly encountered in Sardinia, an island in the Mediterranean Sea. Recent whole genome studies by David Reich[140] revealed that the ancestry of Sardinians originated from farmers from the Near East who migrated to Europe and to this island around eight thousand years ago. The island of Sardinia remained isolated and was not affected by the subsequent ancestry changes that occurred in the rest of Europe. This would link the haplogroup H in India to farmers from the Near East.

1.4.3 Y DNA Haplogroup L

Haplogroup L-M20 probably arose 25 to 30 thousand years bp in South Asia, West Asia or Pamir Mountains. It is further subdivided into L-M22 (L1) and L-L595 (L2) that are split into additional subclades.

L-M20 can be found throughout South Asia, principally in Balochistan (28%), Northern Afghanistan (25%) and Southern India (19%). It also occurs in Tajikistan and Anatolia and at lower frequencies in Iran.

It has also been present for millennia at very low levels in the Caucasus, Europe and Central Asia.

1.4.4 Y DNA Haplogroup J

Haplogroup J-M304 was formed more than 40 thousand years ago in Western Asia. It has two subclades J1 and J2 that are further split into a number of subclades.

Its greatest concentration is in the Arabian peninsula and it can also be found in North Africa and the Horn of Africa. The J-M410 (J1) subclade is common in Anatolia, Greece and Southern Italy and can be encountered also in Central Asia .The subclade J-M172 (J2) predominates in South Asia including India. J2b2 has been discussed in detail in the earlier chapters of this book.

The interested reader can find details on all the Y DNA haplogroups including their own in:
- International Society of Genetic Genealogy, Y DNA Haplogroup Tree, online at https://isogg.org/tree/
- YFull, online at https://www.yfull.com/tree/
- Charles Kerchner's YDNA Haplogroup Descriptions & Information Links, online at http://www.kerchner.com/haplogroups-ydna.htm

2. Peopling of Goa

Parashurama, the Lord warrior with the axe (*parashu* means axe in Sanskrit), the sixth incarnation of Lord *Vishnu*, is credited with having reclaimed land from the ocean by shooting an arrow or throwing his axe, depending on the version, into the ocean that sent the water rolling back. His name, however, would indicate that an axe would be the preferred weapon used for the purpose. He brought from Trihotrapura, modern day Tirhut in upper Bihar, Brahmins belonging to ten *gotras* and those who settled in sixty-six villages called their settlement *Sasashti* or *Shat-sashti* meaning sixty-six that has now evolved to Salcete. Thirty other groups of families from Tirhut followed who settled in *Tiswadi*, literally meaning thirty villages. The *Baradesh* (twelve villages) settlement, today's Bardez, was settled later.[141]

Was *Parashurama* a mythological figure or is there any corroboration from genetic genealogy of the detailed description in the *Sahyadri Skanda*?

Genetics seems to indicate that *Parashurama* actually existed. The description of the Yamnaya and other cultures from the Steppes that evolved from them such as the *Sintashta* culture leads us to believe that *Parashurama* was a powerful *Sintashta* or another *Yamnaya*-related warrior leader. Like the *Sintashta*, his prowess at wielding his axe was such that even the ocean recoiled in fear. His skills and qualities as a warrior were undisputed and he could crush his enemies with ease akin to the *Yamnaya* and *Sintashta* warriors. Like the leaders of these cultures, he was skilled at riding horses and manoeuvring a chariot. And also like them, he spoke an Indo-Iranian language. Sage Valmiki refers to *Parashurama* as Lord *Vimardhana*, the subjugator of kings who punished evildoers and unjust rulers who did not protect their subjects.[142] Such a warrior leader would easily be able to command respect and loyalty and other leaders would follow him, as did the families belonging to the ten gotras who settled in Goa.

No genetic study existed on how and when Goa was populated. The currently available information was based on some archeological findings but factual evidence on this topic was very limited. We now have scientific evidence that my ancestors migrated to Goa around 700 BCE-600 BCE and migrations continued over a large period of time.

The study published by Narasimhan *et al.* discussed earlier contains **whole genome** information on several Indian populations including a Brahmin Catholic from Goa. The qmAdm analysis shows that this individual's ancestry consists of 18.3 percent *MLBA_Steppe* that as we know corresponds to Yamnaya-related Ancestral North Indian ANI, 53.1 percent Indus_diaspora-related corresponding to Ancestral South Indian ASI and 28.5 percent Onge (Ancient Ancestral South Indian AASI)-related. This compares well with values obtained for a Brahmin Bhatt for example and could probably be representative for all Goan Brahmins, Catholic and Hindu.

As already discussed in previous chapters, my Y DNA Haplogroup is **Jb2b** and further downstream J-FT14805*.
Through matches with my DNA, it was possible to discover several Goans from Aldona belonging to the same or related *vangad* including those whose ancestors migrated to Karnataka. This explains why this haplogroup is overrepresented in this study:

Hector Fernandes
Errol Pinto

Eric D'Cunha

Alan Machado

Anil Ferris

The *comunidade* of the neighbouring village of Moira consists of 5 *vangads*. I had the privilege of obtaining genetic information on members of two of the *vangads* and permission to divulge the haplogroups:

Late Professor Teotonio R. de Souza of Moira's 5th *vangad* harboured the Y DNA haplogroup **J2b2**.[143] It is not a surprise that Len Mendes from Moira settled in Calgary, Canada also shares the same haplogroup since he also belongs to Moira's 5th *vangad*. As we have already discussed in Part I, Chapter 7, all members of a specific vangad are descendants of the common founder of this clan and consequently share the same ancestral name and Y DNA haplogroup.

John Nazareth of Moira's 1st *vangad* belongs to Y DNA haplogroup **R-M124 or R2a** according to the YCC nomenclature. Sengupta *et al.* state that the source of this haplogroup that was formed around 14700 years bp is Southwest Asia and migration to India occurred in several waves.[144] It could be hypothesised that individuals belonging to the Y DNA haplogroup R and who were linked to the Yamnaya or their descendants were chosen preferentially to form the 1st *vangad* and lead the settlement of a village. More genetic research on the haplogroups of the 1st clan of several comunidades would be required to validate this hypothesis.

An interesting question that arises is if there is a close relationship between the 4th *vangad* of Aldona and the 5th *vangad* of Moira, since both share the same Y DNA haplogroup J2b2. One reason why this is not the case is the fact that the founder of Moira's 5th *vangad* was Kamat - Professor Teotonio R. de Souza's ancestor's name was Shantappa Kamat - whereas Aldona's 4th *vangad* was founded by a Prabhu. Thus, their professional specialisations were quite different because a Kamat was an agriculturist and the expertise of my Prabhu ancestors was in land reclamation and the building and maintenance of embankments. I was privy to the Y DNA results of late Teotonio R. de Souza and could thus compare his detailed results with mine. Since the tests were carried out by different companies, many of the markers tested differ but from those that were in common, the number of differences led to the conclusion that we shared a common ancestor more than 2 thousand years ago.

Moving on to the village of Saligão whose *comunidade* consists of 12 *vangads*, as part of this project, a sample belonging to noted Church historian, late Father Nascimento Mascarenhas of Saligão's 11th *vangad* was tested and found to belong to Y DNA haplogroup **H-M69**. This haplogroup has been discussed in Part II, chapter 1.4.2.

I was also privy to data on the Y DNA test results of Rohit Menezes, a gaunkar of Malar in the island of Divar, who belongs to Y DNA haplogroup **L** (cf. Part II, chapter 1.4.3).

The village of Assagão has 13 *vangads*. The ancestors of Melvyn D'Souza from Toronto, Canada, who belong to the 7th *vangad* and whose ancestral name was Prabhu as orally transmitted to him, migrated to Karnataka in 1740 CE. He harbours the Y DNA haplogroup **L-M27 (L1a1** according to YCC nomenclature). This haplogroup was formed about 17100 years bp and his L sub-clade is found in about 15% of Indian males. It is also encountered in 20 percent of Balochi in Pakistan, and has also been reported in Kirghiz, Pashtun, Tajik, Uzbek, and Turkmen males across Central Asia.[145]

The whole genome and Y DNA data of Goans mentioned above are random and not collected systematically. They nevertheless allow us to draw some interesting conclusions.

My own whole genome analysis by Family Tree DNA's Family Finder test is biased towards Europeans but it does place my Ancient Origin results as 12 percent Farmer, 63 percent Metal Age Invader, and 25 percent non-European. The 12 percent Farmer contribution corresponds to the Neolithic period (8000 to 7000 ybp) when people from the Iranian Zagros Mountains moved to the Indus Valley Civilisation region. The 63 percent Metal Age Invader contribution is connected to the Bronze Age Yamnaya-related population. That this proportion is higher than expected can be attributed to the fact that in addition to the Yamnaya-related ancestry admixture in the Indian population, my maternal ancestry is also Yamnaya-related. The 25 percent non-European contribution further identified as 53 percent South Central Asia and 45 percent Central Asia could be attributed to the indigenous hunter-gatherers related to the Onge Andaman Islanders inhabiting the Indian sub-continent prior to the arrival of the Iranian farmers. These results fit well with the findings of Narasimhan *et al.* Similarly, the whole genome study of the Goan catholic Brahmin corresponds with other findings for the region.

The data above have identified the presence of Y DNA haplogroups R-M124, H-M69, L including the subclade L-M27 and J2b2, all expected in the Indian population. No R1a has been found but we know from the admixture in the two whole genome results that they will certainly be present in Goa.

The fact that J2b2 has been found in an over-proportional amount in this study can be ascribed to matching. Since this haplogroup was brought by the Iranian farmers who populated the Harappa region, it confirms that after the extinction of IVC, the population moved towards the Gangetic plane where admixture with the Steppe population occurred as shown by the Narasimhan *et al.* study.

From the *comunidade* of Moira's 5th clan, we have a confirmation from what we have already concluded from the 4th *vangad* of Aldona's *comunidade* namely that each *vangad* was founded by one individual and that all members of that *vangad* share the same haplogroup as the founder of the clan and also his ancestral name. Thus, all the members of Moira's 5th *vangad* bore the pre-conversion Hindu name of Kamat and those of the 7th *vangad* of Assagao were Prabhu and harboured the Y DNA haplogroup L-M27.

It is matter of great regret that no systematic study on the genetics of Goa's population has been carried out so far and it can only be hoped that this lacuna will be soon removed.

3. A Comparison with Dhume's Findings

It can be expected that the findings of Sahoo *et al.* with regard to Western India will be valid for the Goan population as well; we recall that their study identified the main haplogroups in Western India to be **C* (5.39%), J2 (11.27%), H (33.33%), L (11.76%), R2 (6.37%) and R1a1a (25%)**, with negligible amounts of F, K, T (each 0.49%), R* (0.98%) and P* (2.45%). The migration route of haplogroup O would not be expected to lead to Goa and this appears indeed to be the case. Regrettably, the paucity of publicly available data with regard to the genetic ancestry of the inhabitants of Goa is appalling.

It would be of great interest to compare genetic genealogical findings with the results of research emanating from other approaches. A. R. S. Dhume published in 1986 a book entitled *The Cultural History of Goa* based on an extensive nine-year research, which went quickly out of print. Fortunately, a second edition was recently published that has enabled an attempt at such a comparison (Anant Ramkrishna Sinai Dhume, *The Cultural History of Goa*, Broadway Book centre, Panjim, Goa, second edition 2009). In the absence of wider DNA-related data on Goa's inhabitants, we can venture to compare Dhume's findings with those of Sahoo *et al.* for Western India and other published results as a first approximation.

Dhume's conclusions are that the Sahyadri and Nilgiri ranges resulted from seismic activity about 10,000 BCE and Goa became suitable for habitation ca. 8,500 BCE.[146] Genetics cannot obviously provide a clue to confirm or disprove this assertion.

The first inhabitants were hunter-gatherers called **Mhars** who arrived from the foothills of the Sahyadri range ca. **5,000 BCE**.

The next to arrive were buffalo-rearing **pastoral tribes** ca. **4'000 BCE** who eventually divided into two groups, one belonging to the Naik caste, and the other practicing the matriarchal system consisting of Chedvans, Bhavins and Kalavants and their brothers. They initiated the worship of female and male elements symbolised by stones.

Around **3,500** BCE the **Asura** tribe arrived from around Chota-Nagpur of Madhya Pradesh. He attributes to them the basic use of copper and spongy iron. These dates cannot be correct because the bronze age started around 2200 BCE and the iron age from around 800 BCE. They introduced the cut-and-burn (*kumeri*) agricultural method to produce cereals and worshipped deities denominated Khaman-Rouduro, Gana-Rouduro and Dhawaj-Rouduro. They were subdued by the Kol tribe and adopted professions of blacksmiths and potters, and labourers of the vani caste. The Bharvankar caste in the Christian community belongs to the Asura tribes.

Next, ca. **3'000 BCE** came the **Kols** from the same area as the Asuras. The Kols were paddy-field cultivators, introduced a village socio-economic administration, and established villages consisting of twelve hamlets each (*barazans*). Their main goddess was "Ro-en" (anthill) later transformed under Aryan influence into Santer and Bhumika. They are represented by a caste named Satarkar, which name is probably derived from Santer.

The **Mundaris** came after the Kols, accepted the hegemony of the Kols and worshipped a forest tree named Kel.

Along with the Mundaris came the **Kharwis** who took to the fishing and boating profession.

Around **2,400 BCE**, Goa was settled by a **first wave of Aryans** who co-habited with the existing inhabitants.

About **2'000 BCE Sumerians** settled in Goa, introduced profound changes such as land-ownership by the village god or goddess, dedicated places of worship (temples), the village commune system.

Ca. 1,400 to 700, a second wave of Aryans, accompanied by non-Aryans arrived. They interacted closely with the Sumerians, introduced titulary and family deities (*Palavi-devata and Kula-devata* respectively), the consultation of oracles and other changes.

It is immediately apparent that the dates proposed by Dhume would need to be revised since the bronze and iron usage he relates do not correspond to the epoch when these metals were first introduced.

This comparison does not extend to the earlier and later dynasties that ruled Goa as described by Dhume. The question of interest here is whether it is possible, based on what can be derived from the migration routes attributed to specific haplogroups by Sahoo *et al.* in Western India, to corroborate Dhume's account of the waves of migration to Goa. We must, however, keep in mind that genetic genealogy is a relatively young science and still evolving rapidly; consequently, in many cases, the information available does not suffice to unravel all the mysteries.

The fact that so many different haplogroups have entered India through diverse routes and entry points makes it evident that this subcontinent was not populated in four single distinctive events, with people speaking a specific language family entering the country from the North, one after the other, in an orderly fashion and driving the existing inhabitants towards the South; the peopling of India was a far more complex process. In fact, as discussed above, David Reich, Vasant Shinde and their respective teams have demonstrated through genetics the identities of the ASI and ANI and how admixture has occurred in multiple waves; we now know that the ancestors of today's inhabitants entered India at different times, both as migrants and invaders in numerous small and large waves.

Thangaraj *et al.* who have conducted mitochondrial and Y DNA studies of Andaman Islanders found that they belong to the mtDNA haplogroup M, found in East and South Asia and associated with the migration of modern humans from eastern Africa towards Southeast Asia, Australia and Oceania. The Y DNA of the Andamese belong to a unique subgroup of haplogroup D namely M174 that split from the main lineage D.[147] We know that Onge-related hunter-gatherers populated India before other major migrations and interbreeding occurred.

Whether the Mhars or the Kharwis better fit the description of seafarers and were the first inhabitants of Goa could be resolved by determining the haplogroups of these communities. They would be expected to also belong to the mtDNA haplogroup M and the YDNA haplogroup D-M174. Also, because of interbreeding with migrants and invaders, their appearance will differ substantially from the Onge or Andaman Islanders.

Dhume claims that the Semitic races did not migrate to India but fails to justify this claim. Genetic genealogy does not sustain this exclusion since Jews who are descendants of the Semitic tribes belong to a large proportion to haplogroups J1 and J2, the frequency being greater in the latter but as we have seen earlier the J2 subclade is very much present in Western India and in the Indian subcontinent.

Dhume castigates B. D. Satoskar among other reasons for his conclusion that Naga people existed in Konkan and Karnataka and also in Goa.[148] Using genetic genealogy, it would be facile to verify these claims.

Cordaux *et al.* have shown that Y DNA haplogroup O (M134) predominates in the Naga population and they migrated to India from the Northeast. All that is necessary, therefore, would be to test for the Y DNA haplogroup of Goan individuals who could be of Naga origin.[149]

Neither Sahoo *et al.* nor Gaikwad & Kashyap found any subjects with haplogroup O in Western India; should this finding be confirmed for Goa as would be expected, Dhume would stand vindicated.

4. Genetic Genealogy and Castes: Separated by Common Haplogroups

The word "caste" is not Indian; it is derived from the Portuguese word "casta" meaning lineage, race or breed. Even though Portuguese colonialism belongs to a bygone era, the term caste is deeply ingrained in Indian society.

The Indian terms for the stratification of society are in Sanskrit: *varna* and *jati*.

The earliest reference to the formal division of society in four classes is found in the *Purusha Sukta*[150] according to which *Brahman, Ra-*

119

janya (instead of *Kshatriya*), *Vaishya* and *Shudra* classes form the mouth, arms, thighs and feet at the sacrifice of the primordial *Purusha*. The *Bhagavat Gita* describes the duties of the *varnas*: The control of the mind and the senses, austerity, purity, forbearance, and also uprightness, knowledge, realisation, belief in a hereafter are the duties of the Brahmins; prowess, boldness, fortitude, dexterity, and also not fleeing from battle, generosity and sovereignty are the duties of the *Kshatriyas*; agriculture, cattle-rearing and trade are the duties of the *Vaishyas* and action consisting of service is the duty of the *Shudras*.[151]

The laws of Manu or *Manusmriti* that is also written in Sanskrit describes in detail the caste system and the roles and privileges of the four *varnas*.

Initially, within these four *varnas,* sub-classes named *jati,* meaning birth, were created to denote specific professions akin to the professional guilds that are encountered in Europe. Over time, the *jatis* expanded to include factors such as regions and languages, acquired a life of their own and today several thousand *jatis* coexist alongside the *varnas* under the umbrella of the caste system. *Varnas* and *jatis* are endogamous and as we shall see below, it can have serious implications from a genetic viewpoint.

Where did the caste system first emerge? There are two options: the Indus Valley / Harappa Civilisation that is commonly called Vedic India or the Yamnaya-related or more specifically Steppe population belonging to the Sintashta culture that migrated to India around the time of the extinction of the Indus Valley Civilisation.

The Harappa site in Punjab, Pakistan after which the Harappa or Indus Valley Civilisation is named, was discovered in 1921, followed by the discovery of Mohenjo-daro a year later. In the meantime, hundreds of other towns and villages of different sizes have been discovered revealing that the Indus Valley Civilisation was the most extensive of the earliest three civilisations, the other two Mesopotamia and Egypt being slightly earlier. Five major sites have been excavated to date namely Harappa, Mohenjo-daro, Ganweriwala, Rakhigarhi, and Dholavira.

Archeologists have shown that this population was literate and had a script that is still largely undeciphered, knew how to control the floods of the Indus River Valley and use them to their advantage to produce different kinds of agricultural crops. The expertise of early Goan *Gaunkars* as both agriculturists and land reclamation and embankment construction specialists probably dates back to this time. The population also bred animals such as cattle, domestic fowl, buffalo and others. They had tamed the elephant because ivory was freely used. They were traders and imported minerals from afar with which they could manufacture jewellery. They have left behind many seals depicting animals such as elephants, rhinoceros, tigers and antelopes as well as some mythical ones. They also produced a large number of terra-cotta figures of humans and animals.[152]

The IVC population was peaceful because few weapons have been found. They did not leave behind massive monuments or bury their dead with weapons but rather with pottery that probably contained grains to accompany the deceased to their afterlife.[153]

At the Rakhigarhi site, the largest of all the Harappan sites to date, archeologists have unearthed evidence of a well-established road and drainage system as well as large rainwater storage facility along with additional city infrastructure.[154]

In the absence of any temples that would provide evidence of religious deities or rituals, it has been speculated that the Harappans worshipped a mother goddess who symbolised fertility. The extraordinary uniformity in pottery, seals, weights, and bricks with standardised sizes and weights, suggest some form of authority and governance. The power structure appears to have been a decentralised one. Excavations of skeletons have not revealed differences in health as would be expected from a highly stratified society and very few elite burials have been discovered pointing to a largely egalitarian form of society. Differences in the sizes of houses, however, suggest the existence of different social classes. It is widely believed that the Harappa civilization was a peaceful one but this could be attributed to the absence of natural enemies and the purpose of the few weapons found could be as defense against wild animals.[155]

In short, the people of the Indus Valley Civilisation had a mild form of stratification, if at all.

There has been much debate in the past regarding the language spoken by the IVC population. The Narasimhan *et al.* study has hypothesised that the IVC Ancestral South Indian ASI population spoke Dravidian languages which were dispersed when they moved south and east after the extinction of the Indus Valley Civilisation. It would be possible to attribute Dravidian languages to the pre-IVC Ancient Ancestral South Indian AASI people related to the Andaman Islanders but we know that the Onge tribe and Andaman Islanders do not speak a Dravidian language. Another clear indication that the IVC spoke a Dravidian language is the Brahui language spoken in Central Baluchistan, Southern Afghanistan as well as some parts of Iran and Turkmenistan. Several theories have been postulated as to how the Dravidian language Brahui arrived in a geographic location that is so distant from South India where Dravidian languages are spoken. The fact that it is spoken in some parts of Iran is an indicator of its origin. A clearer picture emerges from the Y DNA Haplogroups of the Balochis that are primarily R1a1a-M17 associated with the early eastern migrations of Indo-Iranian nomads and J, that as we have seen in earlier chapters has its source in the Middle East with subclades occurring in Iran. Full genome data shows that the Onge (AASI) ancestry present in the Brahui speakers is minimal;[156] the language they speak could not therefore have come from AASI. We can thus conclude that the Brahui speakers are a population of Iranian farmers some of whom settled in Balochistan and surrounding areas whereas others migrated further to finally give rise to the Indus Valley / Harappa Civilisation.

The IVC population was not familiar with the horse and archeology has not revealed any evidence of horse drawn vehicles even though clay figurines of wheeled carts drawn by cattle have been found.

In this context, a very interesting archeological find that appears to be a symbiosis of IVC and a warrior population in Sanauli is worthy of mention. Sanauli is located in Baghpat district of Western Uttar Pradesh. Archeologists excavated a burial site dated to around 2000 BCE corresponding to the late Indus Valley Civilisation period at its eastern-most limit. Initially, in 2005, excavations revealed 116 burials with a wide range of antiquities typical of the Late Harappa or IVC period. In mid-2018, however, archeologists discovered unique legged coffins, one of them with a decorated lid with eight anthropomorphic figures, alongside copper-sheathed and decorated chariots.[157] The latter finding is reminiscent of a Yamnaya-related culture. Could this have been a symbiotic population that emerged at the time of the extinction of the IVC and the arrival of the Yamanya-related Steppe warriors, perhaps a model that evolved to the *gaunkari* system prevalent in Goa? Excavations at the site are continuing and we can expect new stunning revelations on India's past history.

Thus, the AASI and ASI population of the Indus Valley Civilisation could not have composed the Vedas on their own because they did not speak Sanskrit, the language of the Vedas. They were largely peaceful, not skilled warriors and not acquainted with horses or spoke-wheeled chariots that are vividly described in the Vedas. There is therefore no justification to label the Indus Valley Civilisation as Vedic India because it was not. The social stratification was by all accounts rather weak. The caste system could not have emanated from the Indus Valley Civilisation.

The Yamnaya and related cultures, as we have seen earlier, prospered by domesticating the horse and introducing spoked-wheeled chariots and other wheeled vehicles. They were skilled warriors and their burial practices show that they glorified violence.

In a dissertation presented to the University of Pittsburg,[158] Igor V. Chechushkov argues that large-scale migrations of the Sintashta compelled the families to stay together to protect the herds from "animal and human predators" and build walled communities to protect themselves and their assets. He notes that "apparently, those who were talented in managing the construction of closely packed villages surrounded by ditches and walls to protect people and livestock from threats from neighbours, and who otherwise served the community in the newly colonised zone became the most prominent members of society" leading to the creation of Sintashta fiefdoms. They did not accumulate wealth but high social prestige that was even transferred to their children as evidenced by special elite burial sites.

Ancient DNA shows that the Yamnaya spread both westward into Europe and to South Asia spreading their Late Proto-Indo-European language from which all the leading Indo-European languages emanate both in Europe and in the Indian subcontinent. Referring to Europe, Marija Gimbutas concludes from her archeological research that the ideology of Old Europe transformed dramatically with the arrival of the Yamnaya-related cultures: a matrilineal, sexually balanced egalitarian learned theocratic society was replaced by a patrilineal order, a militant patriarchy, a male-dominated hierarchy, and transited from a chthonic goddess religion to the Indo-European sky-oriented pantheon of gods.[159] Events in India took a similar turn with the Indus Valley Civilisation ASI culture being overrun by the Steppe ANI culture.

The cultures related to the Yamnaya would speak proto Sanskrit and be at the origin of the Vedas. In fact, the Rigveda describes in detail battles involving chariots. The hymns describing how the war-god Indra destroys with ease the fortresses of the *dasyu* enemies and how the attacking warriors were protected by armours and shields and used bow and arrows, javelin, axe and sword is associated with the destruction of the Harappan site Mohenjo-daro where scattered skeletons were found during excavations though this interpretation has been challenged.[160]

We have seen that the Indus Valley Civilisation flourished on the banks of the Sarasvati and other surrounding rivers and could not have been of importance to the Yamnaya-related people who migrated to the Indian subcontinent from the Steppes at the time of the decline of the IVC around 2000-1800 BCE and are the source of the content of the Rigveda. It is therefore puzzling that the Sarasvati River should be not only mentioned but praised as mother and Goddess and even more so alongside Indra and Chitra in the Rigveda (cf. Part I, chapter 3.1). One possible explanation is that by the time the Vedas were composed much after the mixing of the ANI and ASI had occurred, some elements that were of utmost importance to the the non-Yamanaya related people had become a part of a symbiotic system of beliefs that was integrated into the ancient sacred texts. Sanauli, mentioned earlier in this chapter, that dates back to the time of ANI and ASI admixture, could be one such example.

As we have seen earlier, all Indians, no matter to what caste they belong and including the non-Hindu tribals are mixtures of Ancestral North Indians ANI and Ancestral South Indians ASI albeit in different proportions. The Reich and Shinde teams found that some isolated groups had a minimal amount of ANI or ASI i.e remained relatively unmixed. For example, the South Indian tribal groups *Palliyar, Ulladan, Malayan,* and *Adiyan* had very little ANI ancestry whereas at the other end of the spectrum, the *Kalash* in northern Pakistan have a ASI admixture that is close to the minimum that is mathematically allowed by the statistical model used. The West Eurasian component can vary from 20 to 80 percent.[161] They found that speakers of Indo-European languages had more ANI ancestry and the Dravidian speakers harboured more ASI ancestry indicating the original speakers of these languages.

They also found that people belonging to higher castes had a higher proportion of ANI ancestry even when compared to the population living in the same state and speaking the same language. Brahmins were found to posses a higher proportion of ANI ancestry than other

Indian castes. As Reich expresses it, "the findings are statistically clear, and suggest that the ANI-ASI mixture in India occurred in the context of social stratification".[162] Thus, there is no doubt that societal stratification arrived in India with the Yamnaya-related Sintashta population who introduced their Indo-European languages as well as the *vedas* written in Sanskrit derived from the Proto-Indo-European language spoken by them at that time. It is the regions of Northern India that were primarily invaded by the Yamnaya-related tribes from the Steppes that should be labeled Vedic India and not the Indus Valley Civilisation. We have seen earlier that between 20 and 40 percent of Indians belong to a Y DNA haplogroup transmitted by the Yamnaya-related males whereas 90 percent of the mtDNA that can only be transmitted by females is autochthonous i.e., Indian. What this says is that the Yamnaya-related males migrated massively from West Eurasia into India, leaving their women behind and successfully interbred with the local females leaving their genetic imprint on the sub-continent. My Yamnaya-related maternal ancestry constitutes an exception.

In genetics, a "bottleneck event" occurs when a small number of ancestors produce a large number of descendants and these offspring in turn also have a large number of descendants; thus, these are groups that live in genetic isolation. This has been observed for example in refugia during the Last Glacial Maximum when due to climatic conditions, inhabitants of the refugia could not leave their location neither could newcomers migrate to the region. Reich found that around a third of the Indian groups they studied had experienced bottlenecks that could only be explained by their observation of a strict endogamy, in some cases, for example the *Vysya*, dating back to three to two thousand years ago. Thus they were not caused by any climatic conditions but were entirely self-imposed, related to their caste and with the obvious objective of preventing dilution and maintaining their superior status over other castes that they considered to be inferior to theirs. To quote David Reich, "The Han Chinese are truly a large population. They have been mixing freely for thousands of years". In contrast, "The truth is that India is composed of a large number of small populations."[163]

When two populations admix, their genes or alleles will associate and the frequency of the association of different alleles is independent and random. The occurrence of random combinations at each locus on a chromosome will result in an equilibrium distribution of alleles at each of the loci. If, however, admixture occurs within the same population, as in the case of endogamy, the association of alleles at different loci becomes non-random. We have a situation of allelic association or linkage disequilibrium LD. Linkage disequilibrium decays with further admixture and the expected value of the linkage disequilibrium of the admixture is related to the genetic distance between the single nucleotide polymorphisms SNPs and the time elapsed. By analysing LD and its decay in 571 individuals from 73 well-defined ethno-linguistic groups from South Asia (71 Indian and 2 Pakistani groups), Reich and co-workers found that 1900 - 4200 years BP, major admixture between groups was common and affected even isolated tribes such as the Palliyar and Bhil. There was, however, a major shift when India transformed into a region in which mixture was rare.[164] The authors state that "The shift from widespread mixture to strict endogamy that we document is mirrored in ancient Indian texts", more specifically, the law code of Manu forbidding caste intermarriage and add that the "evolution of Indian texts during this period provides confirmatory support as well as context for our genetic findings".

In a more recent publication, *A. Basu, N. Sarkar-Roy, and P. P. Majumder*, researchers from the West Bengal National Institute of Bio-Medical Genomics NIBMG carried out a deeper analysis of the *Reich et al* study discussed above and concluded that in addition to ANI and ASI, the Indian population also includes an Ancestral Tibeto-Burman (ATB) and an Ancestral Austro-Asiatic (AAA) component. More relevant to the introduction of the varna, jati systems and its consequences, they found that for most upper-caste communities, strict endogamy was introduced during the Hindu Gupta period known as the age of Vedic Brahmanism about 1500 years ago. The Maratha population started the practice of endogamy during the time of the post-Gupta Chalukya (543–753 CE) and the Rashtrakuta empires (753–982 CE) of western India, whereas in eastern and northeastern India, populations such as the "West Bengal Brahmins and the Tibeto-Burman populations continued to admix until the emergence of the Buddhist Pala dynasty during the 8th to 12th centuries CE". Gene flow from ANI to tribal populations continued but not vice versa, "consistent with elite dominance and patriarchy…but their offspring were not allowed to be inducted into the caste."[165]

In conclusion, there is little doubt that stratification of society was introduced by the Yamnaya-related Steppe population and strict endogamy according to the post-vedic scriptures was implemented by ardent Hindu rulers starting around 1500 years before present.

Inspite of the scanty information available, a few interesting conclusions regarding the caste system in Goa can nevertheless be drawn.

The study of Cordaux *et al.* identified haplogroups R-M17 (corresponding to R1a1a according to the ISOGG 2009 nomenclature), J-M172 (J2), R-M124 (R2) and L-M20 (L) as the most prominent in caste populations. Of these, the 6 Goan subjects cover R-M124, J2 and L; additional data from a bigger segment of the Goan population could probably be expected to confirm the findings of these researchers; Goa is thus not any different from the rest of the Indian sub-continent.

As mentioned earlier, the haplogroup of Church historian late Rev. Father Nascimento Mascarenhas, **H (M69),** is very frequent and belongs to one of the earliest migrants to India approximately 30,000 years ago. Fr. Mascarenhas is a Brahmin *gaunkar* of the village of Saligão. The presence of this haplogroup in upper castes is quite rare (10%).[166] Clearly, therefore, it was possible for an original inhabitant of pre-Indo-European Goa, whose haplogroup is commonly prevalent in the Roma gypsy community to become a Brahmin member of the village *gaunkari* system.

Rohit Menezes' haplogroup **L** arrived in the sub-continent possibly also 30,000 years ago and his ancestors eventually became Brahmin *gaunkars* of Malar village in Divar. This would imply that there were several waves of haplogroup L migrants but not all settled in Divar because we know that Melvyn D'Souza from Assagao also belongs to haplogroup L and more specifically to the subclade L-M27.

As discussed in the previous chapters, haplogroup **J** is well represented in Goa: late Professor Teotonio R. de Souza, Errol Pinto, Hector Fernandes, Eric D'Cunha, Alan Machado and the author, all Brahmin gaunkars from neighbouring villages Moira and Aldona resp. belong to this haplogroup. Again, many non-Brahmin Marathas also carry this haplogroup.

In the village of Moira, John Nazareth belongs to Y DNA haplogroup **R-M124 or R2a** that migrated from Southwest Asia in several waves and could have been allies of the Yamnaya-related population. The fact that he belongs to the first *vangad* of the *Gram samstha* of his village could therefore be of significance and is also discussed below (Cf Part III, chapter 3)

The different *varnas* share common haplogroups and it is legitimate to ask the question if caste affiliation was just a matter of being at the right or wrong place at the right or wrong time.

We can conclude from the above that caste-conscious Indians are separated by common haplogroups!

Another conclusion that can be drawn is that the only person belonging to a pure race was the first African Adam or Adams from whom we all descend and even that is doubtful because the emergence of mankind in Africa was very probably the result of encounters of several different hominins.

As the discussion above clearly demonstrates, the so-called Indo-Aryan race does not exist and all Indians irrespective of their caste consist of ANI and ASI mixtures in different proportions belonging to different haplogroups, resulting from ancestors who migrated out of Africa through different routes and at different epochs. There is no justification for the existence of *varna* and *jati* systems in modern India. All Indians harbour the same genetic mixtures and the same ancestry albeit in different proportions and the caste system that was introduced to perpetuate the power of the Steppe invaders over the other populations of the time based on a higher proportion of one ancestry compared to another has only impeded progress and should not find a place in democratic India.

Additionally, any pure race implies inbreeding and in Darwinian parlance would not be fit for survival. The need to avoid inbreeding and ensure survival was possibly the intent of Manu's interdiction of marriage between individuals belonging to the same *gotra* or lineage.

5. Sometimes a Statue, Sometimes a Crow

Very few people knew to read and write in the country of the Portuguese conquerors of Goa in the year 1500. In fact, even to this day, though the literacy rate in Portugal is very high, functional literacy i.e., reading and writing skills to cope with daily life is amongst the lowest in Europe.[167]

By contrast, Goa's villages including Aldona were endowed with *gaunkars* who were literate, not only familiar with Sanskrit but well-versed in the Vedic scriptures, who spoke one or more additional Indian languages, possessed sufficient management skills to run village affairs and educational institutions and the village society had craftsmen with all the necessary skills to cope with everyday life.

The question therefore arises as to why, in spite of all these assets, it was possible for Goa and the Indian sub-continent in general to be conquered by so many different invaders. This is hardly the place to deal with such a vast and challenging topic but one specific aspect that is intrinsic to Goan society merits to be briefly raised.

We learn early in life that sometimes one is a statue and sometimes a crow that treats statues with utmost disrespect.

History tells us that the Indian sub-continent has been a fertile ground for invading crows from all the neighbouring regions. Every conqueror owes his success to superior technology that is acquired through innovation; in other words, a society that does not encourage innovation is doomed to stagnate and be eventually overrun by a more innovative one.

The hunter-gatherers were superseded by the agriculturists who had learnt to control the food chain and thus increase their chances of survival, they in turn were conquered by horsemen who had thus gained great flexibility of movement and could easily attack and subdue. The advent of bronze and later iron technology brought better tools and sturdier stirrups that gave the possessors of this technology a determining edge and so on.

The Portuguese possessed much better vessels and canons with which they could subdue the Moors, the dominant force in the region. It is unhampered promotion of innovation that has enabled the United States of America to boast of the highest number of Nobel laureates in the world.

Whereas the division of labour *per se* is a necessity in every society, the introduction of a strict hereditary system preventing upward or downward mobility to achieve this aim was a major and determining handicap.

The *varna* and *jati* system in India introduced a rigidity within society that stifled all innovation and thus left the sub-continent highly vulnerable to invaders that were not hampered by similar restrictions.

As Gadgil *et al.* express it: "This process of maintenance of large number of communities in isolation from each other has been accom-

129

panied by extreme specialisation of occupation. It is perhaps this spe-cialisation of occupation that has prevented Indians from cross-fertili-sation of ideas and innovations, so that the Indian society has always been at the receiving end of technological innovations."[168]
And at the receiving end of invading and conquering crows.

6. Caste and Disease

Humans, like other sexually reproducing species have two copies or alleles of each gene. Each of these genes produces a protein and de-termines when, where and how much of it is produced by the body. The proteins also determine our traits or phenotypes, for example if we have dark or light coloured eyes. The two copies of the alleles can sometimes vary slightly as the result of a mutation, leading to slight variation in protein activity and thus affect a trait or phenotype.

A recessive allele can produce a recessive phenotype if both mutat-ed copies, one from each parent, are passed on to the offspring. An individual who has just one mutated allele is considered to be a carrier of the recessive phenotype because the recessive trait is not yet present; it can become a recessive phenotype if a second mutated copy is inherited from one of the parents.

A recessive gene that has been well studied is sickle cell disease. In regions in Africa where malaria is endemic, people developed a muta-tion on chromosome 11 as a result of an evolutionary process that gives them partial immunity against this disease through a single mu-tation in one of the allele copies of the HBB gene of this chromosome. If, however, both the alleles of the HBB gene possess this mutation as can happen in the offspring of parents who are both carriers, it leads to sickle cell anaemia.

One of the countries where sickle cell disease is highly prevalent is Nigeria. One of the frequent questions when dating in Nigeria today is related to an individual's genotype. The Anambra state parliament in Nigeria's eastern region requires a genotype test prior to marriage and some churches will not celebrate a marriage unless a couple can prove with genetic tests that they are not carriers and do not run the risk of having children who will contract sickle sell anemia.[169]

Another well-known example is the Tay-Sachs disease that causes brain degeneration and ultimately early death and occurs frequently in Ashkenazi Jews. The Ashkenazi Jews have a history of endogamy and the children of parents who are both carriers of the mutation causing this devastating disease run the risk of inheriting one copy of the mutated allele from each parent and contracting this fatal condition. In order to avoid such an ordeal, members of this group routinely run a genetic screening to check if they are carriers and avoid contracting a marriage with another carrier.

In India, people belonging to the *Vysya jati* that has observed a practice of strict endogamy since several thousand years react to muscle relaxants administered prior to surgery with a prolonged muscle paralysis. Twenty percent of the people of this community carry this recessive gene and four percent have both copies of the mutated allele responsible for the genetic condition.[170] With so many groups of *varnas* and *jatis* practicing endogamy in India, there is little doubt that many similar recessive genes exist in the country. Reich and Thangaraj plead for a project to identify recessive diseases in these groups, something that could be achieved with little effort and using knowhow and technology that is all available in India. It would be even more helpful if a campaign could be initiated to alert all the groups that practice endogamy of the grave risks that such a practice entails and persuade them to discontinue this tradition.

PART III: The Village of Aldona / Haldonna

1. Origin of the Name of the Village

The village of Aldona is located at 15°35'23"N 73°52'24"E.

Minutes of the *comunidade* meetings dating back to the period 1595–1605[171] refer to the village as **Haldonna**, a name that evolved to Aldona under the Portuguese.

Baba Borkar has suggested[172] that the word stems from the Sanskrit words '*Hal*' (plough) and '*Drone*' (cone). The former is plausible considering the fact that Aldona was settled as an agricultural village but the latter alluding to its shape is questionable since the village settlers would not have access to aerial mapping equipment to determine the shape of the village with precision.

Author Maria Aurora Couto, a resident of Aldona, attributed the name of the village to Haldi or turmeric.[173] The village of Aldona is known for the quality of its chillies and onions but not turmeric; this proposal is without merit since it is not based on evidence.

Father Francisco Xavier Vaz who has written extensively on the etymology of Goan villages attributes the name of Aldona to *Vhadd-dhan* meaning great or abundant *("vhadd")* wealth or riches *("dhan")*.[174] This interpretation is untenable both from a linguistic as well as historical viewpoint. There are many examples where the letter "h" or "v" is dropped from a word over the years, as for example in the case of Aldona that evolved from Haldonna or the letter "a" is changed to "o", for example *humann* (curry) is pronounced as *Umonn* by some sections of the Goan population but by no stretch of imagination could *"vhadd"* morph to *"hal"*. Additionally, even though Aldona must have been a prosperous village, it was not a place of pilgrimage that brought great wealth as in the case of Chuddamonnim (Chorao Island) or a very rich village like Cuncolim that could boast not only of surplus agricultural production but had also developed skilled metal works or a permanent bazar at the end of more than one caravan route.[175]

Based on historical evidence and genetic genealogical results, as discussed in the sub-chapter below, The Year of Aldona's Settlement, I submit that the name of the village of Aldona has its roots in the combination of two words: **Hala**, from plough or agricultural land and the Sanskrit word **Daana**, meaning gift, donation or giving away in charity.

Describing the economic conditions of the Candellas who built Khajuraho and ruled an area coinciding with modern Bundelkhand for over 3 centuries from the 10th to the beginning of the 14th century, and where agriculture was one of the principal activities, S. K. Mitra has the following to recount: "The "*hala*" or plough is prominently mentioned as an instrument of cultivation. Land was measured according to the number of ploughs used in cultivating it. The system of measuring land according to its "seed capacity" was also known. Thus 71/2 "*dronas*" of land was identical with 10 *halas*."[176]

As several copper-plates and inscriptions found all over the country amply demonstrate, it was not at all uncommon in those times for kings and rulers to accord generous land grants to Brahmins, for many reasons including as an investment in their own prosperity and eternal salvation for as King Pulakeshin II wrote in an inscription "He who grants land (whether simply) ploughed, (or) planted with seed (or) full of crops, he is treated with honour in heaven, for as long as the worlds, created by the sun, endure."[177]

Instead of *daana*, the word *drona* could also be envisaged but a combination of two words *hala* and *drona* that have a similar meaning is improbable.

2. The Time Window of Aldona's Settlement

As we have seen in Part I, chapter 7, the members of the 4th *vangad* of Aldona's *comunidade* are all descendants of a common ancestor who lived roughly 800 years ago or approximately **around the year 1200 CE and this ancestor was the founder of the 4th vangad.** We do not know when the chief *gaunkar* of Aldona established the 1st *vangad*. It can be speculated that it would have been at the most 50 years earlier (about 2 generations) in view of the need to feed an increasing population and reclaim land and build sluice gates in the village to regulate salinity, avoid flooding and increase the capture of fish as well as to find partners who did not belong to the same *gotra*. But the 4th *vangad* could also have been formed 100 or 200 years after the first 3 *vangads*. For a more precise date, we would need to have the full genome results of four or five members of the 1st *vangad* for a total cost of 400 to 500 US dollars, an insignificant sum compared to the historical value of the information that would be obtained. We can nevertheless conclude that **the village of Aldona was settled anywhere between 1400 and 1150 CE**. It should be noted that these dates are approximate; genetic TMRCA are based on mutation rates on each chromosome based on past experience and this information can vary.

Clearly, therefore, Haldonna was not part of the twelve villages of *Baradesh* / Bardez to be occupied by the initials settlers of Goa who accompanied *Parashurama*.

From the 10th to the 14th centuries, Goa was under the rule of the Kadambas[178] who were Brahmins. The founder of the dynasty conquered *Saxtti* and part of the adjoining Konkan from the Silaharas with Chandrapur, present day Chandor, serving as their capital. Shastadeva I extended the Kadamba-held territory and added Gopakapattana, present day Goa Velha, as his second capital.

The next ruler, Jayakeshi I (1050-1080), expanded his kingdom even further to include North Goa. Other rulers followed; under Jayakeshi II (1125-1148), the Kadamba Empire of Goa reached the pinnacle of its glory.

It is therefore during the rule of the Kadambas that the ruler, wishing to consolidate his rule in the northern part of Goa, gifted agricultural land to an *Adhistani* Brahmin from *Saxtti*, where the Kadambas and the *gram samsthas* were already very well established, to settle what became the village of Haldonna.

3. *Gaunkari* or *Comunidade* of Aldona

The villages of Goa were settled by following a precise process. An experienced and knowledgeable elder known as an *Adistani Brahmin* was first selected to settle the village. He thus constituted the first *vangad* or clan of the village and was regarded as the *Chief Gaunkar*. In the case of Aldona, this *Chief Gaunkar* was a *Kamti* that has evolved to present day *Kamat*, an agriculturist who possessed deep expertise on growing rice and other agricultural products.

It is probable that the chief *gaunkar* of Aldona came from *Saxtti* (Salcete) as suggested both by Chandrakant Keni as well from historical considerations.

The highest-ranking chief *gaunkar* was greatly respected. He enjoyed a certain number of social privileges.[179] The mud walls of his house were the first to be protected from the monsoons with palm leaves, he was honoured with betel and garlanded with a *pachodi* (strip of white cloth) on festive occasions and the dancing girls were required to perform in front of his house before proceeding to other houses. He did not enjoy any political or other advantages and his vote in the village meetings did not carry more weight than that of other village elders or headmen of the other *vangads*.

After assessing the needs of the new village, he invited additional families to join him as settlers and form additional *vangads*. Aldona's second and third clans were also established by Kamat families thus confirming that the village was primarily agricultural. Each of the *vangads* was allotted a ward or *vaddo* to settle and develop. We do not know in which ward of the village the 1st and 2nd *vangads* installed themselves. It is possible that the 3rd *vangad* was asked to settle in Bodiem or Quitula.

Since Aldona is situated on the banks of the Mapusa river and a control of salinity would be of great importance for the maximisation of the production of rice and other agricultural crops, an expert on *khajan* land management and building of sluice gates would have to be enrolled. For more information on *khajan* land cf.[180] This role was fulfilled by the Prabhu settlers of the fourth *vangad* who were offered the island of *Kaluve*, present-day Calvim, as their new home. According to Professor Nandkumar Kamat, the island got its name from *kaluvam* or oysters that must have been abundant in that region. Records of *comunidade* meetings dating to the time 1595-1605 list the Prabhus of the 4th *vangad* as being *Kaluvekars*. We know that the Kaluvekar Prabhus were *khajan* experts from the fact that their services in that capacity were hired by the neighbouring village of Moira, where they were entitled to one half of a *zhon* i.e., one half of a share of the profits of the village, in exchange for their services.

A village that was growing would need an administrator and that is how a fifth *vangad* was established by a Naik family.

Other *vangads* followed over time, 12 in all, with Kamat families constituting the 6th and 9th *vangads*, Prabhu families forming the 7th and 12th *vangads* and a Naik family starting the 10th *vangad*.

The 11th *vangad* belongs to the Seti, present day Xett or goldsmiths who are not original settlers of Aldona, a story worth recounting. The Goldsmiths call themselves *Daivadnya* Brahmins; *Daivadnya* signifies astrologer but the reason for applying this appellation to goldsmiths is not known.[181] The Bosquejo Historico das Comunidades[182] relates that the Seti acquired the 11th *vangad* from a Portuguese who had been gifted the same by a Viceroy; despite orders to exclude the Seti from the *Gaunkari* system, it appears that financial considerations prevailed.

The Portuguese owner of the 11th *vangad* was not an additional clan that was created and added to an existing structure, in which case it would have become the 13th *vangad*, but rather an individual who replaced the rightful *gaunkars* belonging to the 11th *vangad*. This is highly unusual in the history of the *comunidades* in Goa and the causes of such a dramatic event must have been duly recorded in the *comunidade* minutes. Unfortunately these ancient records that have been so badly and thoroughly neglected by past and present governments must have disappeared forever in the digestive tracts of termites. We can, however, draw conclusions from a similar case that took place in the village of Cola close to which the fortress of Cabo de Rama is situated. The *gaunkars* of Cola having refused to pay taxes despite repeated warnings, the Portuguese Viceroy Dom Antonio de Noronha by a decree published on the 30th of April 1573, confiscated the village from the *gaunkars* citing their "act of rebellion" and gifted it to Luiz de Rego as a dowry on the occasion of his wedding to an orphan.[183] This case leads us to conclude that the members of the 11th *vangad* of Aldona's *comunidade* rebelled, refused to pay their taxes or committed some other crime of insurrection as a result of which they lost their *vangad*, position as *gaunkars* as well as their livelihood.

We have seen in Part I, Chapter 7 that Alan Machado shares the same Y DNA haplogroup as 4 other members of the 4th *vangad* and his autosomal DNA shows a relationship with Errol Pinto and myself. The autosomal DNA of the other members of the 4th *vangad* is not available and therefore comparisons with them cannot be made. Sharing the same haplogroup means that we shared the same common ancestor at the time this haplogroup was formed and this time in this case is hundreds of years ago. Consequently, this fact alone is not sufficient to prove that he belongs to the 4th *vangad*; a much closer relationship would be necessary. And this is indeed the case when we compare our autosomal DNA on GEDmatch. Again, it could be argued that since both Errol and Alan are from Mangalore and not being in possession of their genealogical tree, it would be conceivable that their families were linked by marriage in earlier times. But this situation can be ruled out in my case after having studied the paper trail as far as available. There is therefore no doubt that Alan Machado's ancestors belonged to the 4th *vangad*. But we know that he belongs to the 12th *vangad* both from written records handed down to Alan by his ancestor and the fact that the Macedo family name only appears in Aldona's 12th *vangad*. The only logical explanation to this situation is that the 12th *vangad* was not formed by a new settler who was invited by the Chief *gaunkar* or the *gram samstha* but is in fact a branch of the 4th *vangad*. From this finding that we owe to genetics, we can also infer that the 6th to the 12th *vangads* are branches of the first five namely the 6th and 9th *vangads* with the family name Kamti are branches of the 1st, 2nd or 3rd, the 7th, 8th and 12th *vangads* with the family name Prabhu of the 4th and the 10th *vangad* with the family name Naik of the 5th. Since the *gram samstha (comunidade meetings)* was invariably equitable in the distribution of the village's wealth and assets within the *gaunkari*, it can also be inferred that the owners of the 11th *vangad* who were divested by the Portuguese must have belonged to the Naik family. The only way to obtain a definitive proof to this conclusion would be by carrying out DNA tests on members of all the *vangads*, excepting the 4th and 12th for which we already possess this information, when it is still possible to do so keeping in mind that Aldona's 2nd *vangad* is already extinct.

Why did this branching out of the *vangads* occur? The short answer is increase in population and availability of fertile land to be developed. As the village thrived and prospered as a result of an increase in agricultural produce, the population increased and it became necessary to grow more food by producing more agricultural products and increasing the number of fields for rice cultivation, the staple food of the villagers. The work and responsibility for food production had to be shared amongst a growing population and enough land was available to establish more wards in the village; all this was achieved by creating more *vangads* from existing ones without needing to bring in and sharing the village wealth with outsiders.

4. The *Gaunkari* System

Another reason that enabled the settlers to establish themselves in the village (*gaun*) of Aldona (and Goan villages in general) is that they were well organised in quasi-autonomous village republics. The origin of these villages is linked to Northern India with which they bear similarities;[184] the North-Indian origin is corroborated by genetic genealogical findings as discussed in the earlier chapters.

They are known to have existed already "in the early centuries of the Christian era."[185]

Basically agricultural associations that largely shared common property — even though private property also existed — they also exercised municipal, judicial, fiscal and public welfare tasks. They were initially left mostly untouched by the different rulers who, cautious not to destroy the hen that laid the golden eggs, contented themselves with collecting taxes from these associations.

In time, however, tax demands from the rulers, for example from the Adil Shahi became so exaggerated that the settlers welcomed the Portuguese conquerors under Afonso de Albuquerque as liberators.

The Desais also appropriated themselves of land and the state representative tax collector or *parpotdar* was so focused on collecting rent with determination that the *comunidades* were compelled to sell off their common property to meet these demands.[186] With the decline of the Portuguese empire in India and in need of more funds and free labour, the Portuguese conquerors changed the organisational patterns thereby greatly diminishing the importance of the once powerful village republics.

After the conquest of Goa, the Portuguese changed the *gram samstha* to *comunidade* (meaning community) akin to the pattern that could be found in Portugal at the time, transferred all administrative powers of the *gram samsthas* to their own administrators, and the *comunidades* were thus left with the main role of managing common property, paying village taxes from the revenues of these common properties, and also supplying free labour to the Portuguese authorities as required. In short, the erstwhile *gram samstha* village republics were transformed into "*comunidade*" agricultural organisations.

In 1526, the Goa revenue commissioner, Afonso Mexia, promulgated the Charter of Usages and Customs of these *comunidades* after having consulted all concerned including the *gaunkars*.

After the destruction of the temples, properties that had been set aside for the upkeep of these temples and temple servants were transferred to the Church; thus the Church replaced the temples not only from an economic point of view but also in terms of the village rituals, organisation and practices. The latter changes, in addition to the forced conversions and change of names literally ensured an alienation of the converted Hindu population from their historical roots.

The village bodies were further undermined by vicious ecclesiastical greed spearheaded by the Jesuits[187] and to a lesser extent by the Franciscans.

The Goa Tenancy Act passed by the post-liberation Goa State Government in 1964 sounded the death-knell of the *comunidades*.

The revenue of the *comunidades* depended on profits from common properties but with the new tenancy act, common property passed from the hands of the *comunidade* as owners to those of the tillers, thereby pauperising them and rendering them non-functional. For more information on the topic of the *gaunkari* system and *comunidades* see also.[188,189]

5. And Then There Were Two

The village of Aldona is unique not only because its 11th *vangad* was misappropriated by a Portuguese Viceroy but also in the sense that unlike all other Goan village associations or *gaunkaris*, it boasts of not one but two *comunidades*: the *Comunidade Fraternal de Aldona*, consisting of 12 clans (*vangads*), 11 of Brahmins and one of goldsmiths and the *Comunidade de Boa Esperança*, made up of several *vangads* of *kulachari* (servants at the service of the village) dividend holders (*zhonkars*) belonging to the *Chardo* and *Sudra* communities. The latter are not original settlers of the village of Aldona and are therefore by definition not original *gaunkars* of the village.

It is worthwhile describing how this came to be.

According to the *Bosquejo das Comunidades*[190] as well as an analysis of the *Tombo de Aldona* that covers the period 1600-1605, today's *Fraternal* was the original *comunidade* with 12 *vangads*.[191]

As time went by, the *kulacharis* having rendered important services to the village achieved the status of *zhonkars* i.e., a right to a share in the annual village profits generally generated by common property, but only from the age of 19 rather than 11 as was the case for Brahmins.

My grandfather Dr. Honorato Elvino de Sousa, who supported the *Sudras*, attempted to reduce the age at which a *Sudra zhonkar* was entitled to start collecting his *zhon* from 19 to 14 years of age and was greatly maligned in pamphlets written in those times by Brahmins who considered him to be a traitor because of his social conscience.[192]

Speaking of those events, my father recounted that as a consequence of my grandfather's support to the cause of the *Sudras*, a spear was hurled at him when he was on his rounds visiting his patients in his horse carriage but luckily it only damaged his vest and did not cause any other injury.

The fight of the *Sudras* for equal status with Brahmins was a bitter one; one of the approaches used was to alter important documents. Thus, attempts were made to alter the "*Tombo de Aldona*" by interpolating the word "*Sudra*" in various places to try to demonstrate that the original *vangads* included *Sudras* as its members.

These attempts at forgery are crude and Gajanana Ghantkar was able to easily identify and document these interpolations in footnotes in his transliteration of the *Tombo de Aldona*.[193] At no time does the latter specify the caste of the headmen of the clans or other meeting participants, because to do so would have been an oxymoron, so the obvious conclusion is that the interpolations are forgeries.

This fight culminated in the murder of Caetano Soares, a Brahmin lawyer, in Ucassaim, where a cross was erected to mark the spot where he was murdered. It was generally assumed that the *Sudras* caused him to be killed but this has never been substantiated and there is no proof as to the identity of the perpetrators.

Another point to be considered is the fact that the *Sudra* community took their case to court, but lost and could not expect any relief from the Portuguese judiciary.

In view of the bitterness, violence and irreconcilable differences between the Aldona Brahmin and *Sudra* dividend holders (*zhonkars*), in the very year of the afore-mentioned murder, a new *Comunidade of Boa Esperança*, with the *Chardo* and *Sudra kulachari zhonkars* as its members was created. It is important to note that the *kulacharis* who separated were *zhonkars* and not *gaunkars*; hence it is justified to state that in reality, the *comunidades* did not separate but a new *comunidade* was created. The official document in Portuguese published in the official journal, dated October 30, 1924, and signed by the governor general (*Governador Geral*) is translated below:

Legislative Diploma No. 101

Needing to put an end to the known issue of Aldona, constituted by a long and lamentable series of grave incidents and conflicts of various kinds in which, since a long time, two groups of constituents of one of the most important comunidades of Goa are involved, the government of this state resolved to this end to set up a committee of arbitration constituted of officials as well as representatives of both the groups or parties in which the comunidade had been split.

After a thoughtful study, the committee of arbitration agreed on a solution that it judges to be more secure and equitable to resolve the issue and avoid new conflicts: a division of the comunidade of Aldona into two distinct comunidades.

Upon agreement on this point, the committee moved on to divide land, rights, responsibilities , etc., of the current comunidade between the two proposed comunidades, constituted by the two groups of components.

Convoked to take cognisance and deliberate on the work of the committee, the comunidade met in session on October 12 of the current year, and approved quasi unanimously and voted in favour of the conclusions and division made by that committee, as stated in the respective act; and the administrative board (*junta administrativa*), in its session of October 18 of the current year, approved the deliberations of the comunidade.

It being indispensable, necessary and urgent to approve the deliberations approved by the comunidade of Aldona in its session of October 12 of the current year, in order to provide a solution to the old issue that has been debated in its midst, without benefit to anyone and with a manifest damage to its components, but,

In view of the fact that a division of a comunidade into two or more comunidades was not foreseen in the Code of Comunidades (*Código das Comunidades*) this thus constitutes an omission.

The Legislative Council has approved and the Governor General of the State of India gives his accord to this diploma that provisionally takes effect according to the terms of section 2 of Base 30 of Decree no. 7.008, of October 9, 1920.

Article no. 1: The agricultural comunidade of Aldona is divided into two distinct comunidades according to the form and conditions of the decisions taken by it to this end.

Article no. 2: The two comunidades referred to in the former article will have the following denominations: "Comunidade Fraternal of Aldona" and "Comunidade da Boa Esperança of Aldona".

§1. The "Comunidade Fraternal of Aldona" is constituted by Brahmins and goldsmiths, to whom until the year 1909 primary inscription was allowed at the age of 11 years.

§2. The "Comunidade da Boa Esperança of Aldona" is constituted by Chardos and Sudras to whom until the year 1909 inscription was allowed at the age of 19 years

Article no. 3: The division will be effected proportionally to the number of components of each group registered from 1905 to 1914 according to the decision of the comunidade.

Article no. 4: Within a period of three months, from the day of the publication of this diploma, each of the new comunidade will submit its statutes for approval by the government.

Article no. 5: Each comunidade will have its personal clerk (*escrivão*) with salaries fixed by the government.

Article no. 6: The Governor General in Executive Council will take the steps that may be necessary to implement this diploma and the decisions of the comunidade, such that the separate management of the new Comunidade can begin on March 1, 1925.

Article no. 7: Any legislation to the contrary is revoked
To be enforced.

Office of the Governor General, in Nova Goa, October 30, 1924
The Governor General
Jaime de Morais

The implementation of the order was published in Portaria number 557 translated below from the Portuguese original:

Portaria no. 557 – Being known to this government, in accord with the decision of the Legislative Diploma no. 101, of October 30 of the past year, the project of the statutes of the Comunidade Fraternal of Aldona, elaborated by the previously referred to association, (project)

discussed and voted in the session expressly designed towards this end;

In view of the information furnished on this topic by the Administration of the Comunidades of Bardez;

The Governor General of the State of India, in accord with the vote emitted by the Executive Council, in session on the twenty-ninth of last month, approves the afore-mentioned project that has nine articles, and signed by the chief official, interim, of the General Secretariat, in the capacity of Secretary General.

For implementation.

Government general in Nova Goa, June 9, 1925
Responsible for the Government
F. M. Peixoto Vieira.

(Stamp duty and taxes have been paid by the *guias* nos. 3719 and 502/925)

Statutes to which the above portaria refers

Article 1. The old agricultural comunidade of this village Aldona consisted of *gaunkar* components of twelve (12) *vangads*, of which the first (1st) to the tenth (10th) and the twelfth (12th) belonged exclusively to the class of Brahmins and the eleventh (11th) exclusively to that of "goldsmiths" additionally components of the class of Brahmins designated as interested *mumbres, godes, pundits* and registrars (*escrivães*) of the first and second records (*tombos*) and Brahmin *kulacharis* as such, as well as components of the classes of Sudras and Chardos who were designated as interested "first sudra", *cocas, biras, canxes, biums, maindavado, quetris, sonarvado, taris, gentios, camblis, colecars, botos* and *vetios* and interested Chardos is hereby , according to the terms of the first (1st) article and first and second paragraph of the second article of the afore-mentioned diploma, divided into two distinct comunidades in their form and under the conditions resulting from their deliberations couched in their act number twenty nine of folio seventy inclusive to folio eighty two inclusive dated twelfth of October of the past year in the book of acts (decisions) number ten current, denominated "Comunidade Fraternal" of Aldona and "Comunidade of Boa Esperança" of Aldona.

Article 2. The Comunidade Fraternal de Aldona remains thus, in accord with the terms of the same diploma, constituted exclusively by male individuals belonging to the Brahmin and goldsmith classes, erstwhile components of the afore-mentioned Comunidade of Aldona, with land, rights etc. accorded to them in the proportion of fifty six per cent as per the decision of the Provincial Portaria number eight hundred and one of 16th December last, published in the Official Bulletin number hundred and two of the same month.

Article 3. The Comunidade Fraternal of Aldona maintains its old designations, according to which its components were designated in the said comunidade of Aldona.

Article 4. The components of the Comunidade Fraternal of Aldona are designated as follows:

a. *Gaunkars* of twelve (12) *vangads* or votes of which from the first to the tenth and the twelfth are exclusively of the class of "Brahmins", the second *vangads* or vote being extinct since nineteen hundred and thirteen, and the eleventh exclusively of the class of goldsmiths,

b. Interested Brahmins, *mumbres*, *goddes*, *pundits*, registrars of the first and second records and *kulacharis* as such.

Article 5. The age to benefit from the revenues of the personal *jono* is eleven (11) years completed at the time registered in the Code of the Comunidades.

Article 6. Every orphaned son (*varão*) of deceased components will benefit from half a *jono* until reaching the age of eleven, at which time, in his own right, he will earn a whole one.

Article 7. The cash revenue is distributed by whole and half *jonos* and a whole *jono* will annually be accorded to the patron of this community St. Thomas according to the secular uses and customs, the mandatory registration of which will be made without further formalities by the village registrar and which will be collected by the procurator of the confraternity of Our Lady of Conception and the Holy Sacrament.

Article 8. In the primary inscriptions and registrations of the components, the designations mentions in alineas a) and b) of article four (4th) must be strictly adhered to, and if by whatever mistake, the said designations should have been changed or applied one instead of the other, the procurator and the registrar of the comunidade will jointly rectify this mistake with a note in the margin, both in the primary inscription as well as in the annual registration, signed and dated by both, in case of divergencies, the opinion of the procurator of the co-munidade shall prevail.

Article 9. If any mistake or lapse comes to light in the distribution of funds, properties or division of lands according to the applications made to each of the two comunidades, something that is very proba-ble, the agents

of these comunidades should take the required action and correct them, observing the required formalities.

General Secretariat of the Government, Nova Goa, June 9, 1925.

– By the secretary General, the Chief Official, interim

José Pascoal Matias Machado

As it is more than a century ago that the separation of the *comunidades* of Aldona occurred, an unique and unfortunate event in the annals of the Goan *gaunkari* system, recognising the unhelpful effects of the caste system, it would be fitting for today's more enlightened citizens of Aldona to use their wisdom and efforts to correct the existing anomaly and reunite the two *comunidades*.

6. Pre-Conversion Ancestral Hindu Names

According to the *comunidade records*, the Elvino de Sousa clan be-longs to the fourth *vangad* of the *Comunidade Fraternal of Aldona*. Thus, the 1940 register of the *zhonkars* of Aldona (*Comunidade* Fraternal de Aldona, *Matricula dos joneiros do ano de 1940*) lists my father's name as being from Quitula and having an age of 38 years in 1940. My own registration can be found in 2691 fl 17 L7 as being from "Cottarbatta," Aldona and being 27 years of age in 1973 (Annex III). The registry does not indicate the pre-conversion Hindu name.

Cunha Rivara, as referenced by Rui Gomes Pereira, reports that the *gaunkars* of Aldona bore the surnames of Camotim (Kamti or Kamat), Porobo (Prabhu), Naik and Shete (Seti or Shett).[194] An analysis of the *Tombo de Aldona* confirms this information but allows a more specific link with regard to the pre-conversion Hindu names of each of the 12 family clan (*vangad*) members of the village council.

A *tombo* is a Portuguese registry for land and royal revenue. Ga-janana Shantaram Sinai Ghantkar, the first Director of the Goa State Central Library, renamed the Krishnadas Shama Central Library in 2012, discovered in the library archives old partly moth-eaten docu-ments that were, in fact, minutes of the *comunidade* meetings of Aldona, Carambolim and Cortalim covering a span of 10 years from 1595 to 1605 written in *Prakrit* language in the *Gōykannadi* script often used in Goa during the Kadamba rule and thereafter.

Ghantkar salvaged those minutes that had withstood the ravages of time and termites, deciphered the script, transliterated the documents to *Devanagiri* and published them as the History of Goa through Gōykanadi Script. The minutes pertaining to Aldona can be found in his book that can be consulted in Goa's Central Library as manuscript Ms. No. 8000 under the title *Tombo de Aldona*. He has rendered an invaluable service to Goans in general and Aldonkars in particular by thus making these rare documents that open a window onto the lives of the villagers in the early 17th century accessible to the general public.

In *Tombo de Aldona*, the date of the meeting is recorded first; Ghantkar has recalculated the Hindu Luni-Solar calendar and the Jovian cycle used in these records until September 10, 1601. Starting from September 18, 1601, dates according to the Roman calendar are recorded. The venue of the meeting follows, typically the customary banyan tree in the shade of which the discussions took place. The names of the headmen of the individual clans are noted next, in the order of the *vangads* to which they belong; in many cases, when a newly converted headman attends the Gram Samstha meeting, the pre-conversion Hindu name of the father in full or abbreviated is also mentioned. An example of the minutes translated to English by the author can be found as Annex IV.

The number of the *vangad* to which the participants belong are not explicitly mentioned but this can be inferred from the fact that the same names appear in the same order e.g. the clan of the goldsmiths *Seti* always figure in position 11, the number of the *vangad* to which they belong. A further confirmation is furnished by the post-conversion names of the individual *vangads*, provided by Hector Fernandes, president of the *comunidade* of Aldona, since they match the Christian surnames recorded in the minutes.

In order to analyse the *Tombo de Aldona* with the intent of identifying the pre-conversion names of the *vangads*, the date and venue of the meetings, the names of the participants according to the *vangads* to which they belong together with the names or initials of their fathers whenever recorded were set up in a excel spreadsheet, thus greatly facilitating an analysis. This spreadsheet is a key element of this analysis (cf Annex IX); the pre-conversion ancestral Hindu names derived therefrom are recorded below in Table 4.

Vangad number	Pre-conversion name
1	Kamti
2	Kamti
3	Kamti
4	Prabhu
5	Naik
6	Kamti
7	Prabhu
8	Prabhu
9	Kamti
10	Naik
11	Seti
12	Prabhu

Table 4: Pre-conversion Hindu names of the 12 vangads of Aldona's Comunidade Fraternal

This analysis reconfirms that each clan bore the same Hindu name. This can be concluded from the fact that it is invariably the same Hindu name that is recorded for a specific *vangad* even though there are some rare lapses e.g. the headman Seti of the 11th *vangad* has been omitted in the meetings held on May 7 and July 1601. It has thus been possible to identify the pre-conversion Hindu name of each of the 12 *vangads* of the *Comunidade Fraternal de Aldona* as shown in Table 4.

Other Hindu names are known to have existed among the *interessados* — according to Hector Fernandes, *interessados* are *gaunkars* who left the village to avoid conversion but later returned — but these names do not figure anywhere in the minutes of the meetings. It is possible that the individuals bearing these names acquired the *gaunkar* status at a later stage or their surnames have been derived from their honorific titles.

In the case of a converted headman, his father's Hindu name is also mentioned, often only once — there are occasional exceptions — whereas the Hindu headmen are always referred to along with their father's full names or initials. For example, the father's name of Duarte Moniz, one of the headmen of the 4th *vangad*, is mentioned once in 1595 and then never again.

Using a different source, Chandrakant Keni mentions in his book "The Saraswats" that the afore-mentioned Duarte Moniz, son of Kist Prabhu was converted in 1595,[195] thereby confirming the assumption made above. Using this logic, it can be concluded that **Agostinho Sousa, son of Ramu Prabhu** and the first of the Sousa patrilineage of the 4th *vangad*, was converted in the first half of 1601.

An interesting situation arises in which father and son do not always share the same Christian surname: In the 7th *vangad* the Fernandes surname predominates and it is the only surname that subsists today. The
minutes of the meetings held on August 6 and August 31, 1601 state, however, that the participating headman of this clan, Antonio Ferrão is the son of Antonio Fernandes.

7. Post-Conversion Christian Surnames

The penalties to Hindus for not converting to Christianity were very severe ranging from expulsions from the village, loss of all immovable properties, additional taxes (e.g., the so-called "*shendi tax*") and so on. Reverting to Hindu rituals after conversion was equally dangerous because of the inquisition resulting in torture, imprisonment and confiscation of property. Denouncers were encouraged and rewarded with half of the confiscated property.[196]

Consequently many Hindus fled to more hospitable places and often took their deities along with them. Others branched out into revenue farming and still others into trading. One interesting approach that the analysis of the *Tombo de Aldona* seems to indicate is that the elder headmen did not convert but allowed their children to do so, thereby keeping the immovable properties within the clan.

For example, Ramu Prabhu's son converted and acquired the name of Agostinho Sousa and represented his clan (4th *vangad*) in a meeting held on May 7, 1601 where his name appears for the first time. We continue, however, to encounter Ramu Prabhu's name in the minutes of a meeting held on September 18, 1601 as one of the many participants in the triennial auction.

The Seti clan (goldsmiths) seems to have resisted conversion throughout the 10 years that are recorded in the *Tombo de Aldona*. One explanation could be that goldsmiths were greatly in demand both by the Portuguese administrators for their personal jewellery as well as by the ecclesiastical authorities for the Church ornaments and the latter were wary of running the risk of losing these artists by forcibly converting them. At the baptism of the principal jeweller of Goa, the Viceroy personally chose to be his baptismal godfather[197] and before that, from 1518-1520, the jeweller Raulu Chatim (Shett in Portuguese) from Carrem, near Porvorim, was sent by Afonso de Albuquerque to serve the King of Portugal D. Manuel and his work was so highly appreciated that there were 18 Goan jewellers working in Portugal at that time.[198]

No clue can be found as to why the Prabhus of the 12th *vangad* could also resist conversion throughout that period; a possible theory is that they may have been pundits (healers), very much in demand around that time and were therefore "protected," at least initially.[199]

The pre-conversion family name of the fourth *vangad* to which the Sousa family from Calvim that subsequently relocated to Quitula and the Elvino de Sousa clan belong was **Prabhu.**

Prabhu, meaning lord or master in the Sanskrit language, is a common name among Konkani speaking Saraswat Brahmins across the Konkan coast from Maharashtra to Kerala. According to Dhume, it was a title accorded to the representative of the main village of the district (taluka) committee. "The Prabhus might also have occupied official posts in the central administration, without prejudice to their original posts which were hereditary."[200]

Tradition relates that a Prabhu was a landlord and as such a master to the many employees that were needed to cultivate his lands. Nairne's reference to Prabhus employed by the Portuguese in high positions who were compelled to perform their Hindu religious rites secretly and by night whilst others were forcibly converted can also be interpreted as meaning landlord.[201]

Further evidence of this meaning is furnished in a rendition of a resolution adopted on 28th of June 1541 by the leaders of the Hindu community agreeing to use income from land belonging to the temples destroyed by the Portuguese for the upkeep of Christian Churches and missionaries in which several *"Parbus"* are mentioned as landholders, though not exclusively.[202]

Agostinho Sousa must have been a recent convert at the time his name is first mentioned in the minutes of the *comunidade* meetings because the Hindu name of his father is also recorded. We encounter the name of Gaspar Sousa as the representative of the 4th *vangad* in a meeting that took place on November 28, 1604, but his father's name is not mentioned leading to the conclusion that he was not a recent convert. It is thus safe to conclude that Agostinho Sousa was the first of the Elvino de Sousa patrilineage and Ramu Prabhu the last person of this clan to bear the name of Prabhu.

The *comunidade* has maintained the post-conversion Christian names of the Gaunkars belonging to each of the *vangads*, as shown in Table 5 below.

Vangad	Pre-conversion surnames: Source: This study by the author	Post-conversion surnames: Source:Hector Fernandes, President, Comunidade of Aldona, personal communication
1st Vangad	Kamti	Costa, Couto, Sousa, Tavora (fr)om Sangolda
2nd Vangad	Kamti	Extinct
3rd Vangad	Kamti	Afonso (from Chorão and Divar), Ferrão, Lourenço, Lobo (from Bodiem), Rocha
4th Vangad	Prabhu	Cruz, Cunha, Faria, Fernandes, Lobo, Moniz, Noronha, Pinto, Rodrigues, Sousa

5th Vangad	Naik	Carvalho, Correa, Conceição, Fonseca, Gama, Gouvea, Lousado, Mendonça, Menezes, Noronha, Pinto, Rego, Siqueira, Sá, Soares, Sousa, Vás
6th Vangad	Kamti	Drago, Lobo, Sá, Sousa
7th Vangad	Prabhu	Fernandes
8th Vangad	Prabhu	Mendes, Sousa
9th Vangad	Kamti	Alvares, Bocalo or Bocarro, Castelino, Coutinho, Camotim, Fonseca, Fernandes, Lopes, Noronha, Siqueira, Soares, Sousa
10th Vangad	Naik	Comelo, Lima
11th Vangad	Seti	Xete or Chatim, Rocha, Sousa
12th Vangad	Prabhu	Afonso, Macedo, Soares, Sousa
Interessados	Goddés – Lobo, Mumbrés – Monteiro, Cardosa, Nobriga or Nobres, Silva, Sousa Pandit – Nazaré, Santos	
Escrivão	Primeiro Tombo: Siqueira Segundo Tombo: Sacardando, Soares, Toscano, Vás, Batista	
Kulachari	Miranda, Mesquita, Morais, Pereira, Siqueira, Sousa	

Table 5: Name changes in the vangads

Many Hindus became destitute after conversion because they were shunned and no longer helped and supported by the Hindus, as was the case prior to the arrival of the Portuguese since the converts were considered to be polluted and traitors. They were also not helped by the Portuguese conquerors to redress their situation.

The Hindu ecclesiastics or *bhatts*, the teachers (*purohits*) and the temple servants, for example, who depended on the land allotted to the temples as well as the temples themselves for their livelihood and upkeep, lost their means of subsistence once the temples had been destroyed and the lands appropriated by the Church; they were also not accepted into priesthood by the Catholic Church until very much later.

Thus, a combination of abominable economic conditions as well as the potential threat of having to undergo torture, imprisonment or worse at the hands of the Inquisitors compelled not only Hindus but also many converted Christians as well to flee to places such as Karnataka.

Some families chose a Solomonic path: half the family converted and the other half migrated to Karnataka or other more welcoming destinations.[203]

My ancestors chose to convert but Ramu Prabhu himself continued to resist conversion since his name can be encountered in the minutes of later meetings even after the conversion of his son e.g. meeting of 18 September 1601.

8. The Temple

It is not known if Aldona counted Muslim inhabitants at the time of the arrival of the Portuguese; there is no doubt, however, that Hindus formed the vast majority of the population.

Missionary records provide a total number of 556 temples in the old conquests: 116 in Tiswadi (Ilhas), 176 in Bardez, and 264 in Salcete but more probably existed.[204] The first Provincial Council of 1567 had ordered the demolition of "all idols, temples, trees and sites of Hindu worship" and most times, the temples were replaced by churches on the same land. Additionally, land that had been allotted to the upkeep of the temples and its servants was now, after forceful persuasion of the *gaunkar* headmen, reallocated to maintain chapels and churches.[205]

Such an abundance of places of worship is a strong indicator that religion played a primordial role in the life of the Goan villagers. The importance of religion was so intense that Saraswat Brahmins carried along with them their deities from wherever they arrived as settlers.

Professor Pissurlencar lists the following temples as existing in Aldona in pre-Portuguese Goa: Bhagvati, Ravalnath, Narayann, Santeri, Sidnath, Bhutnath, Dadda, Satti, Fulnath.[206] Rui Gomes Pereira confirms this list except that he fails to mention Sidnath and Satti.[207]

Gomes Pereira lists the following affiliates of the latter in Khandola: Dadd, Ravalnath, Lakshimi-Narayna, Gram-purusha, Karia-purusha, Ananta-purusha and Kollos of Santeri.[208]

The main temple dedicated to Shri Bhagvati was possibly located at the site where the church of St. Thomas the Apostle was initially built in Coimbavaddo.

These temples were shifted to Mayem in 1567 out of fear of destruction by the Portuguese and again to Khandola (Ponda) in 1669 where they continue to be located as the temple of Shri Bhagvati Haldonkarin.

According to oral history, Shree Bhagvati, one of the invocations of the goddess Parvati, consort of Lord Shiva, was the main temple located in Cottarbhatt; Bhutnath, Sidhnath, and Fulnath were subsidiary deities. The temple dedicated to Dadd stood in Quitula, the Ravalnath temple was
situated in Calvim, the Narain temple in Carona and the Santeri temple was located in Santerxette from where the name of this ward has been derived (Hector Fernandes, personal communication).

Santeri is a local non-Indo-Aryan deity[209] and its existence in Aldona may be indicative of the fact that this village was inhabited by indigenous people before the village was settled.

Until it was banned by the Portuguese in the 16th century, the custom of Sati or self-immolation of a woman in a funeral pyre along with her deceased husband must have existed in Aldona since a Sati stone can be found in the temple of Shri Bhagvati Haldonkarin.

In 1898, during excavations for the foundations of a building adjoining the present St. Thomas Church of Aldona, a granite slab as well as statues of a Goddess and a cobra were discovered; these were transferred to the Missionary Exhibition of the Vatican.[210] It is not known if these artifacts belonged to the temple or under what circumstances they were hidden at that location. The *Devi* could be the Goddess of rain and snakes are associated with this Goddess.

9. The Church

The first Church of Aldona was built in 1569 in the ward of Coimbavaddo at the request of Father Fernando da Paz during the reign of Archbishop Temudo, head of the Order of Saint Francis. According to tradition, the *gaunkars* chose St. Thomas as the patron of the Church because they wanted the Church to be dedicated to a person who was directly connected to Jesus Christ and they gifted one *zhon* in favour of the Church at this occasion.[211]

The building of the present Church was initiated in 1595 at the cost of the village. The first entry in Ghantkar's *Tombo de Aldona* is a meeting of the Gaunkars that probably took place in September 1595 – the precise day is not extant — approving a sum of 125 Asrupias to be paid in two instalments to the Father Rector towards construction work of the Church.

We find detailed minutes of a meeting that took place on the 23rd of March 1603, where the Gaunkars met under a banyan tree in the Church compound and approved a permanent lease of a plot of land towards the Church. This venerable banyan tree crashed around 2pm on the 16th of July 1915 taking with it memories of a bygone era when 3 centuries earlier, the *gaunkars* of Aldona made a momentous decision sitting in its shade.

At this meeting Father Costa de Priro Miguel de Sao Boavitória addressed the villagers who had gathered and told them that the old Church made of mud was falling down. The villagers were required to provide land and financing for a good and virtuous meeting place of the village in accord with their vow. He added that Father Rector Frei Rodrigo Espirito Santo would help, and the villagers would have to furnish labour and additional support including a contribution from the population. In order to avoid that the villagers become impoverished the people should get together and provide manual labour. He added that an uncultivated plot or *khajan* land would have to be acquired, auctioned off with a permanent lease, the profits of which would go exclusively towards the building project of the Church. The Gaunkars dutifully passed an unanimous resolution approving these measures.

Monies continued to be funnelled towards the construction of the Church. The *comunidade* passed a resolution on 7th July 1603 with regard to collection of money for the construction of the Church instructing the President of the Church Bernardino de Azavedo to auction off land for the purpose. On 10th November 1604 the sum of 97 Asrupiya, and one and a quarter tanga were approved for wood for the new Church. In the same year, a plot of land on the slope of the Church was acquired for 10 Asrupiya. On the 16th of January 1605, 50 Asrupiya were sanctioned to acquire tiles for the Aldona Church. And at every opportunity, for example as a punishment for villagers who had abandoned the village to avoid conversion but subsequently returned, fines were imposed towards the construction of the Church.

It appears that the construction of the Church was met with some violent opposition. The minutes of a meeting on 29th June 1603 relate that a judicial order by the Captain of Bardez required the village to appoint 4 watchmen paid by the *gaunkars* to guard the monuments of the village as a consequence of the violence of the previous night. Residents moving around at night were required to carry a lamp and outsiders coming from across the river would be allowed to spend the night in the village only after intimating the watchmen. The Church is not specifically mentioned but there was no other monument in the village that would call for an immediate intervention of the Captain.

The walls of the sacristy and adjoining rooms were demolished on 13th September 1897 and the reconstruction work initiated on the 30th of the same month to be completed the following year. Various other improvements have been carried out over the years. It is worthy of mention that the construction of the impressive steps leading to the Church was undertaken under the auspices of Father Joao Francisco Lobo who was the vicar from 1918 to 1929.

10. Care for the Environment

The villagers of Haldonna took good care of their environment. On the 20th of July 1605 the village council of Haldonna duly records that wood is being clandestinely collected from khajan land or cut from embankments of white mangroves or big trees located near isolated *khajan* plots or grass from the mangroves is being collected and "the *khajan* lands and embankments are being devastated" and ruined.

Clearly, the appointed watchmen were not doing the work for which they were being paid for by the village. It was therefore decided that the village council would approach the elected village arbiter to assess charges against the watchmen and as punishment would confiscate their woolen blanket, knife, scythe and pickaxe and take them to the Captain of Bardez by whom they would be additionally fined a sum of 5 Asrupiya towards projects of the Government.

The villages of Goa and the whole State would certainly benefit by following the example of our ancestors and adopting a similar approach today.

11. Life Under the Portuguese
The Portuguese Conquerors were aided and welcomed by the Hindus: Wise Uncle Rat

The thought has often plagued me that the popular and well-loved Goan *dulpod* par excellence *Undir Mhojea Mama* had in it the potential to change the course of history.

Undra mojea mama, ani aum sangtam tuca
Tea mazorichea pillea lagim, khell mandinaca.
Undir mama ailo, ani pette pondak liplo
Ani mazorechea piliean taca eka gansan khailo

Freely translated, it means
Uncle mouse, I wish to alert you
Do not get into play, with that off-spring of the cat
Uncle mouse arrived, and hid under the bed
And the off-spring of the cat, ate it with one single bite

This *dulpod* most probably did not exist in the early 16th century, or if it did, Timaya Naayak was either not aware of it or did not heed its words of wisdom. Had he followed the counsel given to uncle rat, he may not have helped Afonso de Albuquerque, the "off-spring" of the king of Portugal, to bite off Goa from the Adil Shahi and chew it for four and half centuries.

Whether the alternative would have been a better option is a matter of conjecture and debate. The Adil Shahi was oppressive, extorting high taxes from the villages to the extent that the Portuguese conquerors were not only strongly supported by Timaya but also by his captain Madhava Rao, the captain of another vessel Monu Naique, Gorca Naique, Malu Naique as well as other prominent collaborators such as Captain Krishna, Raulu Camotim (Portuguese for Kamat) of Divar, Ganda Chatim (Portuguese for Shetti), Krishna Shenoi and Raulu Xette.[212]

Additionally, the conquerors were welcomed by the local Hindu inhabitants as their liberators. The Portuguese were clearly overwhelmed by this indispensable support of the local Hindu population

156

whom they treated well, their murderous wrath being reserved for the Moors.

In 1503, Vasco da Gama had demonstrated his capacity for savagery at a trading station in Calicut (Kozhikode).

The Moors of Calicut had earlier put to death 53 Portuguese traders in retaliation for the seizure of an Arab vessel. Gaspar Correa, who sailed with Vasco da Gama, recounts that the latter ordered the hands, ears and nose of the Brahmin who had been sent by the king of Calicut as a peace messenger to be cut off and strung around his neck.

The same treatment was reserved for some 800 captured Moorish crew of several vessels, whose teeth were additionally knocked out, hands tied and heaped in one of the captured vessels that was then set alight. The peace messenger, burdened with the mutilated parts of the captured crew, was installed in a small vessel and sent ashore with a message to the king of Calicut suggesting that he prepare a curry with the mutilated parts.[213]

Afonso de Albuquerque's first occupation of Goa with the support of Timaya in March 1510 was short lived but equally brutal; Adil Shah recaptured the town of Goa but discovered according to the same Gaspar Correa, that Timaya, renamed Timoja by the Portuguese, had massacred not only the governor but also the Muslim nobility, leaving behind him a trail of "weepings and lamentations".

Afonso de Albuquerque was not to be outdone in savagery by Vasco da Gama when he definitively captured Goa on 25th November 1510. Convinced that his brutality had been enabled by very special blessings accorded to him by the Almighty Himself, he wrote to his king:

"Our Lord helped us to do this job better than we had planned or expected. Over 300 Turks died, and till Benastery and Gandauly the roads were strewn with dead bodies and others who lay wounded and dying. Several died while trying to cross the river with their horses. I had the city put to fire and sword. During four days our men made the city bleed. No Moor was given a chance to escape alive. They were driven into mosques, which were then set ablaze. I ordered that the land cultivators and the Brahmins should not be killed. Nearly six thousand Moors, men and women, were killed... No burial place or houses belonging to Muslims were left standing. Anyone now caught is fried alive."[214]

Braz de Albuquerque, the son of Afonso de Albuquerque, confirms the above and provides a figure of the number of Muslims put to death: "and it was ascertained that of men, women, and children, the number exceeded six thousand". The principle officer in this massacre was Medeo Rao, "the Hindu captain of Timoja's company". Rao was apparently not a native of Goa.[215] With all powers in the region vying with one another as in a beauty contest with regard to their sanguinary excesses, the mirror in Snow White's fairy tale would face an insurmountable task had it been confronted with the question "mirror, mirror, on the wall, who is the bloodthirstiest of them all"? It is horrifying, though, that the Portuguese claimed the patronage, blessing and empowerment of no lesser power than God Almighty Himself when indulging in this wanton savagery.

12. Conversions and Identity Change

As we have seen earlier, the new conquerors exerted massive pressure on the local population to convert.

Not only the Hindu places of worship were destroyed but large scale conversions were also initiated applying equally a carrot and stick approach where admittedly, to paraphrase the pig in George Orwell's Animal Farm, the stick was more equal than the carrot.

The afore-mentioned 1567 Provincial Council of Goa - under the presidency of the first Archbishop of Goa Gaspar de Leão Pereira and after his retirement under that of George Themudo OP, Bishop of Cochin during whose reign the first Church of Aldona was constructed — passed no less than 115 decrees.

One of them declared that Christians in Goa should not be permitted to use their former Hindu names and must instead adopt the name of their Portuguese god-father at baptism; the existing Portuguese settlers, the residing officer or even the officiating priest assumed the role of god-father.

The process of conducting baptisms has been related by St. Francis Xavier himself in connection with the 10,000 souls he converted within a single month in Travancore.[216] After the baptism, each convert was given his new name in writing and asked to send their wives and families to be baptised in the same manner.

Inevitably, mix-ups occurred bearing in mind that the names as well as the language and script in which they were written were without doubt a novelty for the newly baptised. Since fathers and sons were not necessarily baptised in the presence of the same god-father and by the same priest, unusual situations arose.

In 1594, the son of Pero Parras, a *gaunkar* of the village of Raia, acquired at baptism the new name of Sebastião Barbosa. A few years later in 1609, another son of Pero Parras was graced with the baptismal name of João Rangel. Thus, we encounter the piquant case where a father and his two sons share between them three different surnames: Parras, Barbosa and Rangel.[217] This approach also ensured that by a single baptismal stroke, members of the same *vangad* who initially all shared the same Hindu surname ended with very divergent Portuguese catholic surnames.

Different religious orders had been given responsibility for the evangelisation of the regions of Goa. The Dominicans were entrusted with 15 villages in *Tiswadi*, the Jesuits the remaining *Tiswadi* villages, the islands of Chorão and Divar as well as the whole of Salcete and finally the Franciscans were put in charge of Bardez.

The Society of Jesus undertook its declared objective of rapid evangelisation with zeal and vigour. The Jesuits also used their position of power to acquire properties on a large scale inviting the wrath of even the Portuguese settlers who were left with crumbs.[218]

Nobel laureate Bishop Desmond Tutu of South Africa may have been inspired by the Jesuits in Goa in the sixteen hundreds when he describes the role of missionaries in his continent: "When the missionaries came to Africa they had the Bible and we had the land. They said, 'Let us pray.' We closed our eyes. When we opened them we had the Bible and they had the land."

13. Conversions in Aldona

The Franciscans did not proselytise with the same zeal as the Jesuits and conversions occurred at a more relaxed pace that could be termed *sossegado* to borrow a Portuguese word often referred to as a supposedly typical laid back Goan characteristic.

Fr. Manuel de S. Mathias is credited with having baptised 400 persons at Aldona during his four month stay in the first years of the 17th century.

The proselyte productivity increased because in 1619, the number of the converted in Aldona had doubled with "700 communicants, 561 who go to confession and 576 baptised children."[219] Since my last Hindu ancestor was baptised during the first half of the year 1601, the probability is high that it was by the hands of Fr. Manuel de S. Mathias.

The villagers of Aldona did not embrace the new religion brought to them by the Portuguese conquerors easily. Many original settlers (*gaunkars*), village tenants (*kulachari*) and other Hindus preferred to forfeit their possessions and abandon Aldona rather than convert. On occasion, however, they returned to the village sometimes clandestinely.

Minutes of a village council meeting held on 11th September 1604 passed a resolution stating that Hindus who attend catechism classes will be given property of *khajan* land and by becoming Christians can live in the village and be entitled to a *zhon*. Those who decline to do so will become strangers and lose their right to property that they have acquired through the triennial auction. In the case of outsiders i.e., individuals who are not villagers but hold shares of *khajan* land or are members of the tenants' association, if they attend catechism, they will continue to enjoy the benefits but 4 Asrupiya per plot per year will go towards the construction work of the Church of St. Thomas.

At the same meeting, the village elders passed a resolution as a result of a decree by the Judge of the cases of the crown and public property. Some of the *gaunkars* having abandoned the village and migrated to Muslim-held territories legally lost their rights to property and *zhon* but refused to accept this situation. Two Headmen were therefore appointed to obtain information on these individuals in keeping with the Judge's decree, make it known to the whole village that such an investigation has been initiated and also inform the *gaunkars* who have migrated about the consequences that their actions entail.

We learn from the minutes of a meeting held on 15th January 1605, many portions of which are unfortunately moth-eaten or torn, that the Judge of the cases of the crown and public property learned at the time he had come to preside over the triennial auction that some of Haldonna's Hindu landtiller *gaunkars* and *kulachari* had abandoned the village and he consequently confiscated their property. On being apprised of this situation, fourteen of them approached the village's Father Rector, agreed to become Christians and asked for their land to be returned to them. Father Rector in turn intervened on their behalf with the *Gaunkari* Headmen as well as the Judge and the decision was taken to allow them to reside in the village and enjoy their previous privileges from that day onwards but under certain conditions. They would have to apologise for their behaviour, attend Catechism classes as well as contribute towards the construction of the Church. If the contribution is not made, the *khajan* land belonging to them would be confiscated, auctioned off and the proceeds thereof go towards the construction of the Church.

It is interesting to note that one of the 14, an Aldonkar with the name of Antonio Sequeira was a Christian convert.

Not only were those who did not agree to convert forfeit all their possessions and denied residence in the village but additionally resentment against them was incited by proposing to allow outsiders to the village (*Khuntkars*) to acquire the lands confiscated from them.

Some 130 years after Father de S. Mathias' sustained baptismal activity, Christian religious belief of the converts in Aldona, along with several other Goan villages, was seriously vacillating necessitating a muscular intervention of the Inquisition, and the proposal of a strong plea in favour of the eradication of the Konkani language in favour of Portuguese, witness a report of Cunha Rivara:[220]

"One Inquisitor with eighteen years of service in the Inquisition of Goa, proposed to His Majesty, in the year 1731, the following: " The first and the principal cause of such a lamentable ruin (loss of souls) is the disregard of the law of His Majesty D. Sebastião of glorious memory, and the Goan Councils, prohibiting the natives to converse in their own vernacular and making obligatory the use of the Portuguese language: this disregard in observing the law, gave rise to so many and so great evils, to the extent of effecting irreparable harm to souls, as well as to the royal revenues. Since I have been though unworthy, the Inquisitor of this State, ruin has set in the villages of Nadorá (sic), Revorá, Pirná, Assonorá and Aldoná in the Province of Bardez; in the villages of Cuncolim, Assolná, Dicarpalli, Consuá, and Aquem in Salcete; and in the Island of Goa, in Bambolim, Curcá, and Siridão, and presently in the village of Bastorá, in Bardez. In these places some members of village communities, as also women and children have been arrested and others accused of malpractices; for since they cannot speak any other language but their own vernacular, they are secretly visited by *botos*, servants and high priests of temples who teach them the tenets of their sect and further persuade them to offer alms to the temples and to supply other necessary requisites for the ornaments of the same temples, reminding them of the good fortune their ancestors had enjoyed from such observances and the ruin they were subjected to, for having failed to observe these customs; under such persuasion they are moved to offer gifts and sacrifices and perform other diabolical ceremonies, forgetting the law of Jesus Christ which they had professed in the sacrament of Holy Baptism. This would not have happened had they known only the Portuguese language; since they being ignorant of the native tongue the *botos, grous* and their attendants would not have been able to have any communication with them, for the simple reason that the latter could only converse in the vernacular of the place. Thus an end would have been put to the great loss among native Christians whose faith has not been well grounded, and who easily yield to the teaching of the Hindu priests."

It is understandable that the faith of the villagers in their newly acquired religion started to falter, more so in a place where no activity of any significance could take place without a prior appeal to the corresponding deity and where any unpleasant occurrence or calamity was attributed to the displeasure of a deity who had to be immediately appeased with prayers, offerings and sacrifices.

Consider: whereas prior to their conversion, life for the villagers had been peaceful and the *gram samsthas* ensured that sufficient food was available for all the inhabitants of the village, since their conversion at the dawn of the seventeenth century, either their pre-conversion Hindu deities were punishing them or their new Christian God had failed to protect them from a major famine, two cyclones accompanied by earthquakes, food shortages, attacks by the forces of Adil Shah and Shivaji and a renewed subsequent Maratha attack, tax requirements from the Portuguese authorities to finance the defense of Goa and monetary demands by the ecclesiastical authorities to build lofty Churches both of which obliged the *gram samsthas* to sell some of their common property. Thus, there were numerous reasons to placate the Hindu deities who in the past had so well fed and protected them and their villages. But that was not all.

Denunciations were not only encouraged and rewarded with half of the property of the accused but even more so, they were a legal requirement.[221] The fury of the Inquisition spared neither men nor women or children, not even the deceased.

In December 1580, Garcia d'Orta, the best known European physician of his time in India, a converted Jew who had secretly continued to observe the tenets of his religion but who in life had been protected by his friend and patron Martim Afonso da Souza, Governor-general of the Portuguese territories in India from 1542 to 1545, was submitted to the posthumous insult of having his bones disinterred and publicly burnt.[222]

That the inquisitor cited above attributed the root cause of the vacillating faith of the villagers of Goa to the failure to eradicate the Konkani language constitutes a demonstration of an acute lack of what Hercules Poirot terms "those little grey cells". With life and death decisions and their destinies in the hands of such nano-brained individuals as the afore-mentioned veteran Inquisitor, it is a wonder that more converts did not choose the perilous road to exile.

Insecurity persisted for at least another century in the village. In the eighteenth century, tradition as recounted by my father relates that gangs of Bhonsle's men were known to cross the river and march to the beating of drums demanding a tribute from villagers of substance.

On one such occasion, my ancestors who in the meantime had relocated from Calvim to Quitula preferred instead to invest their money in the acquisition of a shot gun that was fired in the air at the arrival of the marauders, thereby persuading the gang to seek other pastures. On another occasion, tradition again relates that another marauding chieftain who had been captured with the help of a bhatt informant is reported to have pronounced the threat *"haunv tori sutton bhotta tuji gompti haunv kaponn"* (should I escape, bhatt, I will slit your throat).

Every Aldonkar knows that October 29 is celebrated as the *choranchem fest* (the robbers' feast). On this day, in 1895, a gang of armed robbers, claimed to have consisted of Ranes and deserters, crossed the river from Corjuem with the intention of plundering the Church treasury but were intercepted and made to beat a hasty retreat by the villagers, primarily by the women of the village armed with pitchforks and other tilling implements, who had been summoned by the tolling of the Church bells.[223]

Some were captured but most of them drowned in the river as they tried to escape the wrath of the populace. It is only after a regular force of 450 soldiers was posted in *Tercena*, a playground adjacent to the house where I was born, a word derived from the Portuguese word *"terço"* or one-third for one-third of a garrison, did life become more secure in Aldona.

In 1780, the Portuguese conquered from the Marathas Pernem, Sanquelim and Satari, and after a treaty signed on January 29, 1788, with the king of Sonda, acquired the remaining districts that together form what became known as the New Conquests.

The influence of the clergy had massively decreased by this time: the Jesuit order had been banned in 1759 and the political clout of the other religious orders had also considerably diminished. More importantly, the Portuguese had realised that forced conversions leading to a departure of Hindus was detrimental to trade and therefore to the exchequer. The religious freedom of the Hindu majority in the new conquests was consequently left undisturbed.

After 1835, many Hindu families from the new conquests were permitted to settle in the old conquests including Aldona and some Christian families were encouraged to take the reverse route with the lure of land for a small annual rent.[224]

A branch of my ancestors from Quitula availed of this opportunity and thus settled in Quepem maintaining there a thriving textile business; their house located in the Church Square of Quepem bears witness to their entrepreneurial spirit. A small structure called a *loja* (shop or store in Portuguese) where goods were stored for the needs of this business between Aldona and Quepem existed by the river close to the ancestral house in Quitula and to this day the place is known locally as *lozar*.

14. Condition of Women

Other than the custom of Sati, the *gram samsthas* and the *comunidades* derived therefrom being patrilineal in structure, not much is documented on the condition of the women of the times.

Education was reserved for males and primarily for male *gaunkars*. In a resolution of the village council of Haldonna dated 25th January 1605, funds were allocated for the education of the sons of the village *gaunkars*; there is no reference whatsoever to the daughters.

Viewed through the eyes of an European, the condition of Brahmin women was pathetic and deplorable; Azevedo provides the following description:[225]

"Marriages are arranged by parents, without the intervention of the betrothed, and the detrimental consequences are not as bad as it may first appear but the unions immediately after puberty result in fatal consequences to children and mothers.

Children are conceived before the parents have attained their own development for procreation, and the mothers, prevented from becoming educated, and losing within a few years all their physical charms, are reduced to a miserable condition.

Recluses in their homes, occupied in the kitchen and with intrigues, and martyrised as daughters in law, they take revenge when they become mothers in law. They eat after their husbands, from plates of leaves from which they (the husbands) serve themselves, and they resign themselves (to their situation) or commit suicide, to see their husbands waste their life and fortune with prostitutes. These are the only Hindu women to whom the art of reading and writing is taught...

But the most deplorable condition of the Brahmin woman is widowhood. Before the body of the husband is taken away for incineration, the widow removes the collar that symbolised the conjugal alliance, as well as all the jewellery, and the barber shaves off her hair. If she has not yet attained puberty, the mourning begins when the union would have been consumed...and the child is condemned to spend her entire life with strangers and see herself repelled everywhere as a bad omen".

The author adds that the Vaishnavas "are less subject than other Brahmins" to these customs and that the "situation of the women of inferior castes is less pitiable."

How does one explain this subjugation of women in Medieval Goa? As we have learned earlier, the Indian population is a mixture of two groups, Ancestral South Indians ASI and Ancestral North Indians ANI mixed in different proportions.

The ASI population was highly developed and founded the Indus Valley / Harappa civilisation. According to the Indus Valley Civilisation expert, Professor Vasant Shinde, the most fortified IVC city Dholavira practiced a panchayat system where every resident supported the city for the common good.[226] This is reminiscent of the way Goa's *gram samsthas* functioned.

ANI consisted of a Yamnaya-related population that became rich and powerful as a result of innovative new technologies that they developed and formed a stratified patriarchal society with power concentrated among a small number of elite males.

The Yamnaya and the cultures that ensued from them such as the Sintashta, who had domesticated the horse and developed wheeled vehicles were highly mobile and migrated towards the west and south leaving their genetic imprint on India and Europe.

The structure of the *gram samsthas* appears to be a symbiosis of both these cultures, with a well-organised planned village organisation inherited from the ASI and a government of a small number of elite exclusively male *vangads* or family clans inherited from the Yamnaya-related ANI.

A similar male dominated society transmitted by the Yamnaya existed in Europe as well but with advent of industrialisation and the ensuing workforce shortage particularly after the Second World War, a concerted effort was progressively undertaken to encourage women to join the workforce. European governments also invested in education finally leading to a change in the mindset of males and an increasing demand for gender equality. Switzerland was one of the last European countries to grant women the right to vote in March 1971. It is the Swiss males, since only they had the right to vote, who approved the law in a national referendum.

Even though today women in Europe can be considered to be emancipated, complete gender equality has not yet been achieved. The World Bank has found that in 2019, only 6 countries in the world (Belgium, Denmark, France, Latvia, Luxembourg, Sweden) achieved the highest score of 100 in gender equality.[227] In many cases differences in salaries between men and women persist; it is estimated to be still around 10 percent in Switzerland in 2018 in disfavour of women who have an equivalent qualification to their male counterparts and 20 percent on average, a vast improvement when compared to 10 years ago but with room for further progress.

India still has a long way to go in gender equality. Women have had the right to vote since independence, much before Switzerland, but without education and emancipation, political rights confer little influence. In urbanised regions where women are as educated and qualified as their male counterparts, there is undoubtedly enormous progress that has been made in gender equality but much remains to be done in rural India.

Equal Measures 2030 is an independent civil society and private sector-led partnership that tracks an index of gender set forth by their 2030 Agenda in 129 countries in five regions and 51 issues ranging from health, gender-based violence, climate change, decent work and others; the criteria differ from those of The World Bank. In their 2019 gender index report, Denmark occupies the first rank with 89.3 percent, followed by Nordic countries; Germany, Canada and Australia are among the top ten, Switzerland occupies rank 12. India occupies rank 95 out of the 129 countries confirming that there is still substantial room for improvement.[228]

Changing the legacy of the Yamnaya-related cultures in India is far from easy; without a strong political will, the elite male mindset and domination inherited from the Yamnaya will continue.

15. Population of Aldona in 1601

The population of Haldonnna was in a flux around 1601, with many *gaunkars* and *kulacharis* migrating to other parts of the Konkan to escape the pressures and perils of conversion at the hands of the Portuguese missionaries. Some astute Haldonnkars migrated to the surrounding Muslim-held territories but clandestinely continued to till the fields and collect their *zhon*. The Captain of Bardez, having become aware of this situation, ordered the revocation of the triennial auctions and summoned all the village male Brahmin *gaunkars* from the age of 12 and *kulachari* from age 20 to present themselves personally for a new auction to be carried out on the 18th of September 1601. A public proclamation was duly made as required by the law and anyone who did not present himself in person would forfeit his rights and privileges in the village.

On this day, in the presence of the Captain of Bardez Manuel Priro, a census was carried out of all those who presented themselves and the names duly recorded. Only those whose names were registered would in future enjoy the privileges reserved for Haldonna's *gaunkars* and *kulachari*.

On final count, Haldonna had a total population of 631 male individuals, *gaunkars* and *kulacharis*, who were 12 years of age or above in the case of the *gaunkars* and 20 years of age or above in the case of the *kulachari*.

Of these 631 villagers, 203 were registered as *Kaluvekar*. Among the names of these *Kaluvekars*, we encounter those of my ancestors and the Headmen of the 4th *vangad* Ramu Prabhu, his son Agostinho Sousa, another Headman of the 4th *vangad* Duarte Moniz among other. The names of the Hindu inhabitants of *Kaluve* (Calvim) were exclusively Prabhu and Naik with one exception, a Shennvi. There is consequently no doubt, as mentioned before, that the 4th *vangad* had been invited to settle in the island of Kaluve and so were the Naiks of one of the *vangads* that bear this name.

The 631 villagers covered by the census consisted exclusively of males from 12 or 20 years of age depending on whether they were *gaunkars* or *kulacharis*. Multiplying this figure by four to take into account females and children below 12 or 20 years of age as the case may be gives us the approximate number of inhabitants: Haldonna including Kaluve (Calvim) can thus be assumed to have had a total population of about 2500 in the year 1601.

We know from past history that the densely inhabited island of Chorao was afflicted by a devastating epidemic caused by insalubrity, lack of drainage facilities and poor hygiene starting in 1766 and then again some 110 years later.[229] The population was decimated and those who could, translocated to healthier villages. *Kaluve*/Calvim must have suffered a similar fate because its population also dwindled and my ancestors moved to the beautiful ward of Quitula.

16. *Gotra* of the Fourth *Vangad*

A *gotra* denotes the lineage of a person and is generally associated with (some believe it was derived from) two Sanskrit words, *Go* = cow and *thra* = shed. It is believed that the *gotra* classification was introduced post-*Rig Veda* during the *Ayur Veda* period. All present-day Brahmins are claimed to be descendants of 7 *rishis* or sages — the *Saptha rishis* — to whom an eight *rishi* Agastya is added: Gautama, Bharadvaja, Vishvamitra, Jamadagni, Vasistha, Kashyapa, Atri and Agastya.

Over time their number expanded from eight to about 49 today. This expansion came about for a number of reasons, for example, the descendants of these *rishis* initiated their own *gotras* or lineages or through marriage with other Brahmins and so on.

Gaud Sarasvat Brahmins are believed to belong to the following ten gotras:

Atri
Bharadvaja
Gautama
Jamadagni
Kashyapa
Vasishta
Vishvamitra
Kaundinya
Kausika
Vatsa

The importance of the *gotra* to genetics is that it could be construed as being the original gene pool of a clan.

A possible source to determine the *gotra* of a *vangad* would be oral history transmitted from parents to children or any data on the office-bearers (*mahajans*) of the relevant temples.

With regard to Aldona, the available information was initially intriguing and confusing. Rui Gomes Pereira relates that in general, the number of *vangads* of a *comunidade* is the same as that of the *mahajans* of the temple wherever it was reconstituted, but Aldona differs in this regard. *Portaria* (Ministerial Decree) No. 258 (Annex VII, original in Portuguese translated by the author) lists in Chapter II, Art 2°, the castes of the mahajans of the temple as follows:

1° Gaud Sarasvat "Brahmins" known as Vaishnavas of the tribes Vaishista and Vats; 2° Prabhu Zoixi (Brahmins) of the Kaushik tribe; 3° Goldsmiths or Sonar known as Shet or Chatim; 4° Sudras, known as Naik Kamblis; 5° Blacksmiths known as Charis or Mesta.

In Art. 6° of the same chapter, the following 7 *vangads* of the (i.e., associations of the representatives of the temples or their descendants) are described (words in italics within brackets are from the author):

1° *Vangad* – Camot (*Kamat*), residents on British territory (were past components of the 1st *vangad* of the comunidade of Aldona).

2° *Vangad* – Naique Camot (*Naik Kamat*), resident in the Ghats, foreign territory (were past components of the 2° *vangad* of the afore-mentioned comunidade of Aldona).

3° *Vangad* – Camotim Vaga (*Kamat Wagh*) from S. Pedro and Camotim Aldoncares (*Kamat Haldonkar*) from Ribandar (are components of the 9th *vangad* of the afore-mentioned comunidade of Aldona).

4° *Vangad* – Pondit (*Pandit*) of Goa and British India (were past components of the 11th *vangad* of the afore-mentioned comunidade of Aldona).

5° *Vangad* – Porobo (*Prabhu*) alias Zoixi from British India (were former components of the 12th *vangad* of the same comunidade of Aldona).

6° *Vangad* – Goldsmiths or Sonars, known as Xete or Chatim and Blacksmiths, known as Chari or Mesta (the Goldsmiths or Sonars being at present components of the 11th *vangad* of the afore-mentioned comunidade of Aldona).

7° *Vangad* – Sudras, known as Naique Camblis (*Naik Kambli*) (are components of the 10th *vangad* of the afore-mentioned comunidade of Aldona)

Clearly, therefore, the structure of the *mazania* i.e., associations of the representatives of the temples or their descendants changed considerably from the time the *Tombo de Aldona* was written and the transfer of the temple first to Mayem in 1567 and finally to Khandola in 1669. We notice that now only the original *comunidade vangads* 1, 2, 9, 10, 11, 12 are represented in the temple's *mazania*, the *vangads* 3, 4, 5, 6, 7, 8 are not specifically mentioned. The reasons for this exclusion can also be found in the afore-mentioned ministerial decree: since membership of the *mazania* was only open to Hindus, it is obvious that no non-converted individuals of the absentee *vangads*, including the fourth, could be located.

Indeed, Art. 5° §1° of Chapter II makes this clear: "In addition to the *mahajans* inscribed in the catalogue to whom this article refers who are residents of Goa and abroad, others are not mentioned because their whereabouts are unknown, who upon presenting themselves and their credentials duly recognised by the assembly, will be inscribed in the afore-mentioned catalogue."

There is another much more plausible explanation to this reduced number of *mazania vangads*. As has been explained earlier, through genetics we have learned that Aldona had originally 5 *vangads* and that the other *vangads* are branches of the original 5 with the exception of the 11th acquired by the Seti/Shett goldsmiths. The *mazania vangads* reflect this original set-up that was probably known to the *mahajans* of the temple: the 5 original *vangads*, the 6th of the Shetts who were not Gaunkars and a new 7th *vangad* of the Naik Kamblis who were kulacharis and belonged to the *Comunidade de Boa Esperança* split off from the original *comunidade* as discussed below.

The reason for the appearance of the name Pandit, generally a North Indian Brahmin name, in the 11th *vangad* can only be speculated; a Pandit is a scholar and the name could have been adopted by a member of any of the *vangads* of the Comunidade Fraternal. The local Hindu physicians or doctors (*vaidyas*) were given the appellation of *pandits*;[230] it is possible that this title was adopted as a surname by some Brahmin *vaidyas* of the original 11th *vangad* of the Aldona *comunidade* and the surname thus found its way in the *mazania* of the Shree Bhagvati Haldonkarin temple.

The name Zoishi (or Joshi) is derived from *jyotishi*, a practitioner of *jyotish* (astrology) and thus denotes an astrologer. It is possible that some members of the 12th *vangad* of the Aldona *comunidade* adopted the trade of astrology and the corresponding surname.

Another curious anomaly is the statement that the Naik Kamblis of the 7th *vangad* of the temple mazania are Sudras belonging to the 10th *vangad* of the original *comunidade* of Aldona; we have seen earlier in Portaria 557, article 1, and elsewhere that the original comunidade consisted of 12 *vangads*, 11 of them Brahmins and one of Goldsmiths. The explanation to this is that the *Mazania* laws were enacted in 1933, about eight years after the creation of the second *Comunidade de Boa Esperança* for the *kulacharis* who were co-opted in the *mazania* and represented by the Naik-Kamblis belonging to its 10th *vangad*.

From the above, it can be inferred that the Prabhu Zoixi Brahmins of the 12th *vangad* of the comunidade of Aldona belonged to the Kaushik gotra. We now know that the 12th *vangad* is a branch of the 4th and by inference the 7th and 8th *vangads* as well. We thus have proof that the Prabhus of the 4th *vangad* belonged to the **Kaushik gotra**.

The *Kuladevata* or family deity of the Prabhu clan belonging to the Kaushik gotra is Damodar Mahalaksmi and Damodar Aryadurga, whose temple is located in Mashel, Goa.[231]

In conclusion, the pre-conversion Hindu name of the Elvino de Sousa clan from Cottarbhatt (and the Sousa family from Quitula) was **Prabhu**, a Brahmin family originally located in *Kaluve* / **Calvim** belonging to the
Kaushik gotra, worshippers of the **tutelary deities Damodar Maha-laksmi** and **Damodar Aryadurga** and who worshipped at the **Shri Ravalnath Temple** in Calvim. The last Hindu of this patrilineage was **Ramu Prabhu** and the first Christian of Ramu Prabhu's patrilineage to bear the surname of Sousa was **Agostinho Sousa**, baptised in the first half of 1601, most probably by Fr. Manuel de S. Mathias.

Concluding Remarks

With the aid of genetics and the support of ancient documents, the route taken by my paternal ancestors belonging to the haplogroup J, subclade J-FT14805* can be traced with a certain degree of precision: African Rift Valley North Africa / Middle East Fertile Crescent / Indus Valley Civilisation site in Punjab / transit through Madhya Pradesh / Goa, possibly Salcete / Calvim–Aldona, Goa.

Also through genetics, it has been possible to trace my maternal ancestry to the Karasuk culture itself descended from the Siberian Steppe Yamnaya.

The story of my ancestors is that of migrants who on many occasions abandoned whatever was home at the time for greener pastures until they found a peaceful haven in Goa. Every time, it was their quest for survival that triggered their migration and specific value adding innovative skills enabled them to set their roots in new surroundings.

Why did they migrate, what triggered their desire to abandon their homes in the Steppes where they were highly successful and occupied a dominant position to move towards Europe and the Indian subcontinent? In the case of the IVC, it was the extinction of the civilisation caused by dramatic climatic changes and with the Yamnaya, it has been postulated that also due to climatic changes, the grasslands that were absolutely essential for their herds dried up forcing them to literally seek greener pastures in order to survive.

The Swiss Federal Office for Migration summarises the reasons for migration as follows:[232]

- Poor living conditions generate the urge to migrate
- The population grows while economic development stagnates
- Violence and abuse of power force people to flee
- The rich industrialised states are becoming more accessible

Each of these reasons has impacted my ancestors as well as most members of my family at some stage of their long trek out of Africa to the modern era.

Emigrants to Goa today are a subject of animated discussions but the basic reasons to migrate from their places of origin to settle in Goa are easily discernible: poor living conditions in their native towns or villages coupled with accessibility to a more developed region that provides jobs, a better quality of life and "benevolent rulers" on the one hand, and on the other their value-adding skills that are either not available in Goa or not sufficiently attractive to the local Goan population.

Since times immemorial, trade between two countries has led the inhabitants to choose between one of them to settle. This is how descendants of my ancestors can be found in Bahrain, keeping in mind that pearls were actively traded between the IVC region and Bahrain in ancient times.

Yet another reason for migration is the fact that the economy of many countries in the Western world is healthy but the birth rates are very low and do not suffice to cover their manpower needs. This situation opens up opportunities for citizens of countries, primarily from India, that have trained experts in many fields and can fill up the vacuum thus created.

Population Division of the UN Department of Economic and Social Affairs (DESA) provides the latest estimates of the number of international migrants by age, sex and origin for all countries and areas of the world. By definition, an international migrant is a person who is living in a country other than his or her country of birth.[233]

India was the leading country of origin of international migrants in 2019 with a 17.5 million strong diaspora, according to new estimates released by the United Nations, which also stated that the number of migrants globally reached an estimated 272 million.

The report said that the top 10 countries of origin account for one-third of all international migrants.

India hosted 5.1 million international migrants in 2019, less than the 5.2 million in 2015. International migrants as a share of total population in India was steady at 0.4 per cent from 2010 to 2019. The country hosted 207,000 refugees, the report said adding that refugees as a share of international migrants in the country was four per cent.

Among the international migrants in the country, the female population was 48.8 per cent and the median age of international migrants was 47.1 years. In India, the highest number of international migrants came from Bangladesh, Pakistan and Nepal. The report added that forced displacements across international borders continues to rise.

Between 2010 and 2017, the global number of refugees and asylum seekers increased by about 13 million, accounting for close to a quarter of the increase in the number of all international migrants.

High-income countries host almost two thirds of all international migrants. As of 2017, 64 per cent of all international migrants worldwide - equal to 165 million international migrants - lived in high-income countries. Thirty-six per cent - or 92 million - of the world's migrants lived in middle- or low-income countries.

In 2017, of the 258 million international migrants worldwide, 106 million were born in Asia. Globally, the twenty largest countries or areas of origin account for almost half (49 per cent) of all international migrants, while one-third (34 per cent) of all international migrants originates in only ten countries.

India with the largest number of people living outside the country's borders ("diaspora") is followed by Mexico, the Russian Federation and China.

Goa of today is not the same as Goa of the past and will not be the same as Goa of the future. But this is the way it has always been except that the pace and rate of change today are very much greater. In the same manner as Goans have migrated to all the corners of the globe, emigration to Goa from other parts of India is inevitable but it could certainly be better managed. The only way to reduce migration is by improving living conditions in the localities from where people migrate, such that they do not feel the need to leave their homes.

We have seen that genetics has evolved dramatically in the last decade moving from basic Y DNA and mitochondrial DNA tests to a very detailed analysis not only of the sex-determining Y chromosome but of the whole genome giving us deep insights regarding our origin and migration patterns going back thousands of years ago. What is more, progress made in DNA retrieval and testing has enabled scientists to unravel the secrets hidden by ancient skeletons initially in the colder regions and now increasingly in the warmer parts of the world. We have discovered different branches of hominins — the Neanderthals, Denisovans, *homo Naledi*, the "hobbits" of Flores Island, *homo luzonensis* — coexisted and interbred with modern-day humans but all of them with the exception of homo sapiens became extinct. There is no doubt that as science progresses, additional Adams and Eves and our links to them will be discovered.

Genetics has now revealed to us that the migrants from the Zagros Mountains of Iran interbred with the locals linked to the Andaman Islanders and established if not the most then certainly one of the most developed civilisations that the world has every known: the Indus Valley or Harappa Civilisation IVC. We now also know that the IVC population spoke a Dravidian language and could not have composed the Vedas alone; this could be accomplished only after imbibing the culture and language of the Yamnaya-related, probably Sintashta population that moved from the Steppes, spread their genes from the north to the south of India and introduced the elements of a male stratified society that unfortunately persists even today.

Genetics has also shown us that practically all Indians harbour in different proportions a mixed ancestry of the Yamnaya-related people from the Steppe, who were themselves mixtures, the inhabitants of the IVC who were forced to migrate after their civilisation collapsed, and the local Onge-related Andaman Islanders. There is no such thing as a pure human breed or ancestry barring perhaps some African tribes that may have somehow not encountered other tribes or populations though this is very doubtful.

Which genetics projects could be envisaged in the future to further elucidate past history in Goa?

We have seen how it has been possible to establish when the fourth *vangad* of Aldona's Gram Samstha was first formed through Y DNA tests of some individuals belonging to this family clan. It would be of great historical
value if we could repeat this process with other *vangads* of Aldona's *comunidade*, in particular the first clan since the founder of this clan was the first *gaunkar* of the village and thereby establish when the village of Aldona was first settled. It can be speculated that the founder of the first *vangad* was directly linked to the Yamnaya / Sintashta population and genetics could easily either prove or disprove this hypothesis by ascertaining that they belong to the Y DNA haplogroup R or one of its subclades. It would be even more important and interesting to determine these approximate dates by replicating the approach used for Aldona's fourth *vangad* in other older *comunidades* in *Saxtti*, *Tiswadi*, and *Chuddanmanni* (Chorão) that are historically claimed to be the first Goan villages to be settled by *Parashurama*.

We now know that the Onge and Jarawa tribes of the Andaman Islands were probably the first inhabitants of the Indian subcontinent and belong to the Y DNA haplogroup D-M174. The *gaudas*, *kunbis* and possibly *kharvi* are claimed to be the aboriginals of Goa. It has also been claimed that the *mhars* were the original inhabitants of Goa from whom the city of Margaum takes its name. By determining their Y DNA and mtDNA haplogroups and comparing the results to those of the Andaman Islanders, we could determine if there is a link between them and the original inhabitants of India.

176

Yet another burning issue would be to determine if there is a connection between *gotras* and genetics: by determining the Y DNA haplogroups of individuals belonging to different gotras, a link between these family clans and Y DNA would be easily discernible. This project would be easy to carry out since most Hindu families and many converted Goan Christians know to which *gotra* they belong.

The prevalence of specific diseases resulting from endogamy has been previously discussed. This would also be another area of interest that would need to be studied not only in Goa but throughout India.

At the end of this genealogical research, my mind wanders with fondness to three persons, two of whom I have never had the privilege of knowing personally. Wherever they may be, I hope that they can see this monograph and that it will elicit a smile of satisfaction from all three.

The first one is my father Dr. Carlos Elvino de Sousa who was keen on discovering our ancestral Hindu name and had been told by a Church historian that it could be either Desai or Gaitonde. He would have been happy to know that we now have an answer to his question.

The second person is my grandfather Dr. Honorato Elvino de Sousa, a man with a social conscience, a *Brahmin gaunkar* who interceded on behalf of the *Sudra* community, and at whom, for this audacity, a spear was hurled when he was in his horse-drawn carriage on a round of visits to his patients, happily without any severe consequences. He would be gratified to know that the Elvino de Sousa patrilineage that he initiated is now thriving.

The third ancestor is Ramu Prabhu.

As a teenager, totally ignorant of Goa's history, I used to consider my ancestors to be cowardly and weak in spirit for having easily succumbed to the attempts of the Portuguese conquerors to convert them to Christianity. I now know better and understand that the options offered to them were very limited indeed.

I admire the resistance and resilience of Ramu Prabhu, who allowed his son to convert but himself resisted conversion possibly to the bitter end. I would very much wish to tell him that I am proud of him. And I am proud of being a descendent of Ramu Prabhu, the last person of his patrilineage to bear a Hindu surname, **The Last Prabhu**.

ANNEX I: GENETICS FLOWCHART

BASE (Adenine A, Cytosine C, Guanine G, Thymine T)

↓ + *Sugar (Deoxyribose)*

NUCLEOSIDE *(Adenosine, Cytidine, Guanosine, Thymidine)*

↓ + *Phosphate*

NUCLEOTIDE

↓ *Polymerisation (i.e., long chain of nucleotides) and double helix due to base pairing*

DNA *(Deoxyribonucleic acid)*

↑ *contained in*

CHROMOSOMES ⟶ **22 AUTOSOMAL + 1 SEX DETERMINING**

↑ *contained in*

GENES

Tests for male and female matches

Female: XX
Male: XY

SNP on Y chromosome is rare, used to determine deep ancestry and to determine **HAPLOGROUPS**

STR on Y chromosome is more frequent, used to determine recent ancestry and determine **HAPLOTYPE**

ANNEX II: Archeological Ages

ARCHEOLOGICAL TIMELINES	
Palaeolithic	3'000'000 - ca 9600 BCE
Mesolithic	ca 9600 - ca 6000 BCE
Neolithic	ca 6200 - ca 2200 BCE
Chalcolithic	ca 5000 - ca 4000 BCE
Bronze Age	ca 2200 - ca 800 BCE
Iron Age	ca 800 - ca 1 BCE

Source: French National Institute for Preventive Archeology (Inrap)
(https://www.inrap.fr/en/periods)

ANNEX III: Gaunkar Evidence

ANNEX IV: A meet at Aldona in 1605

Translation of folio f 190r, document number 44, page 71 of the book HISTORY OF GOA through GŌYKANADI SCRIPT *by Gajanana Shantaram Sinai Ghantkar, Publishers Rajhauns Vitaran, Panaji Goa, 1993, ISBN 81-85339-93-7*

Date 15 of January of the year 1605 Aldona village meeting on the verandah of the old Church. The Aldona village headmen who met are

Bastião Costa 1 vote
(Ra) Francisco Ferrão 1 vote
(A) Lourenço Ferrão 1 vote
(Ma) Gonçalo Pinto 1 vote
(N) Manuel Sequeira 1 vote
Bernardino de Azavedo 1 vote
(A) Antonio Ferrão 1 vote
(A) Jeronimo Sousa 1 vote
(Vi) Anant Kamti 1 vote
(Maha) Paulo Lima 1 vote
Mahatim Seti 1 vote
Miguel Rodrigues 1 vote

This assembly of the 12 twelve clans passed a written resolution in this manner.

For our village's auction, Sir Judge of the cases of the crown and public property attended and carried out the triennial auction. At this time, stating that they were not living in the village, land of our village's Hindu land tillers members of the village founding clans and village servants was confiscated. Some of them went to our village's Father Rector stating to the Father Rector that we will become Christians and to return our land to us. Telling the Father Rector that they agree to become Christians and after having agreed, our village's Father Rector assembled us for a discussion and told us that these, your village's members of the village founding clans and village servant land tillers, by becoming Christians want to be admitted to the House of the Supreme Being (i.e. Church) and that he went and met the Judge of the cases of the crown and public property and having gathered those people obtained his permission, thus accordingly in our village 14 persons after being present at our catechumen, they may from today onwards reside in the village under surveillance with a fixed rent. These 14 fourteen persons will reside in the village and enjoy the property. If amidst those who enjoy this privilege, anyone does not get permission to become a Christian, or if amidst the fixed rent payers x[185] someone .....[186] his property's reclaimed land with a share in the village profits within the fixed rent ....[186] that interested party with a fixed rent .....[187] .....[186] by imposing a village contribution towards the compulsory association of tenants of khajan fields of Asrupiya 4 four Ta?....[186] for the construction work (of the Church), will be charged to that association of tenants of khajan fields. If the holders of the leased land with fixed rent or the association of tenants of khajan land refuse to contribute, we will auction off in our village his piece of khajan land and the rent thereof will go towards the construction project of the Church, this is the decision of the village council. And at that meeting the following written resolution was taken. Our village's Hindu land tillers, members of the village founding clans and village servants no longer live in the village and have taken up permanent residence in muslim-controlled territory. Therefore if they do not return in time according to custom or village council decision regarding property, their property will be confiscated. Those persons affected by the confiscation who do not come back for permanent residence in the village from the fifteenth up to the eighteenth, those who do not return to our village, their property will be confiscated. The property of all the people affected by the confiscation will be collected and leased, in this manner any land tillers of our village who are members of the village founding clans or village servants who have left the village and have taken up permanent residence in muslim-controlled territories, their property will be given to the people of the village, their property auctioned off to the hands of the village, this is the decision of the village council.

		co	+
Sebastião da Costa	Francisco Ferrão's sig-		L
ferr ão			
	nature + cross		

Ma's son[188] Gonçalo Pinto's	+	+
sig	Manuel Se-	r
o do		
	queira	B
din daz		

Cr+oss	Jeronimo Sousa's	Vi
(?) Anant Ka		
Antonio Ferrão	signature + cross	
mti writing		
has signed		

Paulo Lima's sig-   Mahatim Seti's sig
nature + cross   nature   balance

Miguel Rodri-
gues'[189] x

The apology of the 14 fourteen persons according to the resolution registered in the village book

[190]x Ram Naik	1 p	(A) Goyid Na	2p	(Da)
Balugya	1p			
[187]....Bhogann Ka	2p	Mahatim Seti	1p	(Ph)
Anant Prabhu	1p			
[187]Bhogann Nak[191]	1p	(A) Phati Nak	1p	(Gho)
Sate Prabhu	1p			

| [187]Mu Kati | 1p | (Bho) Antu | 1p | [190]x |
| Antonio[185] … Sq | 1p | | | |

---

[184] Sic (Nfta: the text reads „Kistaum" instead of „Kristaum").

[185] Moth-eaten.

[186] Torn portions.

[187] Moth-eaten: 2 letters.

[188] Abbreviation

[189] Indecipherable.

[190] Moth-eaten: 1 letter.

[191] „Nak" is interpolation

ANNEX V: Description of Aldona

Filipe Neri Xavier offers a description of the village, in the Bosquejo Histórico das Comunidades, Vol. II, 1801 – 1901, *p.419-421 (Nova Goa: Imprensa Nacional, 1852). Translation from the text in Portuguese by the author.*

Aldona

Distance from the seat of the government (*concelho*): 10.7 kilometers
Limits: Olaulim, Nachinola, Moira, Mapusa river.
Wards: 11 (Calvim, Carona, Cottarbhat, Ranoi, Quitula, Boddiem etc.)
Water reservoirs: 1 pond (in Santerxette)
Jetties: 3 (Ambarim, Cottarbhat, Quitula)
Parish: village proper; patron saint of the church – S. Thomas (i)
Population: in 1844 – fog. 800, inhabitants 2278; in 1900 – fog. 2090, inhabitants 7958.
Main types of cultures and their production: coconuts 74'330, paddy 405 *khumbe* (nfa: 1 *khumbo* equals 20 *khandy*, and is a measure for paddy), namely 325 of the *comunidade* comprising of fields 35 *khumbe* of seed of the *sorod* variety and 3.5 of *vaingan* (ii)

Comunidade

Components and interested: *gaunkars, kulacharis*, orphans, cult.
Gaunkars: constitute 12 *vangads*, of which the 11th is of goldsmiths (iii) and the remaining are brahmins, in the past all having to agree unanimously, but in recent times a majority or 7, in the communal deliberations for them to be valid; they started taking part in the management after completing 11 years of age, the age at which they begin receiving their *jono* (nfa: share in the annual profits of the village from auction of village fields, quit-rent etc.).
Kulacharis (nfa: village servant): brahmins (clerks of the 1st and 2nd record, *pandits, goddes, mumbres*, and *kulacharis* proper), who could bid on their own in the auctions
Chardos (1st, 2nd, 3rd) and *Sudras* (1st, *calvinkars, sonarvadde, cocas, maindavaddes, biras, cauxes, buins, ketrys, tarys, botts, kamblis, ventios* and non-converts) who had neither voting rights nor a voice in the *gaunkari* (nfa: meeting of *gaunkars*, the latter being representatives of the clans

185

of the original founders of the village); all receive their *jono* from the age of 19.

Orphans: the eldest sons of the deceased recipients of *jonos* earn half a *jono* until they attain the age of being entitled to their own jono.

Properties: are constituted of 16 *khunts* (plots), and these of 23 fields, divided into 950 *bandins* and retail, 46 "plots of *namoxin*" (nfa: Plots of rent-free land provided to village servants in return for services), 140 of legumes, some of them used for rice cultivation, shops in all the wards and services for hire.

Various services: clerk (escrivão) with a salary of Rs.400 and his assistant with a salary of 180 , etc., (iv).

Contributions: *foros* Rs. 1293:01:00 etc. (v) (nfa: *foro* means *quit-rent*)

FINANCIAL SITUATION

Year	Revenue in xerafins	Expenditure in xerafins	Debt
1797	36.015	14.526	-
1807	49.817	26.737	-
1818	33.428	27.843	-
1824	35.295	14.224	-
1830	32.962	14.255	-
1845	33.642	14.511	18.900
1905	Rs. 28.701	Rs. 15.184	-

Distribution of income in cash: is carried out according to the number of *jonos*, subtracting the half *jonos* of the orphans from the whole *jonos*. In the year 1905, a *jono* amounted to 3:05:09.

i.The church was built by Franciscans in 1596, at the cost of the faithful, according to a document dated 1767, registered in the *Livro dos Monções* n. ° 143, page 738. On the occasion of the foundation, the *comunidade* donated a *jono* in favour of the patron saint and contributes annually to the respective *fabrica* (nfa: trusts established to manage assets belonging to the Church) *xerafins* 962:4:15. It is recorded in the books of the general secretariat that between the years 1801 and 1851, it spent in favour of the church *xerafins* 8605:0:15. The revenue of the *fabrica*, that does not have its own fund, comes, in addition to what it receives from the *comunidade,* from the management of the cemetery, that around 1840 amounted to *xerafins* 90. The village cemetery had some family graves at that time, but none with a legend. The *mestre capella* (the music conductor) was nominated by the *comunidade* and paid by it @ 180 *xerafins* per annum.

ii. The production is regulated by tithes: all the explanations are old.

iii. In spite of it having been ordered to exclude these foreign goldsmiths who had bought the *vangad* from a Portuguese, to whom it had been given as a grant by a viceroy (*see* vol. 1, page 112), it appears that they could hold on to it due to their values.

iv. The two clerks, who in the past belonged to families who owned property by right of office, earned at that time, in addition to their *jonos* as *kulachari*, an additional *xerafins* 150. The monitoring used to cost 100 *xerafins*.

v. Past contributions: Foros of the *comunidade xerafins* 1517:4:40, half *foros* of the same 758:4:50 — *foros* of the pagoda 240:1:12, half of the same 120:0:36 — *foros* of *namoxins* 100:2:45, half of the same 50:1:22 — various 119:2:41; total 2834:1:57 ½; — tithes approximately 16 ½ *khumbs* of paddy.

ANNEX VI: Church construction

Description on the construction of the Church dedicated to St. Thomas in Aldona by Filipe Neri Xavier, Bosquejo Histórico das Comunidades, *Vol. I, p.148 (Nova Goa: Imprensa Nacional, 1852). Translation from the text in Portuguese by the author.*

(409) – The Church of Aldona was built by the Franciscans in 1569, with alms from the faithful, as is recorded in a document of 1767, that is in the *Livro das Monções* no. 143 and p.738, from where we have extracted this, and other notes relative to the foundation of Churches of this district with the exception of those that are specially mentioned.

— the document alluded to does not specify the identity of the faithful and absolutely omits the name of the *gaunkars* and *comunidades*; it is, however, more than certain that the reference pertains to the *comunidades* of the villages that were the only rich corporations, consisting of faithful who could thus contribute, and who did in fact contribute towards those foundations, and even to this day support the cult with practically all the expenses and provide the necessary for its conservation, and maintenance of buildings, with rare exceptions.

The *comunidade* of this village has donated since the foundation of the church a personal and hereditary *jono* to the patron saint of this village.

The *Fabrica* does not have its own funds and its revenues come from what it receives from the *comunidade* and from the management of the cemetery.

ANNEX VII: The Temple

Boletim Oficial do Estado da India (Official Bulletin of the State of India), 1 May 1928, p. 636 – 640. Portuguese text translated by the author.

Ministerial decrees

Nr. 258 – Having present the project of arbitration with the corresponding catalogue of the *mahajans* of the temple Shri Bhagvati Haldonkarin and its affiliates, in Khandola, and it having been demonstrated that measures in force pertaining to similar institutions have been considered;

The Governor General of the State of India, using the rights conferred in nr. 3° of article 26° of the organic law in force, approved by decree nr. 12.499-A, of October 4, 1926, and in agreement with the Government Council, in its session of August 8 last, approves the afore-mentioned agreement (*compromisso*), with the deletions indicated by the same Council, consisting of 47 articles and the corresponding catalogue that have been duly signed by the Director of Services of Civil Administration.

To be enforced.

General Government of Nova Goa, 16 February 1928.
The Governor General
Pedro Francisco Massano de Amorim
(The dues have been paid, authorisation nr. 115/1928)

Agreement with reference to the preceding ministerial decree

CHAPTER 1. ON THE TEMPLE AND ITS AFFILIATES

Article 1. The temple of Shri Bhagvati Haldonkarin, in Khandola, was in the 16th century, in 1567, transferred from the village of Aldona, in Bardez, to that of Mayem, in the district of Sanquelim, and from this village to its present locality, in the Aldonvadi ward of Khandola, in 1669, together with its affiliates.

§ One. The affiliates of this temple are the following small temples

1° Shri Dadd

2° Shri Ravalnath

3° Shri Sidnath
4° Shri Lakshimi Narayan (in the temple of Shri Bhagvati)
and the following *Purushas*:
1° Gram Purusha
2° Ketria Purusha
3° Anant Purusha; in addition to a Kolos of Shri Santeri existing in the
sanctuary of Shri Bhagvati

CHAPTER II: ON THE MAZANIA

(Note from the author: Mazania is an association of the *mahajans* of
the temple; *Mahajans* are the founders of the temple and their descendants)

Art. 2° The mahajans of the temple belong to the following castes:
1° Gaud sarasvat "Brahmins" known as Vaishnavas of the tribes
Vaishista and Vats;
2° Prabhu Zoixi (Brahmins) of the Kaushik tribe;
3° Goldsmiths or Sonar known as Shet or Chatim;
4° Sudras, known as Naik Kamblis;
5° Blacksmiths known as Charis or Mesta.

Art. 3° The Mazania composed of the descendants of the five classes mentioned in the preceding article, constitute an association gov-
erned and administered by general laws and special accords included
in the present agreement and by the regulation on the *mazanias*.

Art. 4° The right to a *mazania* is hereditary and perpetual for the male
descendants and is transmitted from generation to generation by con-
sanguinity or adoption, effected according to the Code of Usages and
Customs of 16 December 1880.

§ One. All the Gouda Sarasvat Brahmin *mahajans* mentioned in 1° of
art. 2° are founding *mahajans* of the temples of Shri Bhagvati and its
affiliates, having borne the costs of construction, conservation and cult
of these temples up to now.

Art. 5° The *mahajans* of the temple, to whom this agreement refers,
are those who have been listed in the accompanying catalogue that
will be revised annually according to the terms of the present regulation.

§ 1° In addition to the mahajans inscribed in the catalogue, to whom this article refers who are residents of Goa and abroad, others are not mentioned because their whereabouts are unknown, who upon presenting themselves and their credentials duly recognised by the assembly, will be inscribed in the afore-mentioned catalogue.

§ 2° *mahajans* who are resident in foreign territories may vote in the deliberations and elections of the *mazania* but are not allowed to be elected or nominated to positions of the administration committee of the temple.

Art 6° The *mazania* of this temple consists of seven *vangads*, the first five consisting of Brahmins; the sixth of goldsmiths or Sonars and Charis or Mesta; and the seventh of Sudras or Naik, namely:

1° *Vangad* – Camot (Kamat), residents on British territory (were past components of the 1st *vangad* of the Comunidade of Aldona).

2° *Vangad* – Naique Camot (Naik Kamat), resident in the Ghats, foreign territory (were past components of the 2° *vangad* of the afore-mentioned comunidade of Aldona).

3° *Vangad* – Camotim Vaga (Kamat Wagh) from S. Pedro and Camotim Aldoncares (Kamat Haldonkar) from Ribandar (are components of the 9th *vangad* of the afore-mentioned comunidade of Aldona).

4° *Vangad* – Pondit (Pandit) of Goa and British India (were past components of the 11th vangad of the afore-mentioned comunidade of Aldona).

5° *Vangad* – Porobo (Prabhu) alias Zoixi from British India (were former components of the 12th *vangad* of the same comunidade of Aldona).

6° *Vangad* – Goldsmiths or Sonars, known as *Xete* or *Chatim* and Blacksmiths, known as Chari or Mesta (the Goldsmiths or Sonars being at present components of the 11th *vangad* of the afore-mentioned comunidade of Aldona).

7° *Vangad* – Sudras, known as Naique Camblis (Naik Kambli) (are components of the 10th *vangad* of the afore-mentioned comunidade of Aldona)

Art 7° The rights consigned in article 4 are imprescriptible and inalienable and begin on the date of the inscription in the catalogue unless it occurs by way of a sanctioned appeal, because in this case it will begin on the day of refusal that gave rise to the appeal.

Art 8° All *mahajans* will enjoy their rights in accord with the decisions of the present agreement.

Art 9° Every *mahajan* can warn any servant found wanting in the accomplishment of his duties and denounce to the committee of *mahajans* the malversation or irregularities committed by the servants or functionaries of the corporation.

Art 10° All *mahajans* are free to examine the accounts of receipts and expenses of the corporation and assist decently attired all religious and festive acts when they are present in the temple, the *mahajans* of each *vangad* taking a seat in the temple in the order of their respective *vangads* in this agreement.

Art 11° *Mahajans* of any *vangad* who are able will be indistinguishably elected or nominated to constitute the administrative committee.

CHAPTER III: ON THE FUND

Art 12° The fund of the mazania consists of movable and immovable property, jewels of gold and silver, precious stones, furniture and utensils and other objects of the inventory recorded in the corresponding book.

Art 13° The receivables consist of

1° rent on immovable property

2° subsidies of comunidades and other corporations

3° offerings to divinities or the cult; results of fines levied according to the terms of the present agreement and regulations on *mazanias*;

4° any pecuniary assistance offered by the *mahajans* and devotees;

5° fees due to the temple for religious ceremonies that may be celebrated;

6° any other eventual receivables.

Art 14° The Mazania may accept any donations in cash, jewels, clothes or any other articles that are voluntarily offered to them, without the donors at any time, as a consequence of their donations, consider themselves to have the right to interfere in the affairs of the temple.

Art 15° The offerings or their value are to be returned to the coffer.

Art 16° The *tulabar* made of any kind of metal, pearls and precious stones will be returned to the coffer; should it consist of coconut, sugar, sandalwood, rice or other edibles, it will be distributed among the servants of the temple.

§ One The distribution of edible offerings will be made as follows: two parts to the *pujari bhatts* (ecclesiastics celebrating the rites) and gurus, and the third part in equal shares to the other servants of the temple, receiving in return one rupee for the coffer.

Art 17° The donations and other offerings will be verified by the administration committee and in its absence by the registrar or the *pujari bhatt* and will subsequently be registered by the registrar in the corresponding book or notebook.

Art 18° Donations consisting of clothes and other objects unnecessary for use shall be sold by the administrative committee by auction, according precedence to legal formalities, taking advantage for this of occasions of great affluence to the temple, as on the occasion of the *zatra* festivities in the month of *Falguno* and its revenue added to the fund.

Art 19° The fees that will be collected for religious acts that the *mahajans* or devotees may wish to celebrate, are the following for the coffers of the temple:
1° for abeshek-nevedea Ponchistam 0:02:03
2° for Shri Bhagvati or affiliate 0:01:03
3° for Cuncumarjan 0:01:03
4° for Ecadasni 0:01:03
5° for Lagurudra 0:08:03
6° for Maharudra 3:00:03
7° for Navachandi simple   0:08:03
8° for dito Sahapalavi 1:00:03
9° for Homadvara 1:00:03
10° for Xatachandi   5:00:03
11° for each Rangapuja 1:00:03
12° each simple puja 0:08:03
13° for each Tulabar 1:00:03
14° for each Gantvol 1:00:03
15° for each marriage 1:00:03
16° for each Senso 1:00:03
17° for each adoption or barso 1:00:03
18° for each prasad or wise counsel (oracle) 0:01:03
19° for each Vonty   0:02.03

Art 20° The *mahajans* are required to pay annually a fee to the coffers of the temple, in the presence of the administrative committee, in exchange of a receipt, two rupees per *mahajan*.

§ One. Should the fee not have been paid punctually by the end of December of each year, the defaulter shall be considered to be a debtor to the coffers of the temple.

Art 21° The *mahajans* and other devotees may provide funds to the coffers of the temple in order to, with their interest at the rate of five per cent, institute new festivities and ceremonies, preference being given, however, to the reestablishment of those that have been suspended due to lack of funds, mentioned in art. 30°.

§ One. Equally, *mahajans* and other devotees who up until now have instituted annual festivities or any other cult in accord with the present agreement bearing the costs, may enter, if they so wish, with the necessary funds in the coffers of the temple.

Art. 22° The expenses of the temple consist of

1° conservation of the temple buildings according to article 1°;

2° celebration of festivities and the daily and ordinary cult;

3° improvement of property;

4° expenses inherent to the administration and management and any other resulting from routine or unforeseen contingencies, provided they have been approved by the hierarchy;

5° salaries of the servants of the temple.

CHAPTER IV: ON CULT AND FESTIVITIES

Section I: Daily and ordinary cult

Art. 23° The daily ceremonies in the temple of Shri Bhagvati and its affiliates are:

1°. Tolling of *Nouboto* at 6 hours

2°. *Nirmalia visarjan* from eight to nine hours

3°. *Abixek, puja, artis* and *nevedia* from eleven to twelve hours according to the observed practice

4°. Tolling of *Nouboto* at ten and eight hours

5°. *Artis, nevedia, garanis* , etc., from twenty to twenty-one hours. The *nevedia* mentioned will consist of rice in the morning and at night to Shri Bhagvati and Shri Lakshmi-Narain and only during the day to Shri Dadd and Shri Ravalnath.

Art 24° Lights called *Nandadipa* and *zoti* shall be lit permanently, the former only in the sanctuary of Shri Bhagvati and Shri Dadd and *zotis* for Shri Lakshmi-Narain and the *purushas*.

§ One In addition to the ceremonies mentioned in this article, other shall take place, when instituted by *mahajans* or devotees and paid by them, which must be celebrated according to the conditions stipulated by them, or by the temple if financed from its coffers.

Art 25° The rice that is used for the *nevedia* ceremony, after having been offered to the divinities, will belong to the respective performing ecclesiastics (*bhatts*) *pujaris* and *gurus*. On occasions of festivities and other, when twelve *neivedias* take place, five of these will belong to the respective *pujari* and *guru* ecclesiastics (*bhatts*) and the remaining seven to the *mahajan* devotees (*kulavis*) of the respective *purushas* according to custom.

Art 26° The *mahajans* and other devotees who wish to celebrate ceremonies or religious acts declared below have to pay to the respective *pujari* or *guru* ecclesiastic the following fee in addition to paying a fee for the coffers mentioned in art. 19° with a receipt:

1° For the ceremony of *abixek neivedia* at *Ponchistan* or for *Devi-suncta* ...1:04:00

2° Ditto for only one goddess...0:10:00

3°For *Kunkumarjan*...1:00:00

4° For *Ecadosnim*...0:04:00

5° For *Lagurudra*...3:12.00

6° For *Maharudra*...75:00:00

7° For *Navachandi* simple...10:00:00

8° For ditto *Sahapalavi*...16:00:00

9° For ditto *Homadvara*...75:00:00

10° For ditto *Xatachandi*...400:00:00

11° For each *Rangapuja*...20:00:00

12° For each simple puja or *Devi Avartana*...5:00:00

13° For each prasad or wise counsel...0:04:00

Art 27° The above fees paid for the corresponding ceremonies will be distributed by the officiating *pujari bhatt* between himself and other temple servants, each of them paying a fee according to custom towards the temple coffers to the administrative committee that will issue a receipt.

Art 28° Under the penalty of having to pay for the costs of *Archashudri* or *Samproshan* along with the loss of their rights with regard to the temple, it is expressly prohibited for *mahajans* or any other individuals who are not Brahmins or corresponding *pujari bhatts* to celebrate on their own ceremonies mentioned above or any other in the sanctuaries of the temples of Shri Bhagvati, Shri Dadd, Shri Sidnath, Shri Lakshmi-Narain and Purushas, the guru requiring to celebrate them in that of Shri Ravalnath.

Art 29° Any other Brahmin or *bhatt* ecclesiastic who so desires may perform on their own religious acts in the sanctuaries of the temples with permission from the *pujari bhatt* and the administrative committee.

SECTION II: FESTIVITIES

Art 30° The festivities that must be celebrated annually in the temple as well as acts of public devotion are as follows:

In the month of Sravan (August)

1° The festivities in the month of Sravan (August) of Rangapuja on all Mondays of this month instituted and paid for, on the first Monday by the Hindu inhabitants of the village of Aldona in Bardez; on the second by Atmaram Sitaram Pandit, from Palem in Siridão, on the third by Bhargava Seguna Kamat Wagh, from S. Pedro; on the fourth by Siurai Pundulik Shett from Pomburpa.

§ One In years when there are five Mondays, the costs of the fifth shall be borne by the servants of the temple as is the custom.

2° The festivity "Navaratra and Dasera" from the first to the tenth day, in the month of *Asvin* (October) *Gatasthapana* in the principle temple of Shri Bhagvati; from the first day onwards until the nineth day the ceremonies of appropriate manner, i.e., at eight at night *puja purana* (sacred poems) and artis etc and on the tenth day dasera, at seventeen hours palanquin of the same goddess with her insignia and two *tarangans* of Shri Ravalnath and Bhutnath, in the direction of Sima-Olungon and then returning to the temple, *artis, garanis, prasad* etc shall be celebrated according to custom, and the costs of which will be borne by Narain Sitaram Pandit of Mormugaum.

3° The festivity of *Tulachi vivaha* that falls on the twelfth day of the month of Kartik (November); the appropriate ceremonies shall be performed by the *pujari bhatt* and other servants until 9 hours at night.

4° The festivity of *Kambarpuja* and palanquin on the 30th (*Antavassia*) in the month of *Kartik* (November); this festivity is suspended due to lack of funds.

5° The festivity of *Kallo* on the 2nd of the month of *Margachircha* (December) is also suspended due to lack of funds.

6° The festivity *Varauni* of the Kolos of Shri Santeri on the 2nd of the month of *Magha* (February) is also suspended.

7° The festivity of *Mahaparvani* or *Maliachi zatra* that takes place on the 2nd of the month of *Falgun* (March) and the costs of which are borne by Bhargava Seguna Kamath Wagh of S. Pedro.

8° The ceremony *Holi* that takes place on the 15th of the month of *Falgun* (March) is carried out by the servants of the temple.

CHAPTER V: ON THE SERVANTS OF THE TEMPLE AND THEIR DUTIES

Art 31° Are servants of the temple individuals of both sexes

a. *Pujari Bhatts* of the Brahmin sacerdotal class
b. *Gurus*
c. Five families of other servants, *poirekars* or *vorsolkars, vazantris, diuttis, murdongis,* female singers, dancers, *bhavinas, katkars ,* etc., these live on the temple grounds as well as other *cambis* and *farazes* who will all provide services according to their competence daily and as needed by the temple.

Art 32° The servants referred to in the preceding article are subordinate to the *mahajans* and administrative committee and are required to loyally perform their duties with all respect and perfect harmony in the following manner, receiving the remuneration specified in the budget and additional to which they may be entitled:

§ 1° It is of the competence of the *pujari bhatts* and *gurus* to discharge their duties in the temple sanctuary

a. Observe every day without interruption the daily ceremonies, *nirmalia vissarjan* and other in their competence mentioned in chapter 4;
b. Decorate for all festivities the images with clothes and jewels; decorate the palanquin, *puja* in the sanctuary and preserve under their responsibility jewel of the images, clothing and other objects;
c. Take *prasad* (wise counsel, oracle);
d. Celebrate on their own ceremonies within their competence
e. Be present in the temple every day, maintain complete cleanliness, observe all the precepts of this agreement and inform the administrative committee of any irregularity that they may notice.

§ 2° It is of the competence of the *poirekars* to sweep and keep completely clean the precincts and sondies of the temples, in the morning, as well as

    a. clean the vases, utensils and lights used in the temple;

    b. keep ready the *artis* at the appointed time;

    c. light after sunset the lights at the exterior of the temple;

    d. set up chairs on festive occasions for *purana, girton,* and for the assistants on the occasion of ceremonies and remove them upon completion of these acts;

    e. be with the *chinvor* on ceremonial occasions, accompany the palanquin and perform other services within their competence at the times fixed in the preceding chapter.

§ 3° It is of the competence of the *katkar* to be under the orders of the *mahajans* and administrative committee, to assist decently attired in the festivities and perform other services within their competence.

§ 4° The other servants, in addition to those mentioned in the preceding numbers, *vazantris*, female singers, *diutes, cambis* and *farazes* are required to regularly provide services within their competence on occasions of festivities and religious ceremonies.

CHAPTER VI: GENERAL AND TRANSITORY DISPOSITIONS

Art 33° All the *mahajans*, adorers and devotees shall contribute towards the benefits of the temple according to their individual ability in order to increase the funds of the coffer.

Art 34° Every *mahajan* is required to pay any fees that may be established according to the resolutions of the *mahajans.*

Art 35° The *mahajans* who are goldsmiths, *charis* or *mesta* and Sudras or Naik Kamblis, mentioned in the *vangads* 6° and 7° of article 6° shall pay a fee of ten rupees per *mahajan* as contribution to the fund of the temple, payable within a non-deferrable period of one year.

§ One This fee demanded from *mahajans* in this article is due to the fact that none of them have thus far contributed to the fund of the temple.

Art 36° The *mazania* reserves the right to revise or change the present agreement, in part or in total, according to the requirements of time and circumstances with the exception of articles 8° and 28° of this agreement.

Art 37° At no time and under no circumstances can the *mazania* alienate the basic property, images of silver and other metals, jewellery of gold, silver and precious stones and any utensils and furniture of the temple.

Art 38° It is prohibited to discuss in the precincts of the temples any alien topics unless they are related to the interests of the temple, in a low voice and outside of the hours when the ceremonies take place.

Art 39° The *mazania* is subject to the laws and regulations in force and that may be enacted in the future with regard to *mazanias* and temples and as in the statutes of the present agreement.

Art 40° Three per cent of the cash revenues will be used for charitable purposes, and if additional funds are remaining, if necessary to subsidise primary education, with agreement of the *mazania*.

CHAPTER VII: PENAL DISPOSITIONS

Art 41° The *mahajans* who do not pay their fees to the tune of ten rupees established in article 35° of this agreement within one year of its publication in the *Official Bulletin* and do not collect the corresponding payment receipt will be struck off from the respective catalogue and will no longer be considered to be *mahajans* of this temple.

Art 42° A *mahajan* or any adorer who creates disorder, proffers insults on occasions of festivities or otherwise shall pay a fine of five to ten rupees, imposed by the administrative committee or *mazania*.

Art 43° A *mahajan* or any adorer who by any means causes or attempts to cause damage to the temple shall be deprived from assisting in ceremonies in the temple, for a period of one month or more up to one year, depending on the gravity of the fault.

§ 1° The rights of the *mahajan* or adorer who usurps land belonging to the temple shall be suspended until he voluntarily restitutes the usurped land, without prejudice to eventual prosecution.

§ 2° A repetition of the fault will be punished with a triple of the fine established in this article, and if, in spite of this, the fault continues without remedy, it will be punished with a suspension for life of the rights of the *mahajan* or adorer.

§ 3° The punishment of life suspension of the rights shall be moderated if the suspended individual shows remorse and the *mazania* considers him worthy of pardon.

Art 44° Servants who have stopped performing their services and duties according to their competence will for the first time be warned, for the second time pay a fine of five Rupees to be deducted from their salary, for the third time suspended for one month, for the fourth time suspended for one year and for the fifth time termination of employment without prejudice to eventual criminal proceedings.

§ One. The salary and other perquisites of the punished person shall be given to whoever substitutes him, the substitution being always made with a person of the same class.

Art 45° A *mahajan* who is excommunicated by the respective prelate remains prohibited from being a part of the *mazania* or religious services and if he is a servant, from providing services, during the time of his excommunication.

Art 46° The punishments described in the preceding articles cannot be applied without previous authorisation of the administrator.

Art 47° This agreement, after having been approved by the competent authority, shall be registered in the corresponding book of the temple along with its translation in Marathi and will enter into force 10 days after its publication in the *Official Bulletin*.

Catalogue of Mahajans

OF THE 1ST VANGAD
1. Atmarama Camat Aldoncar, from Malvan.
2. Ramachondra Camat Aldoncar, from Malvan.
3. Xantarama Camat Aldoncar, from Malvan.
4. Rogunata Camat Aldoncar, from Malvan.
5. Ananta Camat Aldoncar, from Malvan.
6. Narana Camat Aldoncar, from Malvan.
7. Hori Camat Aldoncar, from Margão.
8. Maruti Camat Aldoncar, from Margão.
9. Naraina Camat Aldoncar, from Margão.
10. Manguexa Camat Aldoncar, from Bombay
11. Ganexa Camat Aldoncar, from Bombay.
12. Sridar Camat Aldoncar, from Bombay.
13. Sitarama Camat Aldoncar, from Araundem
14. Manguexa Camat Aldoncar, from Araundem
15. Datatraia Camat Aldoncar, from Araundem
16. Visnum Camat Aldoncar, from Araundem
17. Loximona Camat Aldoncar, from Araundem
18. Bascora Camat Aldoncar, from Araundem

19.Venctexa Camat Aldoncar, from Karvar
20.Trimboca Camat Aldoncar, from Vingurla
OF THE 2ND VANGAD
1. Datatraia Naik Camat, from Murgodo
2. Anant Naik Camat, from Murgodo
OF THE 3RD VANGAD
1. Bargova Camotim Vaga, from S. Pedro
2. Seguna Camotim Vaga, from S. Pedro
3. Vamona Camotim Vaga, from S. Pedro
4. Purxotoma Camotim Vaga, from S. Pedro
5. Ananta Camotim Aldoncar, from Ribandar
6. Narana Camotim Aldoncar, from Ribandar
7. Mucunda Camotim Aldoncar, from Ribandar
8. Panduronga Camotim Aldoncar, from Ribandar
9. Govinda Camotim Aldoncar, from Ribandar
OF THE 4TH VANGAD
1. Atmarama Pondit, from Palem
2. Narana Pondit, from Mormugão
3. Panduronga Pondit, from Sanquelim
4. Visnum Pondit, from Palem
5. Anant Pondit, from *ditto*
6. Vinaica Pondit, from Mormugão
7. Sacaram Pondit, from *ditto*
8. Vamona Pondit, from Sanquelim
9. Purxotama Pondit, from *ditto*
10.Govinda Pondit, from *ditto*
11.Ananta Pondit, from Araundem
12.Sadassiva Pondit, from *ditto*
13.Ramachondra Pondit, from *ditto*
14.Esvonta Pondit, from *ditto*
15.Vassudeva Pondit, from *ditto*
16.Panduronga Pondit, from *ditto*
17.Vitol Pondit, from Vingurla
18.Sitarama Pondit, from *ditto*
19.Manguexa Pondit, from *ditto*
OF THE 5TH VANGAD
1. Sadassiva Zoxi, from Araundem
2. Malu Zoxi, *idem*
3. Esvonta Zoxi, *idem*

4. Bicagi Zoxi, *idem*
5. Damodara Zoxi, *idem*

OF THE 6TH VANGAD

1. Siurai Xete Aldoncar, from Pomburpa
2. Sitarama Xete Aldoncar, *idem*
3. Xamba Xhatim, from Aldona
4. Venctex Chatim, from Britona
5. Xamba Chatim, from Aldona
6. Purxotama Chatim, from Piedade
7. Xamba Chatim, *idem*
8. Govinda Chatim, from Assonora
9. Sadassiva Chatim, *idem*
10. Mucunda Chatim, from Piedade
11. Data Xete Aldoncar, from Pomburpa
12. Vinaica Xete Aldoncar, *idem*
13. Vamona Xete Aldoncar, *idem*
14. Govinda Xete Aldoncar, *idem*
15. Bicu Xete Aldoncar, *idem*
16. Pundolica Xete Aldoncar, *idem*
17. Vitol Xete Aldoncar, *idem*
18. Suba Xete Aldoncar, *idem*
19. Xencor Xete Aldoncar, *idem*
20. Purxotama Xete Aldoncar, *idem*
21. Roguvir Xete Aldoncar, *idem*
22. Pundolica Chatim, from Ribandar
23. Esvonta Chatim, *idem*
24. Purxotama Chatim, from Margão
25. Vassudeva Chatim, from Canolim
26. Balchondra Chari, from Assonora
27. Babulo Chari, *idem*
28. Babu Chari, *idem*
29. Xamba Chari, *idem*
30. Saunlo Chari, *idem*
31. Raia Chari, *idem*
32. Vinaica Chari, *idem*
33. Nanda Chari, *idem*
34. Subrai Chari, *idem*
35. Nanum Chari, *idem*

36.Siurama Chari, from Porvorim
37.Xencor Chari, *idem*
38.Xamba Chari, from Mapuça
39.Ananta Chari, from Verem
40.Vamona Chari. *idem*
41.Datarama Chari, from Nerul
42.Siurama Chari, from Pilerne
43.Sacarama Chari, from Uscoi

OF THE 7TH VANGAD

1. Babli Naique, from Moula
2. Gonexa Naique, *idem*
3. Arzuna Naique, *idem*
4. Visnum Naique, *idem*
5. Siva Naique, *idem*
6. Narana Naique, *idem*
7. Gopal Naique, *idem*
8. Banu Naique, *idem*
9. Loximona Naique, *idem*
10.Ramachondra Naique, *idem*
11.Kolu Naique, *idem*
12.Xanum Naique, *idem*
13.Govinda Naique, *idem*
14.Atma Naique, *idem*
15.Crisna Naique, *idem*
16.Narana Naique, from Palem
17.Sitarama Naique, *idem*
18.Govinda Naique, *idem*
19.Poto Naique, from Dongrim
20.Usno Naique, *idem*
21.Xabi Naique, from Santa Cruz
22.Babi Naique, *idem*
23.Roulu Naique, *idem*
24.Tilu Naique, *idem*
25.Vitu Naique, *idem*
26.Nadu Naique, from Ribandar
27.Gonexa Naique, *idem*
28.Rama Naique, *idem*
29.Babli Naique, *idem*

30.Esso Naique, from Pangim
31.Budu Naique, *idem*
32.Custam Naique, *idem*
33.Custam Naique, from Chorão
34.Joganata Naique, *idem*
35.Sitarama Naique, from Aldona
36.Xencor Naique, *idem*
37.Tucarama Naique, from Bicholim
38.Dajiba Vaircar, from Malvan
39.Ananta Vaircar, *idem*
40.Vitoba Vaircar, *idem*
41.Panduronga Vaircar, *idem*
42.Sitarama Aldoncar, *idem*
43.Xencor Aldoncar, *idem*

Directorate of the Services of Civil Administration, in Nova Goa, 16 February 1928 – The Director of Services of Civil Administration, Alfredo Rodrigues dos Santos

(The cost of publication of this agreement and catalogue was paid on 10-1-1928)

ANNEX VIII: *Gaunkar* name-changes

Name changes in the vangads

1st Vangad	Kamti	Costa, Couto, Sousa, Tavora (from Sangolda)
2nd Vangad	Kamti	Extinct
3rd Vangad	Kamti	Afonso (from Chorão and Divar), Ferrão, Lourenço, Lobo (from Bodiem), Rocha
4th Vangad	Prabhu	Cruz, Cunha, Faria, Fernandes, Lobo, Moniz, Noronha, Pinto, Rodrigues, Sousa
5th Vangad	Naik	Carvalho, Correa, Conceição, Fonseca, Gama, Gouvea, Lousado, Mendonça, Menezes, Noronha, Pinto, Rego, Siqueira, Sá, Soares, Sousa, Vás
6th Vangad	Kamti	Drago, Lobo, Sá, Sousa
7th Vangad	Prabhu	Fernandes
8th Vangad	Prabhu	Mendes, Sousa
9th Vangad	Kamti	Alvares, Bocalo or Bocarro, Castelino, Coutinho, Camotim, Fonseca, Fernandes, Lopes, Noronha, Siqueira, Soares, Sousa
10th Vangad	Naik	Comelo, Lima
11th Vangad	Seti	Xete or Chatim, Rocha, Sousa
12th Vangad	Prabhu	Afonso, Macedo, Soares, Sousa

Interessados		Goddés – Lobo, Mumbrés – Monteiro, Cardosa, Nobriga or Nobres, Silva, Sousa Pandit – Nazaré, Santos
Escrivão		Primeiro Tombo: Siqueira Segundo Tombo: Sacardando, Soares, Toscano, Vás, Batista
Kulachari		Miranda, Mesquita, Morais, Pereira, Siqueira, Sousa

(*Source of pre-conversion names*: this study by the author; *source of the post-conversion names*: Hector Fernandes, President, *Comunidade* of Aldona, personal communication in October 2008)

ANNEX IX: Attendance at meetings

Tables of attendance at the Gram Samstha meetings of the Aldona gaunkars, from which the pre-conversion names of the vangads can be derived.

Pre-conversion name		Vangad 1: Kamti	Vangad 2: Kamti	Vangad 3: Kamti	Vangad 4: Prabhu	Vangad 5: Naik	Vangad 6: Kamti	Vangad 7: Prabhu	Vangad 8: Prabhu	Vangad 9: Kamti	Vangad 10: Naik	Vangad 11: Seti	Vangad 12: Prabhu
Meet date	Meet venue												
N/A	N/A	125 Asrupiya towards construction of the Church was approved											
Sept 22, 1595	Nerul	Bastiao de Costa	Bhogann Kamti	Lourenço Ferrão	Duarte Moniz vote to the village	Manuel Sequeira	Manuel Pinto	Antonio Ferrão	Cristão de Sousa	Purukhe Kamti s/o Bho	Maha Anant	Vitt Seti	Dame Prabhu
Dec 5, 1600	Aldona village intersection under banyan tree	Mateus Carvalho	Ganne Kamti s/o Rou	Antonio Ferrão s/o Ph	Dumi Antonio Fernandes	Manuel Sequeira s/o Nar	Purukhe Kamti s/o Bhogann Kamti	Belchior Fernandes s/o Ato	Diogo Soares s/o Deugo Soares	N/A	Lakh Naik vote to the village	Bhogann Seti s/o Vi	Dame Prabhu
Dec 7, 1600	Aldona village intersection under banyan tree	Mateus Carvalho	Ganne Kamti s/o Roulu Kamti	Antonio Ferrão s/o Vi	Antonio Fernandes s/o Dumi	Manuel Sequeira s/o Nar	Purukhe Kamti s/o Bho	Belchior Fernandes s/o A	Diogo Soares s/o Deugo Soares	N/A	Lakh Naik	Bhogann Seti s/o Vi	Dame Prabhu
Dec 9, 1600	Aldona village intersection under banyan tree	Mateus Carvalho	Bhogann Kamti s/o R, vote to the village	Antonio Ferrão s/o Ph	Vittal Prabhu s/o Phatiye Prabhu	Phati Naik s/o Anant Naik	Purukhe Kamti s/o Bho	Belchior Fernandes	Jeronimo Sousa s/o A	Anant Kamti s/o Vi	Lakh Naik vote to the village	Bhogann Seti	Dame Prabhu vote to the village
Dec 11, 1600	Aldona, Antonio Ferrão's house	Kalu Kamti	Bhogann Kamti vote to village	Lourenço Ferrão s/o A	Duarte Moniz s/o Ph	Manuel Sequeira s/o N	Pedro de Azavedo	Antonio Ferrão s/o A	...nio Sousa	Anant Kamti s/o Vi	Bhogann Naik s/o Maha	Bhogann Seti s/o Vi	Paunte Prabhu s/o Da
Dec 11, 1600	Shrivadi village, Panaji, office of Province Tax Collector	Satu Kamti s/o Ka	Bhogann Kamti vote to the village	Pedro Ferrão s/o A	Duarte Moniz	Goyid Naik s/o A	Pedro de Azavedo	Balthazar Fernandes	Jeronimo Sousa vote to the village	Anant Kamti	Bhogann Naik s/o Maha	Bhogann Seti vote to the village	Miguel Rodrigues s/o Bho
Dec 12, 1600	Nerul village near the jail	Kalu Kamti	Bhogann Kamti s/o R vote to the village	Pedro Ferrão s/o A	Duarte Moniz	Goyid Naik s/o A	Pedro de Azavedo s/o R	Belchior Fernandes	Diogo Sequeira s/o A	Anant Kamti s/o Vi	Paulo de Lima s/o Maha	Bhogann Seti vote to the village	Miguel Rodrigues s/o Bho
Dec 13, 1600	Madhkol near the jail	Kalu Kamti	Bhogann Kamti vote to the village	Pedro Ferrão s/o A	Duarte Moniz	Phati Naik s/o A	Bernardino de Azavedo s/o R	Belchior Fernandes s/o A	Diogo Sequeira s/o Da, A	Anant Kamti s/o Vi	Paulo Lima	Bhogann Seti vote to the village	Miguel Rodrigues
Dec 14, 1600	Shrivadi village, Province tax collector's father's office	Kalu Kamti	Ramu Kamti s/o R vote to the village	Lourenço Ferrão s/o A	Duarte Moniz	Goyid Naik s/o A	Pedro de Azavedo s/o R	Belchior Fernandes	Diogo Sequeira s/o A	Anant Kamti s/o V	Paulo de Lima s/o Maha	Bhogann Seti vote to the village	Miguel Rodrigues s/o Da Bho

Pre-conversion name		Vangad 1: Kamti	Vangad 2: Kamti	Vangad 3: Kamti	Vangad 4: Prabhu	Vangad 5: Naik	Vangad 6: Kamti	Vangad 7: Prabhu	Vangad 8: Prabhu	Vangad 9: Kamti	Vangad 10: Naik	Vangad 11: Seti	Vangad 12: Prabhu
Meet date	Meet venue												
Dec 17, 1600	Aldona village intersection under banyan tree	Mateus Carvalho	Francisco Ferrão s/o Ramu Kamti	Antonio Ferrão s/o Po	Vittal Prabhu s/o Phatiye Prabhu	Phati Naik s/o Anant Naik	Purukhe Kamti s/o Bhogann Kamti	Belchior Fernandes s/o A	Jeronimo Sousa s/o A	Anant Kamti s/o Vittal Kamti	Lakh Naik s/o Mahalap Naik	Bhogann Seti s/o Vi	Paunne Prabhu s/o Da
Dec 20, 1600	Aldona village intersection under banyan tree	Mateus Carvalho	Ganne Kamti vote to the village	Ramu Kamti s/o Bhogann Kamti	Vittal Prabhu s/o Phatiye Prabhu	Phati Naik s/o Anant Naik	Manuel Pinto s/o Roulu Naik	Pedro Fernandes s/o Antonio Fernandes	Jeronimo Sousa s/o Anant Prabhu	Anant Kamti s/o Vittal Kamti	Lakh Naik s/o Mahalap Naik	Bhogann Seti s/o Vitte Seti	Paunne Prabhu s/o Daye Prabhu
Jan 2, 1601	Shrivadi village, Panaji, Province Tax Collector's father's office	Kalu Kamti s/o Ve	Bhogann Kamti s/o R vote to the village	Lourenço Ferrão	Duarte Moniz	Goyid Naik s/o A	Bernardino de Azavedo	Antonio Ferrão s/o A	Diogo Sequeira s/o Ku A	Ganne Kamti s/o Ki	Paulo de Lima	Bhogann Seti s/o Vi vote to the village	Paunne Prabhu s/o Da
Feb 2, 1601	Aldona village intersection under banyan tree	Mateus Carvalho	Ganne Kamti s/o R	Balthazar Ferrão s/o Jo	Antonio Fernandes s/o Du	Manuel Sequeira s/o N	Purukhe Kamti s/o Bhog	Belchior Fernandes s/o Ato	Diogo Sequeira s/o De	Ramu Kamti s/o Bho	Mahalakh Naik s/o L	Bhogann Seti s/o Vi	Dame Prabhu s/o Poko
Feb 7, 1601	Aldona village intersection under banyan tree	Kalu Kamti	Ganne Kamti s/o Rau Kamti	Phati Kamti	Nagann Prabhu	Phati Naik s/o A	Purukhe Kamti s/o Bho	Belchior Fernandes s/o A	Jeronimo Sousa s/o A	Anant Kamti s/o Vi	Lakh Naik	Bhogann Seti	Paunne Prabhu s/o Da
Feb 16, 1601	Aldona village intersection under banyan tree	Kalu Kamti s/o Venu Kamti	Ganne Kamti s/o Roulu Kamti	Purukhe Kamti s/o Phugre Kamti	Nagann Prabhu s/o Madu Prabh	Goyid Naik s/o Anant Naik	Bhanu Kamti s/o Pruruse Kamti	Vittal Prabhu s/o Dame Prabhu	Diogo Soares s/o Deugo Soares	Bhogann Kamti s/o Ramu Kamti	Bhogann Naik s/o Mahalap Naik	Vitt Seti s/o Bhogann Seti	Dame Prabhu
April 9, 1601	Aldona village intersection under banyan tree	Mateus Carvalho	Ganne Kamti s/o Rau	Antonio Ferrão	Antonio Fernandes s/o Domingo Fernandes	Manuel Sequeira s/o Naras Naik	Purukhe Kamti s/o Bhogann Kamti	Belchior Fernandes s/o Antonio Fernandes	Diogo Soares s/o Deugo Soares	Bhogann Kamti s/o Ramu Kamti	Lakh Naik s/o Mahalap Naik vote to the village	Bhogann Seti s/o Vitt Seti	Dame Prabhu
April 12, 1601	Aldona village intersection under banyan tree	Mateus Carvalho	Ganne Kamti s/o Kalu Kamti	Lourenço Ferrão	Antonio Fernandes s/o Du	Manuel Sequeira s/o N	Purukhe Kamti s/o Bhogann Kamti	Belchior Fernandes s/o A	Diogo Sequeira s/o De	Jeronimo Sousa s/o A	Bhogann Naik s/o Maha	Bhogann Seti s/o Vi	Paunne Prabhu
May 7, 1601	Aldona near river crossing	Bostião Costa	Ganne Kamti vote to the village	Purukhe Kamti s/o Fugure Kamti	Agostinho Sousa s/o Ramu Prabhu	Manuel Sequeira s/o Naras Naik	Bernardino de Azavedo s/o R	Pedro Fernandes s/o Ato Fernandes	Jeronimo Sousa s/o Anant Prabhu	Yeugi Kamti s/o Vittal Kamti	Paulo Lima s/o Mahalap Naik	Phati Seti s/o Vitt Seti	Meque.. Rodrigues s/o Bhane Prabhu

Pre-conversion name		Vangad 1: Kamti	Vangad 2: Kamti	Vangad 3: Kamti	Vangad 4: Prabhu	Vangad 5: Naik	Vangad 6: Kamti	Vangad 7: Prabhu	Vangad 8: Prabhu	Vangad 9: Kamti	Vangad 10: Naik	Vangad 11: Seti	Vangad 12: Prabhu
Meet date	Meet venue												
May 7, 1601	Aldona near river crossing	Bostião Costa	Ganne Kamti vote to the village	Purukhe Kamti s/o Fugure Kamti	Agostinho Sousa s/o Ramu Prabhu	Manuel Sequera s/o Naras Naik	Bernardino de Azavedo s/o R	Pedro Fernandes s/o Ato Fernandes	Jeronimo Sousa s/o Anant Prabhu	Yeugi Kamti s/o Vittal Kamti	Paulo Lima s/o Mahalap Naik	Phati Seti s/o Vitt Seti	Mique... Rodrigues s/o Bhane Prabhu
July 5, 1601	Panaji, office of the Province Tax Collector	Kalu Kamti	Bhogann Kamti vote to the village	Lourenço Ferrão	Duarte Moniz	Goyid Naik s/o Aa	Bernardino de Azavedo s/o R	Damu Prabhu s/o De? Vi	Diogo Sequeira	Anant Kamti s/o Vi	Paulo Lima	N/A	Miguel Rodrigues
Aug 6, 1601	Aldona village intersection under banyan tree	Mateus Carvalho	Francisco Gomes s/o Narse Kamti	Antonio Ferrão s/o Ph	Manuel Pinto s/o Vittal Prabhu	Phati Naik s/o Anant Naik	Manuel Pinto s/o R	Antonio Ferrão s/o Antonio Fernandes	Manuel Pinto s/o Narse Prabhu	Anant Kamti s/o Vittal Kamti	Lakh Naik s/o Maha vote to the village	Bhogann Seti s/o Vi	Dame Prabhu
Aug 31, 1601	Aldona village intersection under banyan tree	Kalu Kamti s/o Venu Kamti	Francisco Ferrão s/o Ramu Kamti	Balthazar Ferrão s/o João Ferrão	Agostinho Sousa	Manuel Sequeira s/o Naras Naik	Bernardino de Azavedo s/o Raulu Kamti	Antonio Ferrão s/o Antonio Fernandes	Balthazar Sousa s/o Kistu	Anant Kamti s/o Vittal Kamti	Paulo Lima s/o Maha	Bhogann Seti s/o Vi	Ramu Prabhu s/o Po
Sept 3, 1601	Capital city of Goa, in union with the jewellers, house of Phodd Seti	Kalu Kamti	Francisco Ferrão s/o Ramu	Antonio Ferrão s/o Francisco Ferrão	Vittal Prabhu s/o Ph	Manuel Sequeira s/o Nar	Kist Kamti s/o Bhanu	Antonio Ferrão s/o Ato	Jeronimo Sousa s/o A	Anant Kamti s/o Vi	Bagann Naik s/o Maha	Vitt Seti s/o Bho	Miguel Rodrigues
Sept 16, 1601	At the house of Sir Captain	Mateus Carvalho	Francisco Ferrão s/o Ramu	Antonio Ferrão s/o Francisco Ferrão	Nagann Prabhu s/o Made	Manuel Sequeira s/o Nar	Bernardino de Azavedo	Antonio Ferrão s/o Ato	Balthazar Sousa s/o Ph	Anant Kamti s/o Vi	Paulo Lima s/o Maha	N/A	Dame Prabhu s/o Ra
Sept 18, 1601	Aldona St. Thomas Church under banyan tree	Kalu Kamti s/o Venu Kamti	Bhogann Kamti s/o Raulu Kamti	Lourenço Ferrão	Agostinho Sousa	Goyid Naik s/o Anant Naik	Bhanu Kamti s/o Pru	Antonio Ferrão s/o A	Balthazar Sousa s/o A, Ki	Vittal Kamti s/o Ye	Paulo Lima s/o Maha	Bhogann Seti s/o Vitt	Ramu Prabhu s/o Po
Sept 20, 1601	Aldona Church	Ka...	Bhogann Kamti s/o R	Lourenço Ferrão s/o A	Agostinho... s/o Ra	Goyid Naik s/o A	Bhanu Kamti s/o Pru	Antonio Ferrão ...	Balthazar Sousa	Vittal Kamti s/o Ye	Paulo Lima s/o Maha	Bhogann Seti ...	Ramu Prabhu s/o Po
Dec 6, 1602	Aldona village under banyan tree	Bastião Costa	Francisco Ferrão s/o Ra	Lourenço Ferrão	Agostinho Sousa	Manuel Sequera	Bernardino de Azavedo	Belchior Fernandes s/o A	Jeronimo Sousa	Kist Kati s/o Ye	Paulo de Lima	Vitt Seti s/o Bho	Dame Prabhu s/o Ra

Pre-conversion name	Vangad 1: Kamti	Vangad 2: Kamti	Vangad 3: Kamti	Vangad 4: Prabhu	Vangad 5: Naik	Vangad 6: Kamti	Vangad 7: Prabhu	Vangad 8: Prabhu	Vangad 9: Kamti	Vangad 10: Naik	Vangad 11: Seti	Vangad 12: Prabhu
Meet date / Meet venue												
Jan 12, 1603 / Aldona village under banyan tree	Bostião Costa	Paulo de Sa s/o R vote to the village	Lourenço Ferrão	Agostinho Sousa	Manuel Sequeira	Bernardino de Azavedo	Antonio Ferrão s/o A	Diogo Sequeira	Pedro Bogalo	Paulo de Lima	Bhogann Seti vote to the village	Dame Prabhu s/o Po
Mar 4, 1603 / Pileme, Province Tax Collector's office	Kalu Kamti, vote to the village	Pedro Ferrão, vote to the village	Pedro Ferrão	Duarte Moniz, vote to the village	Phati Naik s/o A	Bernardino de Azavedo	Antonio Ferrão s/o Ato, vote to the village	Balthazar Sousa, vote to the village	Anant Kamti s/o Vi	Paulo Lima, vote to the village	Bhogann Seti, vote to the village	Dame Prabhu s/o Ra Pr
Mar 20, 1603 / Aldona village under the banyan tree	Mateus Carvalho	Ganne Kamti	Pedro Ferrão	Duarte Moniz	Phati Naik	Bernardino de Azavedo	Antonio Ferrão	Kesti Prabhu	Rui de Melo	Paulo Lima	Mahal Seti	Dame Prabhu
Mar 23, 1603 / Aldona Church under banyan tree	Bhanu Kamti s/o Balo Kamti	Paulo de Sousa	Lourenço Ferrão	Duarte Moniz	Manuel Sequeira	Bernardino de Azavedo	Belchior Fernandes	Diogo Sequeira	Pedro Bogalo	Paulo de Lima	Gopal Seti s/o Vitt Seti	...ra Prabhu s/o Pokuli Prabhu
Apr 12, 1603 / Aldona Church under banyan tree	Satu Kamti s/o Kalo Kamti	Paulo de Sousa	Lourenço Ferrão	Agostinho Sousa	Manuel Sequeira	Bernardino de Azavedo	Belchior Fernandes	Diogo Sequeira	Anant Kamti s/o Vittal Kamti	Paulo de Lima	Vitt Seti s/o Bhogann Seti	Da Prabhu s/o Pokuli Prabhu
Apr 14, 1603 / Aldona village under banyan tree	Bhanu Kamti s/o Balu Kamti	Ganne Kamti s/o Raulo Kamti	Pedro Ferrão	Duarte Moniz	Manuel Sequeira	Manuel Pintz	Salvador Fernandes	Jeronimo Sousa	Anant Kamti s/o Vittal Kamti	Pau de Lima	Bhogann Seti s/o Vitt Seti	Dame Prabhu s/o Ra
Jun 29, 1603 / Aldona village under banyan tree	Bostião de Co	Francisco Gomes	Lourenço Ferrão	Agostinho Sousa	Phati Naik s/o Anant Naik	Adrião d'Alicarpo	Balthazar Fernandes	Jeronimo Sousa	Rui de Melo	Bhogann Naik s/o Mahalap Na	Mahal Seti s/o Vitt Seti	Miguel Rodrigues
Jul 7, 1603 / Aldona village under the banyan tree	Satu Kamti s/o Kalu Kamti	Francisco Gomes	Balthazar Ferrão	Manuel Pinto s/o Ra Prabhu	Manuel Sequeira	Domingo Lobo	Antonio Ferrão s/o Antonio Fernandes	Valentino Pinto	Vittal Kamti s/o Yeu	Bhogann Naik s/o Mahalap Frier...	Bhogann Seti s/o Vitt Seti	Martino Popo
Aug 11, 1603 / Aldona village under banyan tree	Satu Kamti s/o Kalu Kamti	Paulo Sousa	Lourenço Ferrão	Duarte Moniz	Phati Naik s/o Anant Naik	Bernardino de Azavedo	Balthazar Fernandes	Belchior Sousa vote to the village	Yeugu Kati s/o Vittal K	Paulo de Lima	Bhogann Seti	Bhogann Prabhu s/o Ra Prabhu
Nov 10, 1604 / Aldona Church under banyan tree	Bastião Costa	Paulo de Sousa	Lourenço Ferrão	Duarte Moniz	Manuel Sequeira	Bernardino de Azavedo	Antonio Ferrão	Balthazar Sousa	Rui de Melo	Paulo de Lima	Bhogann Seti s/o Vitt	Miguel Ridrigues

Pre-conversion name		Vangad 1: Kamti	Vangad 2: Kamti	Vangad 3: Kamti	Vangad 4: Prabhu	Vangad 5: Naik	Vangad 6: Kamti	Vangad 7: Prabhu	Vangad 8: Prabhu	Vangad 9: Kamti	Vangad 10: Naik	Vangad 11: Seti	Vangad 12: Prabhu
Meet date	Meet venue												
Sep 11, 1604	Aldona Church	Bastião Cost s/o H	Paulo Sousa s/o R	Lourenço Ferrão	Bernardino Lo... s/o Go	Manuel de Sequeira s/o N	Bernardino de Azavedo	Antonio Ferrão	Balthazar Sousa	Anant Kamti s/o Vi	Paulo Lima	Bhogann Seti s/o Vi	Paurne Prabhu s/o Da
Sep 12, 1604	Aldona Church under banyan tree	Bastião Costa	Paulo Sousa s/o R	Lourenço Ferrão	Bernardino Lourenço s/o Go	Nuno de Mendonça	Bernardino de Azavedo	Balthazar Fernandes	Diogo Sequeira	Anant Kamti	Paulo Lima	Damu Seti s/o Vi Dha	Paurne Prabhu s/o Da
Nov 28 1604	Aldona village under the banyan tree	Bastião Costa	Francisco Ferrão s/o Ra	Pedro Ferrão s/o A	Gaspar Sousa	Manuel Sequeira	Bernardino de Azavedo	Pedro Fernandes s/o A	Diogo Sequeira	Naru Kamti s/o Bho	Paulo Lima	Bhogann Seti vote to the village	Ramu Prabhu s/o Po vote to the village
Dec 30, 1604	Aldona village under banyan tree	Satu Kamti	Francisco Ferrão vote to the village	Pedro Ferrão	Gonçalo Pinto s/o Ma	Phati Nak s/o An	Ye... Lobo	Balthazar Fernandes	Valentino Pinto	Anant Kamti s/o Vi	Paulo Lima	Bhogann Seti vote to the village	Bhogann Prabhu vote to the village
Meeting date, venue, list of participants not extant. Minutes, however, signed by ten gaunkar attendees													
...15, 1604	Aldona village under banyan tree	Bharu Kamti	Francisco Ferrão s/o Ra	Pedro Ferrão s/o A	Sapte Prabhu s/o Jo	Manuel Sequeira s/o N	Bernardino de Azavedo	Antonio Ferrão	Jeronimo Sousa s/o A	Naru Kamti s/o Bho	Paulo de Lima	Damu Seti s/o Dha	Paurne Prabhu s/o Da

Pre-conversion name		Vangad 1: Kamti	Vangad 2: Kamti	Vangad 3: Kamti	Vangad 4: Prabhu	Vangad 5: Naik	Vangad 6: Kamti	Vangad 7: Prabhu	Vangad 8: Prabhu	Vangad 9: Kamti	Vangad 10: Naik	Vangad 11: Set	Vangad 12: Prabhu
Meet date	Meet venue												
Jan 15, 1605	Aldona veranda of old Church	Bastião Costa	Francisco Ferrão s/o Ra	Lourenço Ferrão s/o A	Gonçalo Pinto s/o Ma	Manuel Sequeira s/o N	Bernardino de Azavedo	Antonio Ferrão s/o A	Jeronimo Sousa	Anant Kamti s/o Vi	Paulo Lima s/o Maha	Mahafim Set	Miguel Rodrigues
Jan 16, 1605	Aldona Church	Bastião Costa	Francisco Ferrão	Lourenço Ferrão	Bernardino Lourenço s/o Ga	Goyid Naik s/o A	Bernardino de Alvedo	Antonio Ferrão	Jeronimo Sousa	Anant Kamti s/o Vi	Paulo Lima	Bhogann Set	Miguel Rodrigues
Jan 25, 1605	Aldona Church	Satu Kamti s/o Ka	Paulo Sousa	Balthazar Ferrão	Francisco Coutinho	Phati Naik catechumen s/o A	Domingo Lobo	Pedro Fernandes	Jeronimo Sousa	Rui de Melo	Paulo de Lima	Phati Set s/o Bho	Ramu Prabhu
Jul 7, 1605	Aldona village under banyen tree	Mateus Carvalho	Francisco Ferrão	Lourenço Ferrão	Manuel Pinto	Ja de Sousa	Manuel Sousa	Vittal Prabhu	Jeronimo Sousa	Pedro Bogalo	Bhogann Naik	Phati Set	Paurne Prabhu
Jul 20, 1605	Aldona veranda Lourenço Ferrão	Bastião de Costa	Ganne Kamti s/o R	Bagann Kamti s/o Bho	Duarte Moniz	Phati Naik s/o A	Bernardino de Azavedo	Antonio Ferrão s/o A	Jeronimo Sousa s/o A	Anant Kamti s/o Vi	Paulo de Lima	Bhogam Set vote to the village	Paurne Prabhu
Jul 20, 1605	Aldona veranda Lourenço Ferrão	Bastião Costa	Ganne Kamti, Christian	Bagann Kamti	Duarte Moniz	Phati Naik	Bernardino de Azavedo	Antonio Ferrão	Jeronimo Sousa	Anant Kamti s/o Vi	Paulo Lima	Bhogann Set	Paum Prabhu

Bibliography

1. Charles Darwin, *The Origin of Species*, 1859, Woodsworth Editions Ltd. 1998, Chapter XIV, p.368, ISBN 978-1-85326-780-2
2. Charles Darwin, *The Descent of Man, and Selection in Relation to Sex*, London: John Murray; 1871
3. L. Pray (2008) Discovery of DNA structure and function: Watson and Crick, *Nature Education* 1(1):100; NIH National Human Genome Research Institute
4. https://www.genome.gov/25520880/deoxyribonucleic-acid-dna-fact-sheet/
5. Svante Pääbo, A Draft Sequence of the Neanderthal Genome, *Science*, Issue of May 7, 2010
6. Genographic Project, "Why am I a Denisovan" https://genographic.nationalgeographic.com/denisovan/.
7. Fahu Chen *et al.*,*Nature* **569**, 16-17 (2019)
8. Matthew Warren, https://www.nature.com/articles/d41586-019-01395-0
9. http://isogg.org/wiki/CentiMorgan
10. V. Slon, F. Mafessoni, B. Vernot *et al.*, *Nature* 561, 113-116 (2018)
11. K. Donka, V. Slon, Z. Jacobs *et al.*, *Nature*, Vol 565, 640-644 (2019)
12. S. López *et al.*, *Evolutionary Bioinformatics* vol 11, p 57-68 (2016);10.4137/EBO.S33489
13. Amanuel Beyin, *International Journal of Evolutionary Biology*, vol. 2011, Article ID 615094, 2011. https://doi.org/10.4061/2011/6150949
14. Katerina Harvati *et al.*, *Nature*, 10 July 2019
15. Daniel Richter *et al.*, *Nature* **546**, 293–296 (08 June 2017).
16. N. Rohland *et al.*, *Nat. Protoc. 2*, 1756–1762 (2007); https://www.eva.mpg.de/documents/Nature, Rohland_Extraction_NatProc_2018_3007574.pdf)
17. L. R. Berger *et al.*, https://www.ncbi.nlm.nih.gov/pmc/articles/PMC5423770/
18. F. Détroit *et al.*, *Nature* **568**, 181–186 (2019)
19. David Reich, *Who we are and how we got here*, Oxford University Press, UK, 2018, ISBN 978-0-19-882126-7, p.43-9
20. C. W. Marean, *Scientific American*, August 2010, p.41
21. M. Tallavaara *et al.*, *PNAS* vol 112 (27), p 8232-8237 (July 7, 2015)
22. Charles Darwin, *The Origin of Species*, 1859, Woodswoth Editions Ltd., 1998, Chapter XIV, p.364, ISBN 978-1-85326-780-2
23. K. E. Prehoda *et al.*, *eLife* 2016;5:e10147

24. Sarah Kaplan, *Washington Post*, January 2016 https://www.washingtonpost.com/news/morning-mix/wp/2016/01/11/startling-new-discovery-600-million-years-ago-a-single-biological-mistake-changed-everything/?noredirect=on&utm_term=.ee93b60c627a
25. Lynn B. Jorde, Ph.D., Department of Human Genetics, University of Utah School of Medicine, https://www.ashg.org/education/pdf/geneticvariation.pdf
26. Chromosome map, https://www.ncbi.nlm.nih.gov/books/NBK22266/
27. R. A. Sturm *et al.*, *Pigment Cell Melanoma Research*, Oct 22(5):544-62. doi: 10.1111/j.1755-148X.2009.00606.x. *Epub* 2009 Jul 8
28. Fan Liu *et al.*, *PLOS Genetics*, May 6, 2010, https://doi.org/10.1371/journal.pgen.1000934
29. Póspiech *et al.*, *J. Hum. Genet.*, 2011 Jun; 56(6):447-55. doi:10.1038/jhg.2011.38. *Epub* 2011 Apr 7
30. Making SNPs Make Sense (Internet). Salt Lake City (UT): *Genetic Science Learning Center*, 2016 (cited 2019 Jan 16) Available from https://learn.genetics.utah.edu/content/precision/snips/
31. T. Kyndt *et al.*, *PNAS* May 5, 2015, 112 (18) 5844-5849
32. P. K. Dash *et al.*, *Nature Communications* vol 10, Article number: 2753 (2019); https://www.nature.com/articles/s41467-019-10366-y
33. X. Wei & R. Nielsen, *Nature Medicine* (2019)
34. Neue Zürcher Zeitung, March 5, 2019, https://www.nzz.ch/zuerich/gentest-genetiker-aus-schlieren-loest-raetsel-ld.1463846?mktcid=nled&mktcval=107&kid=_2019-3-5
35. https://www.familytreedna.com/learn/glossary/
36. https://isogg.org/tree/index.html
37. Y Full phylogenetic tree (https://www.yfull.com/tree/
38. https://www.yfull.com/faq/definitions/
39. Y DNA Haplogroup Tree 2019 https://isogg.org/tree/
40. *The National Geographic* Genographic Project https://genographic.nationalgeographic.com/about/
41. *Family Tree DNA* https://www.familytreedna.com/?idev_id=1760&utm_source=1760&utm_medium=affiliate
42. Charles F. Kerchner, Jr., *Genetics & Genealogy*, http://www.kerchner.com/books/introg&g.htm
43. The International Society of Genetic Genealogy ISOGG at https://isogg.org

44. Semino *et al.*, *Am J Hum Genet.* 2004 May; 74(5): 1023–1034. Published online 2004 Apr 6. doi: 10.1086/386295 *PMCID*: PMC1181965 PMID: 15069642
45. 45. Sengupta *et al.* (*Am J Hum Genet.* 2006 Feb; 78(2): 202–221. Published online 2005 Dec 16. doi: 10.1086/499411
46. *PNAS* January 24, 2006, 103 (4) 843-848; https://doi.org/10.1073/pnas.0507714103
47. https://www.eupedia.com/europe/Haplogroup_J2_Y-DNA.shtml
48. Hunter Provyn, https://phylogeographer.com
49. Diehan Southard, https://www.familytreemagazine.com/premium/big-y-700/
50. Caleb Davis *et al.*,https://blog.familytreedna.com/wp-content/uploads/2019/03/big-y-700-white-paper_compressed.pdf
51. https://isogg.org/wiki/YFull
52. John C. Chambers et al.; *PLoS One,* 2014; 9(8): e102645
53. Vasant S. Shinde *et al.*, Archaeological and anthropological studies on the Harappan cemetery of Rakhigarhi, India, 2018; https://doi.org/10.1371/journal.pone.0192299
54. V.N. Prabhakar, Harappan and their Mesopotamian Contacts, IIC Occasional Publication 48, p.8
55. Vasant Shinde *et al.*,Exploration in the Ghaggar Basin and excavations at Girawad, Farmana (Rohtak District) and Mitathal (Bhiwani District), Haryana, India, p.77, 2008, ISBN 978-4-902325-16-4
56. Vasant Shinde, https://www.sindhulogy.org/cdn/articles/harappan-civilization-current-perspective-and-its-contribution-vasant-shinde/; https://www.academia.edu/37168651/Inscriptions_Indus_Script_on_two_seals_of_Rakhigarhi_translated._Harappan_-Civilization_Current_Perspective_and_its_Contribution_By_Dr._Vasant_Shinde?email_work_card=title
57. Michel Danino, ISBN 0143068644, Penguin Books India, 2010
58. https://en.wikisource.org/wiki/The_Rig_Veda/Mandala_8/Hymn_21
59. L. Giosan *et al.*,*PNAS* June 26, 2012 109 (26) E1688-E1694
60. Thomas H. Maugh II, May 28, 2012, https://www.latimes.com/science/la-xpm-2012-may-28-la-sci-sn-indus-harappan-20120528-story.html).
61. https://en.wikipedia.org/wiki/Sumer
62. *Encyclopaedia Britannica*, https://www.britannica.com/topic/Semite
63. Nadia Al-Zahery *et al.*, *BMC Evol Biol.* 2011; 11: 288. Published online 2011 Oct 4. doi: 10.1186/1471-2148-11-288

64. Vasant Shinde, https://www.sindhulogy.org/cdn/articles/harappan-civilization-current-perspective-and-its-contribution-vasantshinde/
65. Anant Ramkrishna Sinai Dhume, *The Cultural History of Goa, Broadway Book Centre*, Panjim, Goa, second edition 2009, p.2-28
66. Teotonio R. de Souza, *Medieval Goa*, Concept Publishing Company, New Delhi, 1979, p.56
67. Chandrakant Keni, *The Saraswats*, chapter I, The Origin of Saraswats, published by V. M. Salgaocar Foundation, Vasco da Gama, Goa, 2008, p.15-35
68. Sharma *et al.*, *Journal of Human Genetics* (2009) 54, 47–55; doi:10.1038/jhg.2008.2; published online 9 January 2009
69. Brower, Barbara; Johnston, Barbara Rose, *Disappearing Peoples?: Indigenous Groups and Ethnic Minorities in South and Central Asia*, Routledge, 2016, ISBN 9781315430393
70. Chandrakant Keni, *The Saraswats*, chapter 1, The Origin of Saraswats, published by V. M. Salgaocar Foundation, Vasco da Gama, Goa 2008, 15-35
71. Chandrakant Keni, *The Saraswats*, The Origin of Saraswats, published by V. M. Salgaocar Foundation, Vasco da Gama, Goa,2008, p 34
72. https://www.familytreedna.com/mtDNA-Haplogroup-Mutations.aspx
73. S. Maji, S. Krithika and T. S. Vasulu, *Int. J. Hum Genet* 8(1-2) 85-96 (2008)
74. T. Kivisild *et al.*, *Current Biology* 1999, 9:1331-1334
75. Gail Tonnesen, https://www.familytreedna.com/groups/u-5b/about/results
76. A Revised Timescale for Human Evolution Based on Ancient Mitochondrial Genomes, *Current Biology* 23, 553–559, April 8, 2013; http://dx.doi.org/10.1016/j.cub.2013.02.044
77. Pedro Soares *et al.*, *Am J Hum Genet.* 2009 Jun 12; 84(6): 740–759
78. https://www.esd.ornl.gov/projects/gen/nerc.html
79. Richards *et al.*, *Am J Hum Genet.* 2000 November; 67 (5): 1251-1276 Published online 2000 October 16
80. W. Haak *et al.*, *Nature* vol 522, p 207–211 (11 June 2015)
81. M. E. Allentoft *et al.* Population genomics of Bronze Age Eurasia. *Nature* 522. 167-172. 10.1038/nature14507
82. file:///Users/Bernardo/Documents/Geni%20-%20Queen%20Elizabeth%20II%20of%20the%20United%20Kingdom%20is%20related%20to%20Bernardo%20Elvino%20de%20Sousa,%20Dr.%20rer.nat..webarchive

83. https://isogg.org/wiki/List_of_DNA_testing_companies
84. gedmatch.com
85. Lizzie Wade, *Science Magazine*, https://www.sciencemag.org/news/2014/10/oldest-human-genome-reveals-when-our-ancestors-had-sex-neandertals
86. L. Deng *et al.*, *Hereditas*. 2017;155:1. Published 2017 Jun 15. doi:10.1186/s41065-017-0036-2
87. Natural History Museum, Cheddar Man FAQ, http://www.nhm.ac.uk/our-science/our-work/origins-evolution-and-futures/human-adaptation-diet-disease/cheddar-man-faq.html
88. Judy Russel, *The Legal Genealogist*, March 26, 2017; https://www.legalgenealogist.com/2017/03/26/updated-look-at-gedmatch/
89. NCBS News; https://www.nbcnews.com/news/us-news/just-beginning-using-dna-genealogy-crack-years-old-cold-cases-n892126
90. https://www.innocenceproject.org/dna-revolutionary-role-freedom/
91. Madeline Holcombe, CNN.com, August 18, 2019, https://edition.cnn.com/2019/08/18/us/coral-springs-cold-case-rape-dna-arrest/index.html
92. https://www.wsj.com/articles/two-sisters-bought-dna-kits-the-results-blew-apart-their-family-11549037904
93. https://eu.azcentral.com/story/opinion/op-ed/2018/12/08/dna-test-ancestry-birth-parents-adoption-family-love/2212817002/
94. Jacob Koshy, Genome sequencing to map population diversity, *The Hindu*, 19 April 2019; https://www.thehindu.com/sci-tech/science/genome-sequencing-to-map-population-diversity/article26880217.ece
95. A. Caspi *et al.*, *Science*. Aug 2002;297(5582):851-854 ; A. Caspi *et al.*, Sugden K, Moffitt TE, *et al.*,*Science*. Jul 2003;301(5631):386-389
96. D. W. Belsky *et al.*, *PNAS* July 31, 2018 115 (31) E7275-E7284
97. Alan Machado, personal communication
98. Teotonio R. de Souza, *Medieval Goa*, Concept Publishing Company, New Delhi, 1979, p 54
99. A. K. Priolkar, *The Goa Inquisition*, Bombay, 1961
100. http://www.usccb.org/bible/genesis/2
101. B. T. Lahn *et al.*, *Science* 286, 964 (1999); DOI: 10.1126/science.286.5441.964
102. D. Cortez *et al. Nature*, vol 508, p 488–493 (2014); https://www.iflscience.com/plants-and-animals/evolution-y-chromosome/9

103. Doris Bachtrog, *Nat Rev Genet.* 2013 Feb, 14(2): 113-124; doi: 10.1038/nrg3366

104. J. K.Abbott *et al.*, *Proc Biol Sci.* 2017 May 17; 284(1854): 20162806; doi: 10.1098/rspb.2016.2806

105. http://en.wikipedia.org/wiki/Human_vestigiality#Coccyx

106. MedlinePlus, US National Library of Medicine, online at http://www.nlm.nih.gov/medlineplus/ency/article/001669.htm

107. K. Thangaraj *et al.*, *BMC Genomics* 2006 7:151

108. Sengupta *et al.*, *Am. J Hum Genet* 2006, Feb; 78(2): 202-221

109. T. Kivisild *et al.*, *Am J Hum Genet*, 2003, 72:313-332

110. S. Sahoo *et al.*, *PNAS* January 24, 2006, 103 (4) 843-848; https://doi.org/10.1073/pnas.0507714103

111. Cavalli-Sforza L. L. , Menozzi P., Piazza A., *The history and geography of human genes*, p 241, Princeton University Press, 1994

112. Gadgil,M., Joshi, N.V., Shambu Prasad,U.V., Manoharan,S. and Suresh Patil 1997, p 100-129, *The Indian Human Heritage*, Eds. D.Balasubramanian and N. Appaji Rao, Universities Press, Hyderabad, India, http://ces.iisc.ernet.in/hpg/cesmg/peopling.html

113. David Reich, *Who we are and how we got here*, Oxford University Press, UK, 2018, ISBN 978-0-19-882126-7, p128ff

114. David Reich *et al.*, *Nature* 461 (7263), 489-494 (2009); https://www.ncbi.nlm.nih.gov/pmc/articles/PMC2842210/

115. Tony Joseph, Who built the Indus Valley civilisation?, *The Hindu*, December 23, 2017; https://www.thehindu.com/news/national/who-built-the-indus-valley-civilisation/article22261315.ece

116. V. S. Shinde *et al.*, Archaeological and anthropological studies on the Harappan cemetery of Rakhigarhi, India, February 21, 2018, accessible online at https://journals.plos.org/plosone/article?id=10.1371/journal.pone.0192299

117. 4500-year-old DNA from Rakhigarhi reveals evidence that will unsettle Hindutva nationalists, https://www.indiatoday.in/magazine/cover-story/story/20180910-rakhigarhi-dna-study-findings-indus-valley-civilisation-1327247-2018-08-31

118. Tony Joseph, Who built the Indus Valley civilisation?, *The Hindu*, December 23, 2017; https://www.thehindu.com/news/national/who-built-the-indus-valley-civilisation/article22261315.ece

119. Hartosh Singh Bal, https://caravanmagazine.in/vantage/indus-valley-genetic-contribution-steppes-rakhigarhi

120. Sunil Menon, Siddhartha Mishra, https://www.outlookindia.com/magazine/story/we-are-all-harappans/300463

121. Vagheesh M. Narasimhan *et al.*, The Genomic Formation of South and Central Asia, *bioRxiv* March 31, 2018, https://www.biorxiv.org/content/biorxiv/early/2018/03/31/292581.full.pdf

122. Shinde *et al.*; An Ancient Harappan Genome Lacks Ancestry from Steppe Pastoralists or Iranian Farmers, Cell (2019), https://doi.org/10.1016/j.cell.2019.08.048

123. Allentoft *et al.*, *Nature* 2015, Vol 522, Suppl. Materials Section 1, An introduction to the sampled cultures and their dating

124. Lazaridis *et al.*, The genetic structure of the world's first farmers, *Nature* doi: 10.1038/nature19310; https://www.biorxiv.org/content/10.1101/059311v1.full

125. David Reich, *Who we are and how we got here*, Oxford University Press, UK, 2018, ISBN 978-0-19-882126-7, p. 237

126. Amy Goldberg *et al.*,*PNAS* March 7, 2017, 114 (10) 2657-2662; https://doi.org/10.1073/pnas.1616392114

127. Willerslev *et al.*, *Science* 2018 Jun 29;360(6396) http://www.academia.edu/36669320 The_First_Horse_Herders_and_the_Impact_of_Early_Bronze_Age_Steppe_Expansions_into_Asia_including_supplementary_materials_arch._and_linguistic_background_-papers_

128. M. E. Allentoft *et al.* Population genomics of Bronze Age Eurasia, *Nature* 522. 167-172. 10.1038/nature14507

129. W. Haak *et al.*, *Nature* vol 522, pages 207–211 (11 June 2015; https://www.biorxiv.org/content/10.1101/013433v1

130. McDonald Institute for Archeological Research, University of Cambridge, Chapter 31, p.267, ISBN: 1-902937-08-2 (2000)

131. S. Barnabas *et al.*, *Annals of human genetics* 70, Issue 1, p. 42-58 (2006) https://www.ncbi.nlm.nih.gov/pubmed/16441256

132. S. Sengupta *et al.*, *Am J Hum Genet.* 2006 Feb; 78(2): 202–221

133. T. Kivisild *et al.*, *Am J Hum Genet.* 2003; 72:313-332

134. S. Sahoo *et al.*, *PNAS* January 24, 2006, vol 103, no. 4, 843-848, http://www.pnas.org/content/103/4/843.full as well as http://www.pnas.org/content/103/4/843/suppl/DC1 for supporting figures

135. Mugdha Singh, Anujit Sarkar & Madhusudan R. Nandineni, *Nature Scientific Reports* 8: 15421, p. 1-7 (2018); https://doi.org/10.1038/s41598-018-33714-2

136. Maciamo Hay https://www.eupedia.com/europe/Haplogroup_R1a_Y-DNA.shtml

137. https://www.yfull.com/tree/R-Z93/

138. Iain Mathieson *et al.*, *Nature* vol. 528, p. 499–503, Supplementary Data Table 1, (2015)

139.David Reich, *Who we are and how we got here*, Oxford University Press, UK, 2018, ISBN 978-0-19-882126-7, Part II, 6, p. 123ff

140.David Reich, *Who we are and how we got here*, Oxford University Press, UK, 2018, ISBN 978-0-19-882126-7, p 100-103

141.Chandrakant Keni, *The Saraswats*, printed by V. M. Salgaocar, Vasco da Gama, 1998, p. 254

142.J. P. Vaswani, *Desavatara: The ten Incarnations of Lord Vishnu*, Jaico Publishing House, Mumbai 2018, ISBN 978-93-86867-18-6

143.Teotonio R. de Souza, Dying and killing for forged identities, *O Heraldo*, 17 Jan 2009

144.Sengupta *et al. Am J of Hum Genet. 78 (2): 202–21* (2006)

145.Paul Brooker online at https://paulbrooker.posthaven.com/y-haplogroup-l-not-the-r1b-sub-clade-or-mtdna-resource-page

146.Anant Ramkrishna Sinai Dhume, *The Cultural History of Goa*, Broadway Book Centre, Panjim Goa, second edition 2009, p.30

147.Kumarasamy Thangaraj *et al.*, *Current Biology,* vol 13, Jan 2003, p 86-93

148.Anant Ramkrishna Sinai Dhume, *The Cultural History of Goa*, Broadway Book centre, Panjim, Goa, second edition 2009, p. 639

149.*Curr Biol.* 2004 Feb 3;14(3):231-5; http://www.cell.com/current-biology/retrieve/pii/S0960982204000405?_returnURL=https%3A%2F%2Flinkinghub.elsevier.com%2Fretrieve%2Fpii%2FS0960982204000405%3Fshowall%3Dtrue

150.*Rig Veda* 10.90.11-12

151.Swarupananda "Srimat-Bhagavad-Gita", *Internet Sacred Text Archive*, http://www.sacred-texts.com/hin/sbg/sbg23.htm, Retrieved 28 March 2019

152.Encyclopedia Britannica, online at https:/www.britannica.com/topic/Indus-Civilisation

153.Ancient Civilisations, online at http://www.ushistory.org/civ/8a.asp)

154.Shinde *et al. PLoS One* 2018; 13(2): e0192299. doi: 10.1371/journal.pone.0192299

155.Khan Academy, *Indus River Valley civilisations*, online at https://www.khanacademy.org/humanities/world-history/world-history-beginnings/ancient-india/a/the-indus-river-valley-civilizations

156.I. Lazaridis *et al.*, *Nature*. 2016; 536(7617):419–424. doi:10.1038/nature19310

157.Ahluwalia, Disha, "Sanauli's Mysterious Warriors." Live History India, 2018; https://www.academia.edu/38832511/Sanaulis_Mysterious_Warriors?email_work_card=view-paper

158. BRONZE_AGE_HUMAN_COMMUNITIES_IN_THE_SOUT.pdf
159. The Indo-Europeanization of Europe: the intrusion of steppe pastoralists from south Russia and the transformation of Old Europe", *Word* 44 (1993): 205–222 online at https://www.tandfonline.com/doi/pdf/10.1080/00437956.1993.11435900
160. George F. Dales, The Mythical Massacre at Mohenjo-daro, online at https://www.penn.museum/sites/expedition/the-mythical-massacre-at-Mohenjo-daro/
161. David Reich, *Who we are and how we got here*, Oxford University Press, UK, 2018, ISBN 978-0-19-882126-7, p.136
162. David Reich, *Who we are and how we got here*, Oxford University Press, UK, 2018, ISBN 978-0-19-882126-7, p137
163. David Reich, *Who we are and how we got here*, Oxford University Press, UK, 2018, ISBN 978-0-19-882126-7, p145-6
164. P. Moorjani *et al.*, AJHG, Vol 93, p422-438, Sept 05, 2013; https://doi.org/10.1016/j.ajhg.2013.07.006
165. A. Basu *et al*, *PNAS* Feb 9, 2016 113 (6) 1594-1599; https://doi.org/10.1073/pnas.1513197113
166. Thamseem *et al.* Genetic affinities among the lower castes and tribal groups of India: inference from Y chromosome and mitochondrial DNA BMC Genet. 2006 Aug 7, On-line at http://www.ncbi.nlm.nih.gov/pubmed/16893451
167. http://www.oecd.org/dataoecd/24/21/39437980.pdf, Table 2.2 shows that about 48% of Portuguese adults had literacy at Level 1, the lowest of 5 levels
168. Gadgil,M., Joshi, N.V., Shambu Prasad,U.V., Manoharan,S. and Suresh Patil 1997, p 100-129, The Indian Human Heritage, Eds. D. Balasubramanian and N. Appaji Rao, Universities Press, Hyderabad, India, http://ces.iisc.ernet.in/hpg/cesmg/peopling.html
169. Aisha Salaudeen, CNN, https://edition.cnn.com/2019/07/10/health/genotype-dating-nigeria-intl/index.html
170. David Reich, *Who we are and how we got here*, Oxford University Press, UK, 2018, ISBN 978-0-19-882126-7, p147
171. Gajanana Ghantkar, *History of Goa through Gõykanadi Script*, Chapter 1 Tombo de Aldona, Publishers Rajahauns Vitaran, Panaji, Goa, 1993)
172. Baba Borkar, on-line at http://www.mailarchive.com/goanet@goanet.org/msg04332.html
173. Aldona Goa – Most beautiful Village in the World, by Anuradha Goyal, June 16, 2016, https://www.inditales.com/aldona-goa-beautiful-village-world/
174. *O Oriente Português*, V17-N03-N04 Vol. V17, p.148, 03 April 1920

175.Teotonio R. de Souza, The Cuncolim Martyrs, http://www.goa-com.com/the-cuncolim-martyrs-paper-by-prof-teotonio-r-de-souza/

176.Sisir Kumar Mitra, *The Early Rulers of Khajuraho*, second edition 1977, p. 179, partially accessible on-line as a google book

177.https://www.jatland.com/home/Chaluky

178.Pratima P. Kamat, *Goa Through the Ages* Vol. II, Chapter 1, p. 11ff, Concept Publishing Company, 1990

179.Teotonio R. de Souza, *Medieval Goa: A socio-economic history*, Concept Publishing Company, New Delhi, 1979, p.54

180.Kamat, Nandkumar, (2004), *History of Khazan land management in Goa: ecological, economic and political perspective*, https://www.a-cademia.edu/38045768 History_of_Khazan_land_managemen-t_in_Goa_ecological_economic_and_political_perspective?auto=download

181.Anant Ramkrishna Sinai Dhume, *The Cultural History of Goa*, Broadway Book Centre, Panjim, Goa, second edition 2009, p 187

182.Filipe Neri Xavier, *Bosquejo Histórico das Comunidades*, Vol. II, 1801–1901, Nova Goa: Imprensa Nacional, 1852, p 419-421, for an English translation, cf. Annex V

183.*O Oriente Portugues*, V17-N03-N04, Vol. V17 - 03-Abr, 1920, p.125

184.Teotonio R. de Souza, *Medieval Goa*, Concept Publishing Company, New Delhi, 1979, p57

185.Teotonio R. de Souza, *Medieval Goa*, Concept Publishing Company, New Delhi, 1979, p56

186.Azevedo, Antonio Emilio d'Almeida, *As Comunidades de Goa: historia das instituições antiguas*, Publishers Viuva Bertrand & C. 1890, p 80-81

187.Teotonio R. de Souza, How the Church Flourished in Goa, O Heraldo, 2009 on-line at http://oheraldo.in/pagedetails.asp?nid=16467&cid=14

188.Baden Powell B.H., The villages of Goa in the early sixteenth century, 1900, online at http:www.archive.org/details/villagesof-goaine00baderich

189.Teotonio R. de Souza, *Goa Through the Ages* Vol. II, Rural Economy and Life, Concept Publishing Company New Delhi, 1990

190.Filipe Neri Xavier, *Bosquejo Histórico das Comunidades*, Vol. II, 1801–1901, Nova Goa: Imprensa Nacional, 1852, p 419-421, for an English translation, cf. Annex V

191.Rui Gomes Pereira, *Hindu Temples and Deities*, entry no. 35, 1978,p 179

192.Rochelle Pinto, *Between Empires: Print and Politics in Goa*, Oxford University Press, 2007, p 160-161, cf also on-line http://osdir.-com/ml/culture.region.india.goa.research/200503/msg00002.html

193.Gajanana Ghantkar, *History of Goa through Gōykanadi Script*, Publishers Rajahauns Vitaran, Panaji, Goa, 1993

194.Rui Gomes Pereira, *Hindu Temples and Deities*, entry no. 35, 1978, p179

195.Chandrakant Keni, *The Saraswats*, Appendix II, printed by V.M.Salgaocar, Vasco da Gama, 1998, p 391

196.Chandrakant Keni, *The Saraswats*, Appendix II, printed by V.M.Salgaocar, Vasco da Gama, 1998, p105

197.Teotonio R. de Souza, ttps://ciberduvidas.iscte-iul.pt/outros/di-versidades/os-descobrimentos-e-eu-2/992

198.S. C. Bhatt, Gopal K. Bhargava, *Land and people of Indian states and union territories*, Vol. 7, p.162, Gyan Publishing House, 2006

199.Pandya SK. Medicine in Goa--a former Portuguese territory, *J Postgrad Med* (serial online) 1982 (cited 2009 Sep 18);28:123. On-line at http://www.jpgmonline.com/text.asp?1982/28/3/123/5573

200.Anant Ramkrishna Sinai Dhume, *The Cultural History of Goa*, Broadway Book Centre, Panjim, Goa, second edition 2009, p 205

201.Reverend Alexander Kyd Nairne, *History of the Konkan*, Asian Educational Services, New Delhi, Second Reprint 2001, p60

202.A. K. Priolkar, The Goa Inquisition, published by Voice of India, New Delhi, second reprint 1998, p 68

203.Mario Cabral e Sa, Is The March Over? *Hindustan Today*, October, 1997, on-line at http://groups.google.co.il/group/sci.lang/browse_thread/thread/3ca83ee7b7a7c1f7

204.Anant Ramkrishna Sinai Dhume, *The Cultural History of Goa*, Broadway Book Centre, Panjim, Goa, second edition 2009 p 237

205.Stephen Neil, *A history of Christianity in India: The beginnings to Ad 1707*, Cambridge University Press, 1984, p 131-133, available as a Google book

206.A. K. Priolkar, *The Goa Inquisition*, published by Voice of India, New Delhi, second reprint 1998, p 88

207.Rui Gomes Pereira, *Hindu Temples and Deities*, entry no. 35, 1978, p 179

208.Rui Gomes Pereira, *Hindu Temples and Deities*, entry no. 188(A), 1978, p 179

209.Azevedo, Antonio Emilio d'Almeida, *As Comunidades de Goa: historia das instituições antiguas*, Publishers Viuva Bertrand & C. 1890, p 38-40

210.F. X. Gomes Catão, *Boletim Eclesiástico da Arquidiocese de Goa*, Vol A15, p.397, 1957

211.F. X. Gomes Catão, *Boletim Eclesiástico da Arquidiocese de Goa*, Vol A15, p.395ff, 1957

212.Alan Machado, *Sarasvati's Children*, Camelot Publishers, 2nd edition 2002, p 56ff

213.http://www.historyguide.org/earlymod/calecut.html

214.Teotonio R. de Souza, Never the same again? *OHeraldo*, 6 December 2008, on- line at http://www.goa-world.com/goa/index.html

215.A. K. Priolkar, *The Goa Inquisition*, Bombay, 1961, 63-64

216.Alan Machado, *Sarasvati's Children*, Camelot Publishers, 2nd edition 2002, p 87

217.Pedro do Carmo Costa, Famílias Católicas Goesas: entre dois mundos e dois referenciais de nobreza, p 12, on-line at http://www.arcip.org/Frames/FamiliasGoesasCatolicas_PedroCosta.doc

218.Teotonio R. De Souza, *Goa through the ages*, Vol. II, Rural Economy and Life, p 107, Concept Publishing Company New Delhi,1990

219.Fr Cosme Jose Costa sfx, Christianity and Nationalism in Aldona, http://groups.yahoo.com/group/aldona-net/message/4362

220.A. K. Priolkar, *The Goa Inquisition*, published by Voice of India, New Delhi, second reprint 1998, p 177

221.A.K.Priolkar, *The Goa Inquisition*, published by Voice of India, New Delhi, second reprint 1998, p 177

222.Pandya SK. Medicine in Goa--a former Portuguese territory, *J Postgrad Med* (serial online) 1982 (cited 2009 Sep 18);28:123. On-line at http://www.jpgmonline.com/text.asp?1982/28/3/123/5573

223.F. X. Gomes Catão, *Boletim Eclesiástico da Arquidiocese de Goa*, Vol A15, p.395ff, 1957

224.Fr Cosme Jose Costa sfx, Christianity and Nationalism in Aldona, http://groups.yahoo.com/group/aldona-net/message/4362

225.Azevedo, Antonio Emilio d'Almeida, *As Comunidades de Goa: historia das instituições antiguas*, Publishers Viuva Bertrand & C.1890, p 61-64

226.https://www.heraldgoa.in/Review/Ahead-of-their-time/83649.html

227.Women, Business and the Law 2019, A Decade of Reform https://openknowledge.worldbank.org/bitstream/handle/10986/31327/WBL2019.pdf

228.https://data.em2030.org/em2030-sdg-gender-index/

229.Con. Francisco Xavier Gomes Catão, *Subsídios para a História de Chorão*, STVDIA separata, Nos. 15 and 17, April 1966, p15

230. Pandya SK. Medicine in Goa--a former Portuguese territory, *J Postgrad Med* (serial online) 1982 (cited 2009 Sep 18);28:123. Online at http://www.jpgmonline.com/text.asp?1982/28/3/123/5573
231. http://gsbkonkanis.coffeecup.com/html5/gotra.html
232. http://www.bfm.admin.ch/bfm/en/home/themen laenderinformationweltweite_mi gration/migrationsgruende.html
233. https://www.un.org/en/development/desa/population/migration/index.asp

Printed in Great Britain
by Amazon